# Media Work

# Media Work

*Language Teaching Through Media Literacy*

Carla R. Chamberlin

University of Michigan Press
Ann Arbor

To Ellie

# Contents

# Note on Illustrations

My collection of photographs for this book—some taken with care, others hurriedly, and none professionally—resulted in inconsistent quality for reproduction. For clarity, the decision was made to have Theodora Dagkli illustrate the photos. As much as possible she has reproduced the signage verbatim. I made decisions to leave out small, unreadable text, and to sometimes change names of local businesses in order to focus on media work, rather than offer commentary on a specific business. On occasion, Theodora gave me illustrations that contextualized signage and included her creative interpretations; these artistic interpretations are clearly identified in the text. I contributed a number of illustrations, mostly focused on pedagogical guidelines and exercises at the end of chapters (figures 2, 6, 9, 10, 11, 19–25, 26a, 28e, 31, 37, 42, 44, 47a, 48, 49a, 52–54, 56, 58, 60, 62, 64–67, 69, 70), and most of these were magically transformed into legible images by Erin Greb. The remaining 70 drawings are the creative and skillful work of Theodora Dagkli.

# Acknowledgments

This book is the result of many people, opportunities, and events that led me to question mediated environments and their connections to culture and language. As a student, I was encouraged to study then live and work abroad by my teachers and mentors who believed in possibilities that I had not yet imagined for myself. Later, I was supported by Penn State Abington College through a Career Development Professorship and other awards that allowed me to go to conferences, conduct research internationally, and procure the artwork for this project. In my years living and working near Philadelphia, I have worked with teachers in various school districts who, despite their long days and overwhelming responsibilities, were always eager to do and learn more. My undergraduate students at Abington College continually open my eyes to new media and interpretations. I am grateful for all of these experiences.

The process of organizing my ideas, recognizing what worked and what didn't, and returning to writing after unexpected interruptions, however, required an intangible type of support that gave me confidence and motivation when I needed it most. I thank my friends and fellow educators Deborah Crusan, Ilze Duarte, Tammy Irvin, Monica Neal, Claudia Payne, and Maria Scalzi Wherley, whose support has spanned thousands of miles and more than three decades to keep me grounded both intellectually and emotionally. I am indebted to Dolores Arevalo, Roxanna Senyshyn, Paula Smith, and Karen Weekes who became more than colleagues over the years. You all listened, cared, and guided me through my personal and professional endeavors. And many thanks to my friend Erin Greb who shared her professional expertise, sharp attention to detail, and calming focus to transform images during the final, frantic stages of preparation.

Through organizations for language teachers, applied linguists, and intercultural educators I have met many caring and inspiring people around the world who helped me to realize that I had something to say, and that others would listen. This book found its form through conversations and explorations of ideas and places with Su Motha, Brian Morgan, Barry van Driel, Nektaria

Palaiologou, Ondine Gage, Muhammad Ali Khan, Stephanie Vandrick, Ryuko Kubota, Yilin Sun, and many, many others that I do not have the space to list. Thank you all for making me think and rethink.

At the University of Michigan Press, my editor Katie LaPlant understood my vision for this book in the early stages and never let me lose sight of what I wanted to achieve. She kept me on track, but was willing to deviate from the norm. When we first looked at a couple of Theodora's drawings together, I remember thinking "What if the entire book were illustrated?" Katie was thinking the same. Thank you, Katie, for your guidance and faith in this project. Theodora came on board and transformed my photos and rough sketches into vibrant and interesting illustrations. I am grateful for her talent, her hard work, and her dedication to this project. Juliette Snyder and Haley Winkle at Michigan dealt with my seemingly infinite list of questions and patiently led me through the production process. Thank you.

I am grateful to my parents, Ray and Stella, who filled our house with books, artwork, poems, newspapers, and yes, televisions (but no cable!). From them, I learned to appreciate my local community and my own history. From my dad, I learned to talk to my neighbors and to look at everything around me with both wonder and healthy skepticism. My brother Dan's relentless and informed critiques of media keep me on my toes and challenge me to continually learn and analyze the world around me. My sister Deni, who tells stories in photographs, taught me to see *more* and to think about semiotics before either of us had even heard of that word. My partner David listened to my developing ideas with patience, gently offered critiques, and provided unwavering, enthusiastic support. Thank you for never doubting my ability to finish this book and for helping me to turn "I'll try" into "I will."

To Patrick who bought yellow "caution" tape and cordoned me off in my home office so I could get my book proposal written ... your heart and your love are a part of this project, though you would not live to see it published. Our daughter Ellie has been my constant inspiration. She has endured hours of commentary about media, and she puts up with the "wait, wait" that I exclaim everywhere we go so I can stop and take a photo of a sign. This book is dedicated to you, love, my pride and joy.

# Introduction

I started writing about media literacy and its relevance to second language teaching in the early 2000s, but my interest in media in classroom settings began long before then. In the late 1980s and early 1990s, while teaching English as a foreign language in France and South Korea, I became keenly aware of stereotypes that traveled around the globe through print media, television shows, and movies, and I saw how these stereotypes cultivated narrow and sometimes damaging mindsets. I incorporated discussions about media representations into my classes, including the questioning of my own impressions of the world that I had gleaned through media. I knew that this critical interrogation was important, but I did not know at that time, almost four decades ago, that it had a name: media literacy.

Fast-forward to the digital age. I have sat through plenary presentations at international language teaching conferences where large audiences are enthralled by projections of flashy, entertaining images. One plenary shared a curated collection of commercials from YouTube. The speaker outlined linguistic structures that could be pulled from each advertisement, made sweeping (mostly negative, trying to be funny) generalizations about the cultures in which these were produced, then said *nothing* about examining the content of the messages or their social implications. At another conference the plenary speaker showed an audience of teachers from an economically challenged school district amazing ways to share information with their students using applications on smartphones and computers. The ideas and resources were innovative and exciting. But, at the time, most of these teachers had limited access to computers for classroom use, and less than half of the population in the school district had internet access in their homes. Although access today is closer to 85% (67% for Spanish speaking households), the digital divide continues to be a challenge in this district (Horrigan, 2021). Despite this incongruency, audience members were smiling, nodding enthusiastically, and playing along on their phones with the presenter (those who could download the app, that is). I successfully downloaded the app only to find the free version very limited and doused with advertisements. All of these challenges, however, seemed to be overshadowed by the mesmerizing attraction of digital media.

Most recently, I attended a packed session at an international conference in which a well-known publisher was showcasing a screen-based methodology. The presentation showed a video of a teacher using the resource on a smartboard with a small group of EFL students. The lesson was teacher-centered and consisted almost exclusively of traditional question-response-evaluation patterns of interaction. Even when students were talking in pairs, they looked at the screen instead of their partners. After showing the video, the presenter asked the audience about the effectiveness and interactivity of the instruction, and the replies were all positive. The inclusion of screens and technology seemed to automatically render that lesson interactive and effective, despite the fact that all patterns of communication signaled the contrary.

In all of these cases, I was more intrigued by the audiences than the speakers. I listened to "ooohs" and "aaahs" as entertaining images flashed on screens. I saw smiling faces. Digital media is impressive. No doubt about it. But no one talked about the pedagogical value of media, how we could make it meaningful, and whether or not teachers and students actually had access to these tools. No one interrogated the stories and ideologies that the media portrayed. I saw this lack of problematization and inquiry as a missed opportunity for teaching and learning.

## What Is this Book About?

This book is not about innovative techniques for incorporating new media technologies into your classroom. This book does not offer foolproof or step-by-step instructions for debunking fake news and images. This book will not assume that you have access to the best digital devices, software, and high-speed connections, or that you keep up with every trend on social media. Instead, this book will encourage you to work with the media that is part of your students' daily experiences, to explore the possibilities and limits of media platforms, and to unravel the literal and social meanings of media content. The overall goal is for you to see media literacy as part of an integrated approach to language teaching and learning that is adaptable to all ages and contexts.

Here's what this book *does* provide:

- an expansive vision of media and literacy;
- a guided yet flexible approach called "media work" for language teaching;

- a focus on local media and recognition of its connection to larger social, historical, and political worlds;

- an understanding of the challenges and opportunities involved with media work.

It will be quickly apparent to readers that I do not limit media to digitally and mass-produced messages but include ephemera such as food labels, maps, job application forms, bumper stickers, community newsletters, and bulletin boards. To look closely at these everyday media, I introduce and apply my approach called *media work*, which entails recursive and overlapping processes of observation, interrogation, interpretation, reflection, and response. Examples of media work are contextualized in the social, environmental, and political conditions in which we live. The challenges we face as educators cannot be ignored, but the opportunities that media literacy bring to language learning are real and substantial. In essence, this book is not about the "ooohs and aaahs" of media, but about the "hmmm" and "aha" moments of teaching.

## Who Should Read this Book?

This book is for all teachers. A fundamental understanding of how language is part of a social semiotic system that creates meaning is as relevant to a children's book about friendship as it is to a graduate school textbook about health care. Media work transcends all disciplines. Language teaching and learning have been part of my life for decades, though, and I have the most to share with language teachers and language teacher educators who are dedicated to creating meaningful and relevant learning experiences for their students.

This book is for language teachers who might not always have elaborate resources at hand and who want students to engage with their local environments and with their peers. I write for teachers who are navigating the challenges of teaching about language, culture, identity, and inclusion in places that increasingly limit or even legally prohibit discussions of these topics. My intention is for you, the reader, to think about how you could adapt each example to reflect the needs of your students, their experiences, and your communities.

Media work evolved during my 35 years of teaching on three continents for a wide range of levels, age groups, and purposes. The examples I share in this book reflect the worlds of my current undergraduate college students, and I believe that educators who read this book will be able to adapt activities to other audiences. No book can cover all circumstances or contexts, but the tools you will learn to use in these pages will serve you well in a wide variety of settings. I focus on examples from my classes and from Philadelphia, its suburbs, and nearby towns. These local examples are not meant to be universal, but the strategies of looking around and exploring routine everyday media as rich pedagogical resources do apply to any context.

The students I work with are linguistically and culturally diverse. Many are first generation college students, from middle to lower income families, hold full or part time jobs, and are first- or second-generation immigrants. They sometimes tell stories of their home languages not being valued in their elementary and secondary schooling. The monolingual speakers in my classes are also culturally diverse, share their experiences, and are curious about language learning. Media work gives all students the chance to see what is important to the person sitting next to them in class. As much as possible, I share examples of media that can be adapted to different groups of students.

## What's Inside?

In Chapter 1, "What is media literacy?" I define media and media literacy education for this book and discuss the basic principles that media literacy education and second language teaching and learning have in common. Chapter 2, "Media Work: The Model," introduces my model "media work" as a pedagogical tool. I share ideas and theoretical approaches from communication, media, and language studies that form the foundation for the model. Chapter 3, "Media Work: The Process," describes the model in detail and illustrates its components by taking readers through an example of media work applied to local newspaper stories about English as a second language in elementary and secondary schools.

The second half of the book is dedicated to illustrating the flexibility and structure of media work for teaching about language and culture. Chapter 4, "Exploring the Language of our Daily Lives," illustrates how everyday media such as labels, bumper stickers, memes, menus, and signs in public places can be examined as linguistically and culturally rich texts. Chapter 5, "Media Work and Storytelling," shifts from a medium-centered to a thematic approach. We move across space and formats to investigate how media construct stories about people, places, and events. The examples of applied media work that you will see in chapters 4 and 5 move from single artifacts and language samples to larger themes and ideas. This progression may align with language proficiency and student readiness, but it does not necessarily imply a progression of analytical complexity. A sign that contains few words, for example, can inspire multiple levels of discussion, ranging from linguistic features and communicative styles, to the representation of voices and identities within a community. In practice, you can move back and forth between these chapters according to the needs of your classes. Chapter 6, "Challenges in Media Work" addresses the social, emotional, and political nature of media literacy education in language teaching. Fake news, misinformation, and propaganda are discussed along with the political nature of media. Finally, Chapter 7, "Opportunities" outlines how media work opens up spaces for engagement with language, culture, and community. Each chapter ends with a list of key ideas, questions for reflection and discussion, activities to explore, and suggested resources for learning more about a specific topic.

Throughout this book I hope to deepen your knowledge of media literacy education and show you how it naturally fits into second language teaching and learning. You may notice that I do not include sections about assessment. This is not an oversight, but a deliberate decision. Different teaching contexts require different outcomes, and I believe that media work lends itself to assessing students' recognition and understanding of grammatical forms, vocabulary, cultural knowledge, and critical thinking. I trust you, the teacher, to decide how to assess student learning. Finally, I want you to believe that media work is not another method or approach to add to your overloaded schedules; instead, it is meant to help you integrate and streamline discussions, activities, and projects that are already part of your teaching practices. I hope that as you read, you say to yourself "hmmm" and "aha" as you think of ways to create your own versions of media work.

# CHAPTER I

# What Is Media Literacy?

What comes to mind when you hear or see the term "media literacy?" Do you think about Instagram, TikTok, or YouTube? Fake news and misinformation? Do you think about your school's new course management system that you have to learn, just when you seem to have mastered the old system? Do you think about opportunities for learning: Building connections across cultures? Taking students on a virtual tour of a museum that is thousands of miles away? Do you think of media literacy as something that students learn outside of your class?

Many people connect "media literacy" to social media, mass media, and tools we need to navigate our increasingly technology-dependent lives. Working effectively with digital resources is crucial to many transactions today, but media literacy involves much more than the digital world and technical skills. Media literacy is a way of engaging with the world around us. In this chapter, I will show you how media literacy and second language studies share some fundamental principles and theoretical perspectives that make their convergence practical and purposeful; but first we need to explore the terms *media*, *literacy*, and *media literacy education*.

## What is Media? Take a Look Around You

As I sit at my desk, ready to write, I look up at the blank page that glows on my screen. Behind it are windows filled with icons, images, texts, and animations—all calling for my attention. In this one small space, there are layers and layers of media. But that's not all. Around me are piles of books, pages of printed and handwritten notes, maps, crossword puzzles, cut outs of New Yorker cartoons, and the wrapper from my take-out lunch that I just finished. All of this is media, with the wrapper being, ostensibly, the least intriguing. I take a closer look. The falafel wrap that I bought at a Mediterranean food stall at a local farmers' market came wrapped up tightly in paper bearing the name and logo of the vendor (figure 1).

**Figure 1**

I notice the highly stylized font that seems to convey an "exotic" vibe, something special, fancy, or out of the ordinary. I see font colors that are deep red and orange, adding a sense of warmth and richness to the logo. The information on the wrapper seems straightforward: the name, address, and opening hours of the business. Why is it called "Mediterranean Café" and not a name that is more culturally specific? And what about the address? Does this suburban, gourmet market, with limited days and hours, cater to a certain clientele? What does going to this market mean to me—a sense of place, belonging, or identity? What do others think of me for shopping here rather than the fast-food places that surround it? Could my actions be seen as snobbish, or even unpatriotic? All this from a wrapper? Yes!

As you might have guessed, I work with a broad definition of media. Media include printed and digital materials and artifacts that convey messages through linguistic and semiotic processes, sometimes augmented by sound, touch, and motion (Kress, 2010). We easily think of news, entertainment, and advertisements and their digital modes of delivery as the media of our daily lives. In many parts of the world, it is quite a challenge to get away from screens and mass media. These platforms are powerful and important, but they are not the whole picture. Media also include the ephemera of our daily lives: the yard signs in our neighborhoods, textbooks and classroom decor, labels on the goods we buy, political pamphlets left in our mailboxes, and yes, even food wrappers. These non-digital, or analog, forms of media are still very much a part of our environments along with the digital. Analog messages that we encounter connect us to the "here and now," to our communities, and to the people who create the messages. This provides a sense of immediacy—a term from nonverbal communication that refers to how we establish a connection to our immediate surroundings. Similar to how nuanced facial expressions and tone of voice can connect us to other people, analog media such as signage, printed materials, and decor can create a sense of connection to a place or community. Media educator Antero Garcia (2019) says:

> Collectively, teachers of English in the United States are expected to guide students to utilize the latest resources for multimodal consumption and production in order to join a globally competitive workforce. However, I would advocate for our field to make an intentional turn toward the local and toward the present. Teachers and learners must emphasize analog literacy practices that center care that addresses inequities and needs in our backyards. We must do so while recognizing that we are also tethered to communities that exist in online and geographically distributed ways. (p. 193)

Garcia reminds us that the local and present are vital to understanding issues relevant to our students. The examples I offer in this book tap into my local resources but are meant to be adapted to your teaching settings. Language learners might be negotiating their places in new communities where messages of welcome or hostility are produced in multiple formats, and opportunities to respond range from face-to-face to online. If my neighbor puts a sign in their yard that conveys a message of hate or prejudice, I might respond by posting a sign with a counter message, and I can try to talk to my neighbor. I might also go to a community website to seek affiliation and advice from members of my local community. I rely on analog and digital pathways. We all rely on this mixture to communicate our ideas, avow our identities, and form relationships. Our definition of "media" needs to be inclusive of different locales and formats. Media in this book, consequently, refers to all forms of textual, visual, and auditory messages that are conveyed through digital and analog modes of delivery, and the examples come from what my students and I see all around us. Becoming aware of these local media messages and what they say about a community and its social relationships is a necessary step to understanding our positions as global citizens.

## What is Literacy? It's More than Reading and Writing

Just as media is about more than electronic or digital forms of communication, literacy is more than measurements of reading and writing skills. Traditional conceptualizations defined literacy as mastery of reading and writing skills based on an idealized, print-centered, language standard. As a result, literacy was determined by the ability to comprehend and produce measurable competencies. What these competencies entailed typically reflected narrow and static visions of what and whose skills were seen as most valuable to a society. Consequently, a student's literacy was contingent on their individual ability to master specific skills. This process left little room for considering individual variations in learning, not to mention cultural, social, and economic factors. Those who used different language varieties, engaged with texts that were not part of an accepted canon, or had life experiences that did not match the standard curricula may not have even been considered worthy of education. Definitions and theories of literacy, thankfully, have evolved over time. While none of the modern and overlapping theories of literacy deny the necessity of basic skills for reading and writing, they all expand the definition of literacy to recognize that changing communication and social contexts necessitate wider, more fluid definitions of literacy, often referred to as multiliteracies.

In their seminal 1996 article in the *Harvard Educational Review*, "A Pedagogy of Multiliteracies: Designing Social Futures," the New London Group[1] pointed out the need for a broader definition of literacy in response to increasingly globalized and diverse societies and to the spread of information through multimodal, multimedia channels (New London Group, 1996; Cope & Kalantzis, 2017). The New London Group proposed a framework for designing social futures that rejected a monolingual, monocultural as well as a print-centered view of literacy. They recognized that if students are to be active participants in the design of their own futures, pedagogy must respond to the changing needs of our *lifeworlds*—that is, our working, public, and private lives. They realized then that new media environments and globalization were blurring boundaries among these *lifeworlds* and that students would need skills to navigate new social spaces and ideas of citizenship:

Local diversity and global connectedness mean not only that there can be no standard; they also mean that the most important skill students need to learn is to negotiate regional, ethnic, or class-based dialects; variations in register

---

1. The New London Group includes ten scholars who came together in New London, New Hampshire in the US in 1994 where they fleshed out ideas for a new pedagogy.

that occur according to social context; hybrid cross-cultural discourses; the code switching often to be found within a text among different languages, dialects, or registers; different visual and iconic meanings; and variations in the gestural relationships among people, language, and material objects. Indeed, this is the only hope for averting the catastrophic conflicts about identities and spaces that now seem ever ready to flare up. (New London Group, 1996, p. 69)

Today in the United States, conflict over contested spaces and identities has flared up. School curricula have been targeted as part of this conflict and have become political battlegrounds, dividing citizens and oversimplifying the complex issues around multiliteracies. Rather than recognizing multiliteracies as a curriculum that builds on basic literacy skills and critical thinking (both traditional dimensions of education), some groups view deviations from prescribed monolingual, monocultural definitions of literacy as a threat. For many educators and students, however, the expansion of literacy to include skills needed to successfully participate in multimodal and intercultural spaces is a positive and practical response to a continually changing world.

Some of these changes involve "new literacies," "digital literacies," "multimodal literacies," and the skills needed to navigate media environments where images, texts, sounds, smells, and tactile elements converge (Jewitt & Kress, 2003; Kress, 2003, 2010; Lankshear & Knobel, 2006; Street, 2017; Warschauer, 2006, 2011). Digital platforms, for example, require different ways of processing grammar than text on a printed page. On screen, text can challenge grammatical and orthographic conventions, move around, and interact with images and sounds (Lotherington, 2004, 2011). Analog media, however, can also challenge conventions through metaphors and language choices, nonverbal elements, and relational interactions. Think about museum exhibits that invite you to look at an object, read about it on a plaque mounted nearby, watch a video, and possibly touch and respond to an exhibit. These visual, auditory, and tactile modes are not uncommon, and literacy today involves multiple processes, various combinations of modalities, and multiple ways of knowing.

## What is Media Literacy?

Media literacy is an old topic but a relatively new academic discipline. Before discussing media literacy specifically, I want to first highlight the relationship between media and information. Modes of communication have always conveyed messages and stories that shape ideas of truth, knowledge, intelligence, and morality—in essence, what we should value and pay attention to. Oral cultures rely on the spoken word and storytelling to convey knowledge, which is often associated with relevant and immediately useful information or stories passed down through generations to teach moral codes. Early writing systems encoded meaning in symbols and created a knowledge base that was more permanent, though not easily transportable or accessible to everyone. Paintings and photography later interpreted visual stories of faraway times or places. The printing press redefined knowledge as replicable text that was not bound by time and space and was thereby accessible to a wider audience. Printed materials told stories around the world and about the world, though not all voices were represented. The telegraph, radio, and television transcended both time and space, and each reshaped what could be conveyed, who could access it, and how much information could be shared. These innovations over time dramatically changed what different communities considered to be valuable knowledge. For example, when the penny press became popular in the late 19th century in the United States, newspapers began to change their content to include more stories for a mass audience. Although gossip, scandals, and social news were not new phenomena, this new means of distribution brought trivial items and entertainment to the forefront. A century later television and its reliance on advertising defined "entertainment," "news," "marketing," and "education," often blurring boundaries as it told stories about people, places, and events.

Then, in a relatively short period of time, the media environment was transformed by digital technologies. The spread of information expanded dramatically and at an unprecedented rate. Stories could be shared around the world and content expanded to capture the attention of new audiences. On one hand, more voices could be heard, and important news could get to audiences immediately. On the other hand, news became more fragmented and decontextualized; entertainment, advertising, and propaganda found new platforms for expansion, and media companies became the gatekeepers of information. Media literacy as a field has evolved as a response to all of these technological changes, though not always with a singular purpose.

As early as the 1920s, educators began to question the role of commercially produced films for classroom use, questioning whether business, entertainment, and education could have common goals. In the 1950s and 60s media literacy was expressed through both "protectionist" and "technicist" approaches. The former focused on raising awareness as a defense against propaganda, commercialization, and corporate aims, the latter on the tools and techniques of media production (Hobbs & Jensen, 2009; Masterman, 1985). The second half of the twentieth century brought more changes to media literacy, influenced by social and critical theories of learning (Freire, 1985, 2000;

Vygotsky, 1986) and articulated by those who challenged mediated representations, corporate interests, and political ideologies in mass media and popular culture (Giroux, 1994; Hall, 1997; Herman & Chomsky, 1988; Lewis & Jhally, 1998; Masterman, 1985). In addition, scholars positioned media as shaping our way of understanding and experiencing the world (McLuhan, 1964; Ong, 1982; Postman, 1986). Media literacy became a critique of the ideological reproduction of the status quo and a means of encouraging more democratic media. These protectionist, technicist, and critical approaches were—and still are—sometimes positioned at odds with one another. But each has something to contribute to a definition of media literacy education (MLE), a theory-driven practice that is being embraced in various places around the world.

Across the globe, non-profit organizations centered on education, journalism, and digital technology are calling for policies and practices that will make media literacy education a required or essential competency in schooling at all levels. Organizations and journalists in the Philippines, Korea, India, and the Middle East frame media literacy education as essential to preparing youth to engage in their increasingly digitized futures and to protect themselves against misinformation and addiction (Center for Digital Literacy, Korea; Center for Media Freedom and Responsibility, Philippines; Korea Press Foundation; *The Times of India*, to name just a few). UNESCO's document *Towards Media and Information Literacy* (Moeller, et al., 2011) positions MIL as a path toward civic engagement and equity:

> The goal of MIL is to give people the power to use their rights of free expression, to defend their access to information, to evaluate content, to secure their participation in the process of governing, and to help all voices be heard. At its best, MIL teaches the global public to evaluate available information—including that provided by both formal and informal media—about the world's needs; to make sense of the solutions that are on offer; and to be able to communicate and engage with others proportionately and responsibly. MIL, in other words, is a bottom-up idea. Locally generated projects that focus on education and training to develop people's capacities to create and use both traditional media and new digital resources are especially effective. (p.12).

Calls for media literacy education around the world make similar arguments and propose various combinations of cultural learning, critical thinking skills, and mastery of digital tools. The Center for Media Literacy Education in the United States offers an educational philosophy with three tenets: 1) Media literacy is education for life in a global media world; 2) The heart of media education is informed inquiry; and 3) Media literacy is an alternative to censoring, boycotting or blaming "the media" (Center for Media Literacy

Education, n.d.). TESOL's standards in technology and teacher education, Common Core Standards for ELA, and the Modern Language Association all call attention to media literacy education in their practices and policies. In addition, in the *International Encyclopedia of Media Literacy*, Haixia He writes:

> To introduce media literacy in the ESL [English as a second language] class-room, teachers should not only consider the presence of media artifacts but also endeavor to teach about the media. It is by questioning these media that ESL students find the opportunity to engage in a critique of the culture while learning how the language works (He, 2019, p. 3).

Varied approaches to media literacy have their strengths and weaknesses. Some approaches reflect the protectionist view and focus on media literacy education as a defense against fake news, misinformation, and addiction to technology, positioning audiences as passive consumers. Others focus on inquiry and individual agency, not holding media conglomerates ethically responsible for their reporting and advertising. The bottom line is that we need a multilayered approach. Sometimes we need to detect unreliable information and harmful propaganda, but we also need to know how we can critically interpret and respond to media for civic good.

A useful and often cited definition of media literacy comes from the *Core Principles for Media Literacy Education* published by the National Association for Media Literacy Education (NAMLE, 2007). NAMLE states that "Media literacy education is the ongoing development of habits of inquiry and skills of expression necessary for people to be critical thinkers, thoughtful and effective communicators, and informed and responsible members of society" (NAMLE, 2023). If you replace "media literacy" with "language teaching and learning" the overlapping objectives become quite clear. Moreover, *The Core Principles of Media Literacy Education* (NAMLE, 2023) outlines ten goals of media literacy education, further aligning this field with second language teaching and learning. I encourage you to visit their website to read the implications for teaching that are listed under each of the following ten goals.

1. Media literacy education *expands* the concept of literacy to include all forms of media and integrates multiple literacies in developing mindful media consumers and creators.
2. Media literacy education *envisions* all individuals as capable learners who use their background, knowledge, skills, and beliefs to create meaning from media experiences.

3. Media literacy education *promotes* teaching practices that prioritize curious, open-minded, and self-reflective inquiry while emphasizing reason, logic, and evidence.
4. Media literacy education *encourages* learners to practice active inquiry, reflection, and critical thinking about the messages they experience, create, and share across the ever-evolving media landscape.
5. Media literacy education *necessitates* ongoing skill-building opportunities for learners that are integrated, cross-curricular, interactive, and appropriate for age and developmental stage.
6. Media literacy education *supports* the development of a participatory media culture in which individuals navigate myriad ethical responsibilities as they create and share media.
7. Media literacy education *recognizes* that media institutions are cultural and commercial entities that function as agents of socialization, commerce, and change.
8. Media literacy education *affirms* that a healthy media landscape for the public good is a shared responsibility among media and technology companies, governments, and citizens.
9. Media literacy education *emphasizes* critical inquiry about media industries' roles in society, including how these industries influence, and are influenced by, systems of power, with implications for equity, inclusion, social justice, and sustainability.
10. Media literacy education *empowers* individuals to be informed, reflective, engaged, and socially responsible participants in a democratic society.

These principles reflect continual changes in the role that media play in our lives. We use media for interpersonal, social, and mass communication, for commercial transactions, for entertainment, for advocacy, and for teaching and learning. These principles also correspond to changes in language, how it is used, interpreted, mixed, and remixed in various modalities and contexts. Teaching *about* language and media as well as how to *use* language and media today relies on an acceptance of multiliteracies as a norm and commitment to building students' capacities for participation in both smaller communities and larger society. Language and media are enmeshed in pedagogically intriguing ways.

## What Do Media Literacy and Language Teaching Have in Common?

In addition to some basic principles, media literacy education and second language teaching and learning share an evolution that begins with transmission and technical points of view, followed by cultural perspectives, and most recently, social and critical perspectives. These represent important shifts in theory and practice. Early perspectives are easy to criticize for their deficiencies, but it is more productive to consider how parts of these older theories are still relevant and how newer perspectives were generated from their weaknesses. I discuss some general perspectives here (I am unable to do justice to the depths of each), but I hope to lay the foundation for a pedagogy that draws on commonalities in language and media studies.

In the 1950s and 60s scholars from several disciplines began to question the influence of commercial Hollywood films and propaganda materials. Earlier critiques existed but did not take hold in educational practices (see Hobbs & Jensen, 2009 for an overview of media literacy history). Media literacy at midcentury, however, began a more concentrated effort to examine the commercial nature of media, particularly film, and the techniques used to tell stories. These techniques, like those from literature, include understanding genre, character, and plot development, as well as cinematic techniques such as dissolve, fade, cut, and zoom (Hobbs, 2005). The goal was not to turn students into film producers, but to give them the chance to understand how stories are constructed through film and to give them the tools to explore this process. This technical approach also applied to advertisements and propaganda as a way to show students how to defend themselves against harmful messages.

Today this skills-based focus is manifest in the imperative for both teachers and students to know how to technically navigate and produce digital media. On one hand, this is a practical approach that gives people the basic tools they need to manage the multitude of digital interfaces confronted each day. On the other hand, this focus can be seen as a "technicist trap" (Masterman, 1985) in which people learn to use technology without understanding the larger contexts of cultural, economic, and social practices in which meanings and representations are created. For example, a local community center might offer a computer skills course for adults that concentrates on using digital devices and protection from scammers. In this technicist approach, successful learners master skills needed to protect themselves. This is a practical objective, but is it enough? Do they also learn which groups are most targeted and vulnerable, and why?

In second language teaching and learning, a parallel "technicist" approach existed in the early part of the twentieth century in which successful language learning was defined by mastery of linguistic structures and production that resembled the accuracy of an "ideal native speaker." Similar to media literacy, a focus on accurate encoding and decoding of messages decontextualized language and measured success through normative standards. Interestingly, as media literacy was concerned with guarding people from the effects of propaganda, foreign language learning in the United States during World War II became an imperative for military defense. Protectionism against subversive or foreign influence was an impetus for both disciplines. Teaching methods at the time stressed memorization, mimicry, and accuracy. Successful learners mastered the linguistic codes of languages.

The "technical" phases in both media literacy and language teaching conceptualize learning as discrete skill sets with measurable outcomes. This focus on usage and production skills is a top-down, teacher-centered approach that ultimately places the burden on individual students to produce content without considering the social processes involved. This also reflects a transmission perspective on communication in which meaning is transmitted from one source to another without negotiation of meaning. These technical perspectives remind us that knowledge of linguistic structures and media production skills are necessary, but inadequate.

In addition to tools, language learning and media literacy rely on processes of meaning-making that recognize the symbolic and socially situated natures of both. Breaking away from the transmission perspective of one-directional influence, media studies began to recognize that "communication is a symbolic process whereby reality is produced, maintained, repaired, and transformed" (Carey, 1989, p. 23). The site of meaning-making was no longer confined to the individual but embedded in the culturally circumscribed symbolic spaces where language takes on meaning. For example, advertisements often draw on cultural contexts, assuming consumers will understand subtle references to popular culture. Memes rely on the symbolic nature of language as they adapt language and imagery in quickly changing cultural spaces by infusing new meanings into old scripts.

In applied linguistics, a similar shift took place that relocated language learning into cultural spaces. In addition to grammatical knowledge, communicative competency expanded to include sociocultural, discourse, and strategic dimensions, bringing cultural contexts and negotiation of meaning among interlocutors to the forefront (Canale & Swain, 1980; Halliday, 1978, 1994; Pica, 1994). Pedagogical shifts from audio-lingual methods to communicative language learning ushered in a new focus on conveying meaning over accuracy in the later part of the 20th century. Research expanded to question the role of interlanguage, student to student interactions, and implicit and explicit feedback (Carroll & Swain, 1993; Duff, 1993; Ferris, 2002; Selinker, 1972; Selinker & Lamendella, 1981), to name just a few of the important lines of inquiry. We began to question individual affect, motivation, and language input (Krashen, 1985; Long, 1983) and to consider the relationship between culture and language in the classroom and beyond (Nieto, 1992, 1999; Scollon & Scollon, 1981, 1995). This orientation toward social interaction, culture, function, and negotiation of meaning advanced both media and language studies, but did not emphasize how much social and institutional structures shape cultural realities.

Critical theories and critical pedagogy began to challenge media literacy education and applied linguistics to unpack the dominant ideologies that define social structures and privilege certain groups over others (Freire, 1970/2000; Giroux, 1994; Giroux & Purpel, 1983; Hall & Du Gay, 1996; Kincheloe, 1993; Sleeter & McLaren, 1995). In media literacy education, this critical turn confronted questions of ownership of media production, misrepresentation, underrepresentation of minorities in media, censorship, profit-making, and socially irresponsible practices. Lewis and Jhally stated that media literacy should be about "helping people to become sophisticated citizens rather than sophisticated consumers" (1998, p. 103). Kellner and Share (2005, 2007) argued that media literacy that does not engage in the critical understanding of ideology, power, and politics dilutes the transformative potential of education, leaving media literacy education vulnerable to reproducing social structures that disenfranchise marginalized groups. This critical turn in media literacy continues to produce an immense body of literature on representations from various fields (see suggested readings at the end of this chapter). For example, Molina-Guzmán (2010) looks at representations of Latina bodies in media as "symbolic colonization" but also discusses challenges to these portrayals as a form of "symbolic rupture." Critical researchers also examine photography (Paakspuu, 2009) and archival media that frame colonial histories of Indigenous peoples (Cohen & Glover, 2014), metaphorical choices used in media to describe climate change, pandemics, inequalities in health care, housing, and criminal justice, to name just a few. In my own critical media analyses, I have questioned why audiences complacently accept portrayals of speakers of a non-prestige variety of American English as lazy, unambitious, and illiterate (Chamberlin-Quinlisk, 2012b).

The critical turn in media literacy education not only challenges representations, but also the institutional forces and corporate monopolies of the media industry. Project Censored, the Media Education Lab, and the Critical Media Literacy Project are just a few examples of concentrated efforts to challenge the media industry by supporting research, conferences, and projects that strive to dismantle corporate power through education and activism.

In applied linguistics, the critical perspective is best defined by Alistair Pennycook's seminal work, *Critical applied linguistics: A critical introduction* (2001). Pennycook says:

> Critical applied linguistics, then, is more than just a critical dimension added on to applied linguistics: It involves a constant skepticism, a constant questioning of the normative assumption of applied linguistics. It demands a restive problematization of the givens of applied linguistics and presents a way of doing applied linguistics that seeks to connect it to questions of gender, class, sexuality, race, ethnicity, culture, identity, politics, ideology, and discourse. And crucially, it becomes a dynamic opening up of new questions that emerge from this conjunction. (Pennycook, 2001, p. 10)

Pennycook sees critical applied linguistics not as a mechanism for simply uncovering social or political inequalities related to language, but as a mechanism for exploring how these inequalities operate in complex ways and in various communities.

Critical applied linguistics positions our work as interdisciplinary, involving critical thinking as a precursor to social change. Engagement and agency can arise from problematizing typically unchallenged norms and assumptions (Pennycook, 2001, 2021). Research from the critical perspective in applied linguistics does, in fact, expose structures of power but situates them within complex local communities and relates them to participants' identities and desires as well as global ecologies. This leads to a deeper understanding of both local and global forces that shape the lived experiences of our students. Examples of critical inquiry in the past few decades include challenges to native-speaker/non-native speaker dichotomies and to hierarchies that associate prestige, opportunities, and higher expectations with speakers of certain varieties of English (Brutt-Griffler & Samimy, 1999, 2001; Davies, 2003; Faez, 2011; Ruecker, 2011). I have known students who, as native speakers of English—though not American English—had been marked as non-native speakers and placed in ESL classes in their elementary or secondary schools. Is it a coincidence that they were also students of color?

Critical applied linguistics also examines intersecting identities. For example, those who are already labeled by their status as language learners might be further categorized by race and ethnicity (Alim, Rickford, & Ball, 2016; Amin, 1997; Kubota, 2020, 2021; Kubota & Lin, 2006, 2009; Motha 2006a). In addition, gender, sex, age, and social class intersect with language learning status and impact educational opportunities (Block, 2014; Heller, 2006; Nelson, 2006, 2009; Vandrick, 2009). A critical lens also sheds light on the effects of post-colonial ideologies and identities in the teaching of English (Canagarajah, 1999, 2008; Motha, 2006b, 2014) and questions the globalization of English as a lingua franca and as a neoliberal construction of social mobility (Edge, 2006; Phillipson, 2009; Piller, 2016; Ricento, 2014, 2019; Skutnabb-Kangas, 2000; Widdowson, 2012, 2021). This critical shift highlights the importance of situating our work within social, political, and historical contexts and replacing hegemonic practices with more inclusive pedagogical norms.

Critical applied linguistics and critical media literacy have both faced challenges over the years. Earlier critiques generally fell into two categories: one is that these critical perspectives imposed narrow viewpoints on students; the second is that they focused on theory and not practice. Today, the idea that critical perspectives impose viewpoints is still prevalent, and ironically the main critique is that they are infiltrating educational practices (López & Sleeter, 2023). Part of this critique is due to a misunderstanding and misappropriation of the word "critical." Critical theories are meant to question assumptions and ways of being that have become normalized to the point of invisibility. In mainstream media, however, "critical" has been used to invoke a sense of threat and fear and to promote pedagogy that does not question how meaning is created and shared. For instance, let's consider an example where media meets language policy. How many stories can you think of (movies, books, videos, biographies, etc.) that promote the idea that if you are an immigrant in the United States, learning English is the key to success and that language learning happens quickly for those who try hard enough? From this perspective, English-only policies (in classrooms, schools, and public realms) would ostensibly help everyone succeed. Perseverance leads to success, right? Not always.

A critical perspective asks, "Wait, a lot of people speak English well, and a lot of people work really hard. Why aren't they all successful? What else is going on?" Here we start asking questions about disparities in socioeconomic resources, allostatic load,[2] learning styles, abilities/disabilities, and much more. In fact, critical approaches to education in the past decades have been profoundly beneficial. They have led to increased access for students with disabilities, brought needed attention to mental health issues, and have even allowed my daughter to take any classes that interest her (I was stuck in home economics when I wanted to be in drafting), to name just a few.

---

2. Allostatic load refers to chronic stress that is caused by life experiences and events. Those living in poverty or facing continual discrimination, bullying, poor nutrition, violence, etc. have shorter life expectancy and negative health outcomes.

Perhaps most familiar to educators is the conceptual term *culturally relevant pedagogy* first introduced by Gloria Ladson-Billings (1995, 2014, 2021) to challenge a curriculum that ignores the cultural practices and languages relevant to students of color, or any students who do not identify with the White middle-class norms of schooling. Ladson-Billings was not the first to respond critically to linguistic, social, and cultural inequities in education, but her work, along with many others, positioned and continues to center culturally relevant and culturally responsive teaching as a foundation in teacher education programs and pedagogical development (Cummins, 1997, 2001, 2010; Delpit, 1996, 2012; Ladson-Billings, 1995, 1998, 2021; Gay, 2002, 2018; Nieto, 1992, 1999, 2010; Sleeter, 1991, 2012; Valdés, 2001). Today this critical stance is advanced in the theory and practice of *culturally sustaining pedagogies* (Alim & Paris, 2015; Paris, 2012, 2021; Paris & Alim, 2014, 2017). Culturally sustaining pedagogy (CSP) builds on the desire to erase inequalities in education that base definitions of success on patriarchal, ableist, heteronormative, Anglo normative, and xenophobic norms. Past responses to these inequalities too often have limited their focus to increasing access and perseverance, rather than critically questioning the definition of success. In other words, students whose language, cultural knowledge, experiences, and diverse thinking are not valued in classrooms are seen as deficient in skills, rather than as possessing skills and knowledge that should be recognized as valuable. CSP calls for educational systems to broaden their expectations for what it means to learn and teach, including understanding culture as fluid, and applying a critical lens to examine all curricular choices, from traditional canons to contemporary studies. Critical pedagogy is expansive, not restrictive.

In media literacy education, the critical approach seeks not only to understand the tools, content, context, and ideologies of media, but to engender closer examination of media that maintain and disrupt social practices. Critical media literacy activates social justice, civic participation, and engagement both locally and globally (boyd, 2014; Garcia & de Roock, 2021; Hobbs, 2020; Jenkins, 2006; Kellner & Share, 2007; Martens & Hobbs, 2015; Mihailidis & Thevenin, 2013). Gordon & Mihailidis (2016) describe an applied approach called civic media literacy as "the technologies, designs, and practices that produce and reproduce the sense of being in the world with others toward common good" (p. 2). More specifically, Mihailidis (2019) describes civic media literacies as a way to rebuild civic relationships that are being dismantled through distrust, fake news, and spectacle. He proposes the integration of *civic intentionality* into media literacy education as a way to reimagine media literacies. Civic intentionality involves caring for one another as a way to develop collective agency, developing a critical consciousness, imagining a better world, persistence in connecting knowledge to action, and emancipation from communication practices that leave out or restrict underrepresented voices (Mihailidis, 2019).

Language teachers understand that caring and persistence, interrogating social inequities, reimagining lives, and helping students to develop their voices is a central part of what they do. In some cases, learning a new language is an act of civic intentionality. Media literacy education as activism and civic participation aligns with critical approaches to language teaching and learning. However, media literacy is not a panacea for social problems, just as learning English does not guarantee access to socioeconomic mobility. What media literacy and language learning both offer is an expanded repertoire of skills with which to engage in communities that will enrich people's lives.

## What Does this Shared Evolution Mean?

Applied linguistics and media literacy are, of course, not the only disciplines to have evolved from technical to cultural, social, and critical perspectives, or from decontextualized to contextualized views. However, their overlapping concerns for language and semiotics, the modalities through which we communicate, and the goals of engagement allow for an integration of theory and practice that enriches second language teaching and learning. I was compelled to write this book, not in order to bring something completely new and unfamiliar to language teaching, but to highlight what the two disciplines share and how media literacy education can enhance language learning. Figure 2 illustrates the stages of development of media literacy (center column) and language teaching and learning (right column), showing how they both widened their perspectives over time.

These perspectives have only directly converged, however, in a relatively small number of calls for incorporating critical media literacy education into language learning (Chamberlin-Quinlisk, 2003, 2012; Egbert & Huff, 2011; Egbert & Neville, 2015; He, 2019; Hobbs et al., 2015). Instead, researchers and practitioners have focused more on incorporating digital literacy skills into learning and assessment, especially in situations that call for online learning. Increasing students' skills and accessibility to digital resources is, without doubt, crucial. However, it is not sufficient.

We need to be asking more questions about media as pedagogical resources, as tools for communication, as symbolic processes, as ideological storytellers, and as cultural artifacts. Remote teaching imposed by the COVID-19 pandemic in 2020 and 2021 brought many questions to the surface: How do media platforms impact classroom interactions? Who has access to resources

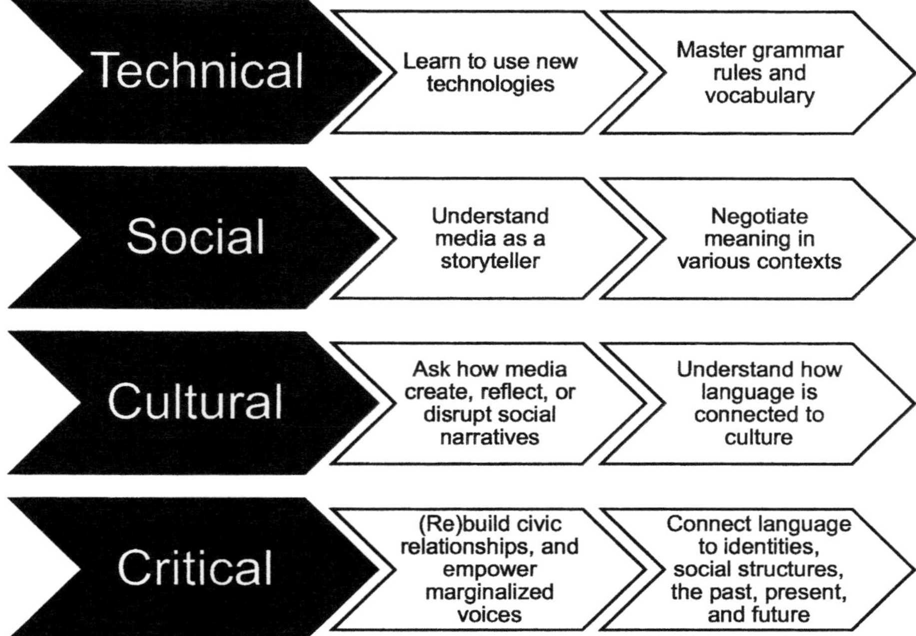


**Figure 2**

and who does not? How does misinformation and propaganda impact the health of communities? And, as we develop our own agendas for media literacy education in our field, we need to be reflexive. Are we focused on digital resources at the expense of other media? How can we teach skills and critical thinking that lead to meaningful learning and participation in community life? And we do not stop with these questions. The critical perspective demands continual questioning of ideas and development of innovative practices, and these processes can happen as long as we do not allow ourselves to be drawn into ambivalent or fear-mongering discourses that pull us back to the technicist view of learning.

## Back to the Food Wrapper

Let's return to that food wrapper and see how the different approaches to media literacy might apply to it. From a *technicist* point of view the food wrapper might not be the most interesting medium we encounter. For those who design, print, and distribute the wrappers, there will be concerns about materials, food safety, and space for advertising. Mostly, a technicist view would focus on the direct messages being conveyed and the effectiveness of these messages on the receiver. Is the business name bold enough? Do you get

**Figure 3**

enough information about the product? Is the wrapper attractive? Is the consumer influenced at all by the information conveyed through this modality? Let's move on to the more intriguing cultural aspects. The style and form of the information printed on the wrapper bring up some interesting linguistic and cultural elements. For example, font choices matter (see figure 3).

The font that I see on the wrapper is an exaggerated stylized form meant to evoke a sense of the exotic. The deep red and orange colors used in the design are considered to be warm rather than cool colors. (You will have to imagine these colors!) What kind of mood or response do the font and colors convey? How does the name Mediterranean Café contribute to a sense of the authenticity of the restaurant and the type of food it serves? Next, we can question how this *form* functions culturally. Is this wrapper intended for food to be eaten by hand or "on the go," something that we find in all communities? The form allows the food to be served hot and ready to eat, but where should it be eaten? Does this form of delivery contribute to or reflect a cultural norm of not having or making time to sit and eat?

The linguistic content of the information printed on the wrapper is informative and symbolic: the name of the food vendor, the address, and phone number. Other vendors might choose to describe their food as "homemade" or "organic" or "all natural," but this one is limited to identifying the vendor and location. What is interesting about the name "Mediterranean Café"? What might these word choices represent in the minds of the customers? It does not serve coffee, so why is this borrowed word used? What is its appeal? Here we can question not only the word "café" but also the choice of "Mediterranean" rather than a more specific name that reflects the cultural identity of the family who owns and runs the business. Perhaps the Middle Eastern family background of the owners in a post 9/11 world cannot be marketed in the same way that the Greek, Italian, and Korean food stalls emphasize their national identities. If this were located in a culturally diverse neighborhood, would a sense of nationality be more present? Instead, this business is located in an Amish farmers' market in a small town, serving a predominantly White middle to upper class population. It is only accessible by car. It is crowded with people toting reusable shopping bags, taking advantage of flexible work schedules, and having enough money to purchase a healthy lunch. This is privilege. This is status. The market vendors are culturally diverse, selling foods from around the world as well as from local farms, but the customers are not diverse. What does this say about the community?

At this point, you might think that I am a bit odd by reading all of this from a food wrapper. I certainly do not examine every artifact I encounter in my life to this degree (most of the time, anyway).[3] This example is only meant to illustrate, however, the possibilities of media literacy for teaching about language, culture, and community based on the artifacts and media we encounter every day. The wrapper shows us that modality and text are important (form, style, content), but the contexts in which messages are read (cultural, social, and personal) profoundly affect the meaning-making process.

---

3. Gunter Kress (2010) describes a bottle of mineral water and a spoon rest in his seminal book on semiotics. I have also attended presentations at conferences that examined the semiotics of individual sugar packets, tea bag wrappers, greeting cards, and other ephemera of our linguistic landscapes.

## What's Next?

Media literacy is something that you probably think about every day, perhaps without even realizing it. As you look at your textbooks, school memos and announcements, professional newsletters, not to mention the thousands of advertisements you see on a daily basis (Story, 2007), you take part in a process of interpretation, evaluation, and response. In this first chapter, I have introduced key concepts of media literacy education along with an argument for its alignment with and role in language teaching and learning. I could provide pages more of arguments to convince you that media literacy education is desperately needed today to deal with the daily avalanche of media that attempt to tell us who to believe and what to fear. I could argue more that media literacy converges naturally with language learning. What matters most, however, is *you*.

You must not think of media simply as a fun way to get students' attention, or as something to avoid or fear. You must believe that media resources can bring variety to your teaching and improvement of language and analytical skills that can be applied beyond the language classroom. You should be committed to the idea that you want to make informed, intentional decisions about cultural stories that you use in your classrooms. You can expand your idea of media to include analog as well as digital, the mundane as well as the spectacular, mainstream as well as alternative, and everything in between. In the next chapter, I review some concepts about language and its intersection with media in greater detail, and introduce "media work" as a model for merging media literacy education with second language teaching and learning.


KEY IDEAS

media

literacy

media literacy education

multiliteracies

multimodalities

digital

analog

technical perspective

social perspective

critical perspective

civic media literacies


QUESTION

1.  Before reading this chapter, what did you already know about media literacy? How different or similar are those ideas from what you read about in this chapter? What do you think media literacy means to teachers, students, parents, and others?

2.  In your experience as a student and/or teacher, what roles have media played in your classroom or formal learning experiences? What media are the most common in your classrooms? Think about what you see in classrooms: texts, images, digital and analog materials. How do you relate to these media as a teacher and/or student? What were the dominant forms of media both in and outside of school when you were growing up? How have these media changed over the years, and how have they remained the same? What media do you think is most beneficial for teaching and learning and why? What do you think present-day students prefer?


EXPLORE

1.  Think about your typical day. From the moment you wake up to the moment you fall asleep, how are media present in your life? Make a list. Is it longer or shorter than you expected? Take a look and make note of which media are imposed upon you and which ones you choose to use. Compare your list and thoughts with those of your peers in class.

2.  Look up media literacy education in the geographical context of your own teaching (country state, province). Are you able to find policy statements or newspaper articles, research articles, blogs, videos, that call for media literacy education? If so, what approaches are reflected in these definitions (technicist, social, critical)? Who supports them? Who challenges them?

3.  Pick an object or collection of objects that you see or use in your everyday experience. Choose something that combines text and imagery. Bring the object or a photo of it to class to share with your peers. What message does the language convey both figuratively and literally? What do the images or other non-linguistic characteristics add to the message?

## LEARN MORE

Here are a few websites and other places where you can learn more about media literacy.

- *Journal of Media Literacy Education* https://digitalcommons.uri.edu/jmle/

  This is the flagship journal of NAMLE and is an open-access journal published quarterly. This journal publishes articles from educators around the world and across disciplines. Simply browsing through the archives will give you a sense of the inspiring work being done in media literacy education.

- Media Literacy Now https://medialiteracynow.org/

  Here you can find resources for parents, teachers, and policy makers. Media Literacy Now provides reports on how US states are responding individually to the need for media literacy in public schools. They publish a "Media Literacy Policy Report" and support research projects and educational initiatives.

- National Association for Media Literacy Education (NAMLE) https://namle.org/

  NAMLE is a professional organization that supports media education in a wide range of contexts around the world. Membership is free, and the website provides links to sources, conferences, and journals.

- UCLA Library: Critical Media Literacy Research Guide https://guides.library.ucla.edu/c.php?g=1108715&p=8084564

  This is an excellent guide to sources in critical media literacy research as well as practice. You can explore subtopics such as movies, science, gender, advertising and consumerism, to name just a few, and they include a page of resources in Spanish.

- UNESCO Institute for Information Technologies in Education: Media and Information Literacy https://iite.unesco.org/mil/

This site provides links to publications, policies, and resources around the world that promote and advocate for MIL. A useful link to resources is https://en.unesco.org/themes/media-and-information-literacy.

If you are interested in learning more about the origins of media literacy and how thoughts about literacy have evolved through the years, the following publications may be of interest to you.

Hobbs, R. (Ed.) (2016). *Exploring the roots of digital and media literacy through personal narrative.* Temple University Press.

Kellner, D. & Share, J. (2007). Critical media literacy is not an option. *Learning Inquiry, 1,* (1), 59–69. DOI:10.1007/s11519–007-0004-2.

Kellner, D., & Share, J. (2005). Toward critical media literacy: Core concepts, debates, organizations, and policy. *Discourse: Studies in the cultural politics of education, 26,* (3), 369–386.

Kress, G. (2000). Multimodality, in B. Cope & M. Kalantzis, *Multiliteracies: Literacy learning and the design of social futures.* Routledge.

Thevenin, B. (2022). *Making media matter: Critical literacy, popular culture, and creative production.* Routledge.

Macedo, D. & Steinberg, S. R. (Eds.) (2007). *Media literacy: A reader.* Peter Lang.

Mills. K. A. (2016). *Literacy theories for the digital age: Social, critical, multimodal, spatial, material, and sensory lenses.* Multilingual Matters.

# Media Work: The Model

In this chapter I am going to present a model with the intention of giving you a way to think about media literacy as a process that can be infused into various aspects of your teaching. This is not a step-by-step or prescriptive approach. Indeed, a common theme in critical media education is that there is not a singular approach. Media literacy can enter spontaneously into a classroom activity or discussion; it can be a collaborative or individual assignment; it could be part of a larger project. In any case, you need to be intentional in your presentation and discussions, link critical media analysis to language and culture, and engage students in meaningful tasks. I call this process *media work.*

We can start with thinking about the basic components of media work. These include content, processes, and context, each with their own components. Content can be described in terms of its *modality*[1] (sensory pathways, formats and platforms), the *symbols* used to convey meaning (text, images, sounds, movement, touch), and the *storyline* that is conveyed both directly and indirectly. These three components (modality, symbols, storylines) are the *content* of media work and overlap and reinforce one another. They constitute the "media" in media work.

Next come the *processes* that constitute the "work" in media work. These processes include observing, interrogating, interpreting, reflecting, and responding. *Observation* is about looking around, documenting what you see, and remaining open to seeing the unexpected. *Interrogation* takes a close, detailed look at media (e.g., printed ads, news, posters, audio podcasts, zines, music, TikTok videos, Instagram posts), potentially questioning and problematizing every dimension of content and context. Through the process of *interpretation*, we ask how individual and social perspectives offer multiple ways of "reading" media, and through *reflection* we think about what shapes our own and others'

---

1. I use "modality" throughout this book to refer to modes of communication. This entails the actual media, their linguistic and nonlinguistic features, and the sensory pathways they draw on.

interpretations. *Responding* is a multifaceted process. It can include classroom discussions, short assignments, or projects. Responding can also include taking action outside of the classroom such as joining a club, creating posters or other media for the school, or attending community events.

The *context*, as you can imagine, is unlimited in scope. The components presented here are intended as guides for thinking about what impacts meaning-making. *Time* and *place* situate media and how they are produced and distributed, connected to social narratives, and embraced or dismissed. *People* refers to the status, authority, and power conveyed through media as well as the interactional dynamics among consumers and producers. *Identities* refers to roles we play, roles that are ascribed to us, and how these roles shape our realities. *Resources* include physical tools for accessing, creating, and responding, as well as social resources that shape one's relationship to media. *Systems*[2] is a large category that refers to culture as a system of shared beliefs, values, behaviors, and histories that profoundly impact what we see, how we act, and how we evaluate and respond to various situations. Systems naturally include ideologies—I use systems here in that broad sense with the understanding that individuals and groups conduct their lives using many different systems, even sometimes in contradiction with one another. Systems can include several cultures and identities through which an individual sees the world. Systems influence what we need and desire. You can think of this as intersectionality, where identities and social roles converge to make our experiences both unique as well as shared with others. The basic model of media work with three main components is visualized in figure 4, with the processes in the middle to emphasize their connection to both content and context.
All three of these components—content, contexts, and processes—consist of layers of elements that interact with one another dynamically. Media work moves around and through these layers, as if they were loose sheets of paper that can be stacked and reshuffled at any time as depicted in figure 5.

Keep in mind that media work is not a singular approach. It takes on many forms (see chapters 4 and 5 for extended examples). For example, my study of anti-racist yard signs in small communities during the COVID-19 pandemic included almost every element in the model, but place and time were

---

2. Hall et al. in their book *Among Cultures* (2022, p. 5), describes systems as "any group of elements that are organized in such a way that the elements are able to do things they couldn't do individually." Systems include norms of behaviors and expectations for places like classrooms and court rooms, for events like weddings and grocery shopping, and for functions like making requests. Media play a large part in systems as they help to create norms as well as recreate and disrupt them.

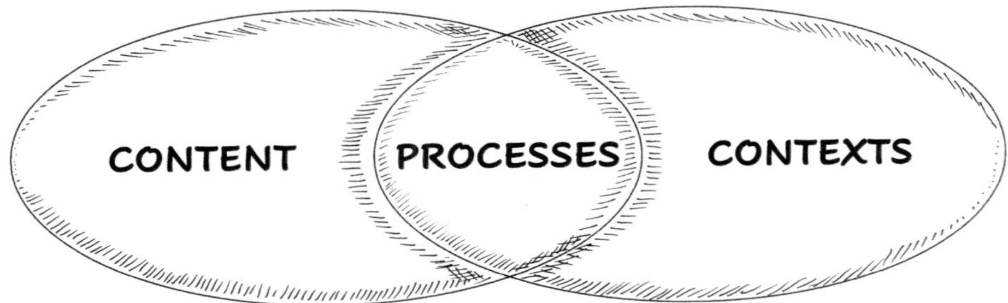



**Figure 4**

particularly important to the meaning-making process. In a time of restrictions to public spaces and events, private spaces such as yards became platforms for messages of solidarity and division in local communities (Chamberlin, 2021). Here's another example. If you look at the content of emails or texts sent to families from schools (see figures 6 and 7), it is important to unravel all of the elements outlined in the model, but it might turn out that modalities, relationships, identities, interrogation, systems, and responses merit the deepest exploration.

The language in these messages raises questions such as who is receiving these emails and texts and why? What is the MCPC? When is the SpringFest and what are "parents" supposed to do for it? Who is included or excluded by the word "parents"? It is not clear from the email that "program planning" refers to course selections for students in their upcoming move to the middle school. Missing out on information about program planning can be detrimental to a student's course of study, but here it is placed in the same sentence as a festival. What if someone cannot make it to this meeting? Will they be left

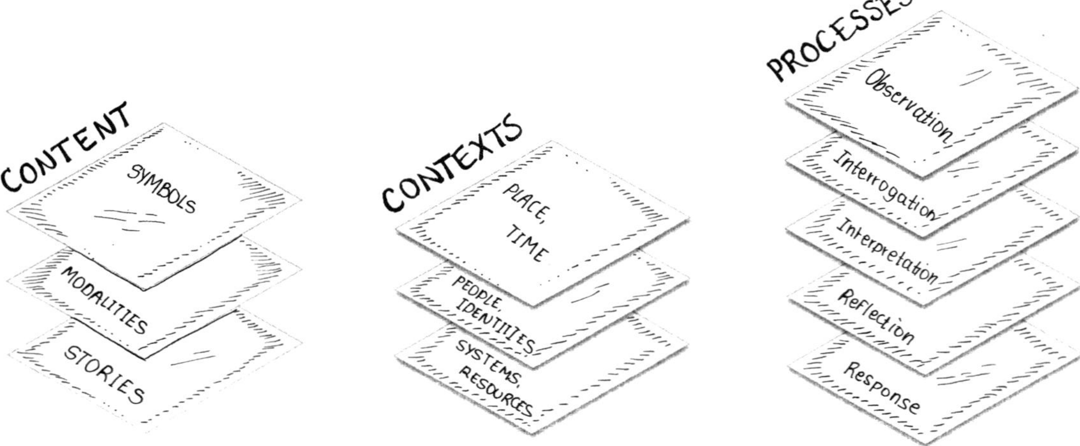



**Figure 5**

<Parent-LISTSERVE@your.school.

To all parents of 6<sup>th</sup> graders:

Don't forget this week's meeting of the MCPC that will be held at Grove Elementary.

All are encouraged to attend as we will be discussing the Spring Fest and program planning for middle School.

**Figure 6**

**Figure 7**

out? Who can be contacted to get more information? The text, sent out in the middle of the day, is another example of a communication that is restricted by its modality (texting) to include a minimum of information. For those who are participating for the first time, where are the old and new rooms? When are the students supposed to eat? Is a dinner provided?

These messages not only assume all recipients are fluent in English, they also assume that everyone knows about certain yearly events or about expectations for involvement. The messages conveyed are not inclusive, and the relationship between schools and families might be affected. This example shows how media work can unravel messages first by observing and interrogating the content, then by interrogating, interpreting, reflecting on, and responding to the context. Any media source, such as a newspaper article, meme, map, movie, song, or video, can be explored through media work, but the process must be fluid rather than prescriptive. How teachers encourage students to apply media work will be informed by their understanding of their teaching contexts and of some key ideas from media studies, communication, and applied linguistics. The ideas I describe in the following sections provide a foundation for how and why I use media to teach about language and culture.

## What Informs Media Work?

The easy answer to this question is "everything." But this is not a helpful answer. To be helpful, I want to share with you the ideas that ground media work. Grounding means that these ideas form the theoretical basis of my pedagogy, and I use them to guide my decision-making. But grounding also means that I can use these ideas in my classrooms to address contradictions, ambiguities, and controversies generated through media work. I draw on these ideas to respond to my students and to teach them about the power of language and media. Discussions about culture and media can bring emotions and values to the surface; many people, after all, have value-based *opinions* about media that they are not hesitant to express. As an educator I want my students to be able to talk about media, language, and culture in informed ways based on their ability to make sense of their social environments through different analytical lenses. Individual opinions cannot be ignored, but they have to be seen as part of more complex and interpretive processes. When we do media work with students, therefore, we need to model a process that is based on more than opinion. When we ground our work in solid theories and concepts, we are showing our students how do to the same.

One way to think about media work is that it can be divided into different types of knowledge. Meyrowitz (1998) discusses the content of media (what we see), the grammar of media (how it is presented), and the medium (how it is delivered to us) as three approaches that are needed in media literacy education. Lewis and Jhally (1998) argue that textual analysis must be accompanied by contextual analysis. They say, "Media literacy, in short, is about more than the analysis of messages, it is about an awareness of why those messages are there" (p. 111). Media work combines the ideas that the content of media are rich resources for exploring language and that the examination of modalities, stories, and contexts connects language to society. Grammar, medium, text, context—all of these can be discussed independently, but media work is about exploring how they intersect and affect each other. As I present the following "big ideas" that anchor media work, keep in mind that they each contribute to different parts of the overall model and that these contributions can shift and overlap.

## The Big Ideas Behind Media Work

To manage the flexible nature of media work, I rely on a foundation of interrelated ideas from language, culture, communication, and media studies. These concepts guide the design of activities, help to maintain focus on communication processes, and can be drawn on as needed to respond to students' needs. These ideas can be organized in three general areas: the symbolic nature of language and media, systematic methods for looking at media, and the potential effects of media. In other words, these ideas answer the questions of what, how, and why?

### *What Does Media Work Look For?*

Language is a symbolic system that depends on both the referential and social to provide meaning. For example, the exact object or idea that a word refers to can sometimes be shown as a tangible object or described in accurate detail (such as in a dictionary). This referential meaning is augmented by social meaning that comes from the context, the status of the communicators, and the knowledge they all bring to the communicative event. We can all find a technical definition of "snow," for example, but what it means to different people in different places and times will vary greatly. And this variation can occur because of the symbolic nature of language and its reliance on social processes and culture to provide meaning. Further, there are words that are more abstract, such as "love," "hate," and "pain." How do you define love? There is no way to absolutely define this word, so we have to do our best with the symbolic resources that we have. Language is not a direct representation of our thoughts or feelings; it is a symbolic system that allows us to express our thoughts and feelings as best we can. It should be no surprise that language is flawed. Sometimes we can describe a feeling in one language more concisely than in another. Sometimes words are inadequate, so we use other means to express ourselves: nonverbal communication, visual and performing arts, poetry, or music. And, sometimes, we miscommunicate because of different interpretations.

In addition, as part of a symbolic system, language is both arbitrary and conventional. In introductory linguistic classes we often learn that language is arbitrary. There is no logical, inherent reason why the letters I am typing on this keyboard represent the sounds and meanings that we connect to them. But of course letters and words have meaning! Of course they do, but the meaning between the "signifier" (that is the symbol such as a letter in our alphabet) and the "signified" (the object or concept that it refers to) is an arbitrary one, deriving not from an inherent relationship between the signifier and signified themselves, but from the meaning that is created through social processes (de Saussure, 1966; Foucault, 1972). In other words, the letters $C$, $O$, and $W$ mean nothing by themselves, but they take on meaning that is constructed through consensus in language communities. This arbitrary relationship makes it possible for the animal to be represented by "cow" in English, "wah-ga" in Cherokee, "krowa" in Polish, and "baka" in Tagalog. Further, this word can connote something sacred, a resource for nutrition, a commodity, a logo for a fast-food company, and different words for "cow" may exist within each language to index the animals' age, role, and type. This arbitrary nature of language allows us to generate richness, nuance, and creativity, whether it be in prose, poetry, song lyrics, or memes.

At the same time, meaning is not haphazard but derives from layers of historic events and complex social processes as well as individual responses. Signs and symbols relate to conventional meanings, allowing those who produce a text or image to assume that those who receive it will interpret it in an intended way. Without this conventionality, language would not be an effective tool for communication. And as signs change over time, new meanings become appropriated by new groups for new conventional usages. Thousands of examples can exemplify this point. *Platform* is a stable, human-made, structure that rises above its surrounding area; or is it a set of ideas that guide a political stance; or is it a new app for your phone? We can guess meaning from context because language is conventional; and we can use the word "platform" in different ways because language is arbitrary.

## How Do We Look Closely at Media?

Depending on your disciplinary background and goals, media can be analyzed in many different ways. For language teaching and learning it makes sense to focus on language, but the complexities of today's media formats offer opportunity for so much more. We can look at, for example, how messages are transformed as they move from one modality or frame to another, such as memes. We can look for language varieties and how they are linked to social class and the identity of communicators. We can look at the order and layout in which information is presented as a reflection of its importance. We notice whose voices are heard and whose are omitted. We can examine relationships among participants (producers, consumers, prosumers), cultural narratives, ideologies, communities, and history. The depth to which analytical methods are taught and applied in media work will vary. I encourage you to explore different methods in order to have a wide repertoire available, but I want to offer you a place to start. Media work can involve combinations of ideas from discourse analysis, semiotics, critical discourse analysis (CDA), content analysis, media ecology, and linguistic landscapes. These approaches all offer perspectives on the relationships among media, audiences, and social factors, and each contribute something unique to media work.

Discourse analysis focuses in detail on linguistic features such as sequences of utterances or sentences, dialect markers, tenses, interruptions, hesitations, turn-taking, intonation, and semantics, to name just a few. We can use discourse analysis to talk to students about variation in grammatical forms, vocabulary, dialects, pronunciation, the selection of pronouns, tense, and many other aspects of speech or texts. Discourse analyses highlight choices that are made to emphasize certain ideas and social norms, validate identities, and shift responsibility and agency of subjects. In media work, discourse analysis informs observation and interpretation, but it does not fully address the social and cultural aspects of interrogation. For that, I draw on ideas from semiotics and CDA.

Semiotics, or the study of signs and their meaning, dives deeper into symbolic representations, recognizing images, gestures, sounds, and other nonverbal dimensions of communication as part of the meaning-making process. Traditionally, semiotics has focused on meaning created through text and images that are presented in printed formats that offer relatively stable representations of meaning. As illustrated in figure 8, a broadsheet newspaper in the 1860s consisted of six narrow columns of small print, no visuals, and barely discernible titles in upper case but not in a large font. Only small amounts of blank space (and not much of it at that) indicated the separation of stories. Readers were expected to search for information and make their own choices

**Figure 8**

about what was relevant. Credibility was grounded in the written word, and the format shaped a publisher–reader relationship in which the publisher was charged with choosing what was important, and the readers were responsible for discerning what they should pay attention to. A certain stability (though not equilibrium) was maintained through this unspoken relationship and from the text-only nature of this printed medium.

In contrast, a modern front page is designed to tell you what you should pay attention to, and the meaning-making process is destabilized. Text does not always dominate; authority can be placed in non-text-based material; and creative layouts with colors, movement, sound, and images organize and highlight information differently. Large bold headlines and images, for example, impose a level of importance. Moreover, the boundaries between producers and consumers, different genres, fact and fiction, experts and novices, knowledge and information, are blurred as never before (Kress, 2010). For example, a news website organizes and presents information through imagery, grabs attention much like advertisements do, and positions viewers as individuals whose specific interests should be met, rather than as community members whose collective needs should be addressed.

Today's media is an unstable semiotic cornucopia of multiple modalities, shifting social patterns, and choices. We can see this play out in blurred formats such as infomercials and edutainment. Nevertheless, the layout of text and images within framed screens or printed materials still organize and direct attention, and language choices carry much symbolic weight. Social semiotics gives us a lens to see these fluid multimodalities, consider the audience as active in the meaning-making process, and link linguistic, visual, and auditory codes to social relationships of power.

CDA looks at media texts (including language, imagery, and nonverbal aspects) as semiotic activities that reflect ideological assumptions and power relations (Fairclough, 1989, 2010, 2011; Scollon & Scollon, 2003; van Dijk, 1993; Wodak, 2012, 2013; Wodak & Meyer, 2016). CDA examines *ideational functions* (representations of what the world is supposed to look like), *interpersonal functions* (who is involved and what are their roles?), and relations (what relationships are established between participants?) (Fairclough, 2010). And CDA goes further. Fairclough (2010) includes "intertextual analysis" in his CDA framework to explore conventionalized practices such as the organization and structure of communicative events, modes of delivery, styles associated with specific genres or mixtures of genres, available cultural narratives, and tensions between public and private domains. Fairclough (2010) refers to "intertextuality" as a way to look at the mediation between texts and contexts. An intertextual analysis might reveal how a popular idiom is creatively and even unpredictably transformed over and over again in a meme, or how politicians change conversational tone to connect with different audiences. In both cases, the transformed texts contribute to changes in discourse practices. Intertextuality is about how the text and context weave together in various patterns, textures, and tensions. If we look again at the 1860s broadsheet, the content is certainly embedded in the historical context, but the form—layout, font, formality—reflects expectations of literacy, confers credibility and authority on authors, and defines social relationships by including or excluding certain voices. As newspapers have transformed into their modern renditions, they both reflect and create changing social relationships, norms, and expectations. (For more on CDA as a methodological approach in applied linguistics, I encourage you to read further from the list at the end of this chapter.) For media work, CDA reminds us that media, audiences, and social factors are dynamic and interrelated.

Although media work is largely qualitative, there are quantitative or descriptive dimensions to it. I sometimes use the method of content analysis in the "observation" process of media work as a place to start. A content analysis is a systematic description of communication or media content in which categories of analysis are clearly defined.[3] For example, we could look at illustrated children's books in a classroom library and make an inventory of what languages and cultures are represented, how diversity is portrayed in images, how families are defined, and so on. The inventory might include details about the characters: gender, age, ethnicity, race, physical attributes, personality attributes, relationship to other characters (family, friend, stranger, student-teacher, etc.), and behaviors or actions. A content analysis can also focus on the text by making a list of the adjectives used to describe each character or the verbs associated with the actions of each character. If you are working with young language learners, you can focus on the observed vocabulary and how students interpret it. Interrogation, interpretation, reflection, and response can be realized informally with class discussions of which characters the students like most or identify with. What do they like about them? Would they change anything about them? What do they think the characters will do next? What other characters would the students like to see in books? Ask students to create and describe characters that they would like to see in a book. This is media work about voice, identity, and representation based on content analysis.

For older learners, a content analysis can be the first step to a deeper qualitative interrogation of actions and behaviors and texts associated with different attributes of characters. Students can interpret the importance of these associations and reflect on their social and personal meanings. Responses can entail replication of the content analysis to another group of books or collection of media, or curation of media samples that provide alternate representations. Whether working with younger or older students, content analysis is a springboard for media work. It encourages observations of details that can be used for later qualitative analyses (see Chapter 3 for detailed questions that guide the processes of media work).

When I first became interested in how accents are used to create identities in Hollywood comedy films, it was easy for me to find examples that fit into my hypothesis that non-North American accented speech was associated with negative stereotypes. In fact, in today's mediascapes we can find examples of almost anything, and we can easily ignore examples that don't support our claims. Looking into a mirror, though, is what we want to avoid. Instead, we need to make objective observations of a well-defined, contextualized sample and provide clear evidence to back up our claims. My study of a character,

---

3. For advanced students I also present Glaser & Strauss' (1967) method of grounded theory in which you begin by looking at data and allow themes and patterns to emerge, rather than beginning with categories a priori.

Nazo, in the internationally successful comedy *Big Daddy* (Dugan, 1999), was inspired by conversations I had had in class about this character (Chamberlin-Quinlisk, 2012). I thought the character was offensive. My students at the time had mixed feelings, but most thought that Nazo was a funny, endearing character who despite being portrayed as inferior was still a representation of an English language learner and immigrant that was "better than nothing." I knew that I simply couldn't go through the movie and pick out convenient examples that would support my claim. I had to look closely at all of Nazo's behaviors (verbal and nonverbal), and try to understand these behaviors and how they can be read as "better than nothing," endearing, or offensive.

I began by transcribing the verbal and nonverbal behaviors of every scene in which Nazo appeared in the movie. I documented the number of lines he had, described the scenes in which he appeared with other characters, and noted the occasions in which his speech contained what might be considered "non-standard" features. In addition, I noted the topics of his speech, the emotional qualities of his utterances, as well as physical dimensions such as clothing, space, and proximity to other characters. This content analysis was a necessary place to start this media work and serves as an example of the observation process. Next, I was able to interrogate, interpret, reflect, and respond to this portrayal based on observable data, rather than selected or anecdotal evidence. I can show how Nazo made fewer errors than his monolingual English-speaking counterparts, yet was referred to as an incompetent, illiterate speaker. I can discuss his status among all the characters and give examples of his childlike behaviors, and his portrayal as unambitious and lazy. I can reflect on why this character is endearing and acceptable to a wide audience. I still use this example in class to introduce the observation process and to elicit conversations related to interrogation, interpretation, reflection, and response: Are representations of accents different in popular media today? Have new modalities contributed to changing or maintaining evaluations of accents and language learners? Is it okay to make fun in the name of entertainment? Do media portrayals of different accents affect attitudes? Each time I share this example with students, their responses are new and insightful. The questions we can ask about even just one media sample continually change. But we still need a place to start.

There are so many things to observe in any given medium, even those that appear simple in design. As I lead students through the processes of media work, I give them a handout (hard copy or digital version), or we generate a list together of what to look for (see figure 9). I emphasize that these concepts vary in their presence and power, are often interrelated or overlapping, and can be interpreted in various ways. I remind them to look closely at language, nonverbal communication, and elements of design.

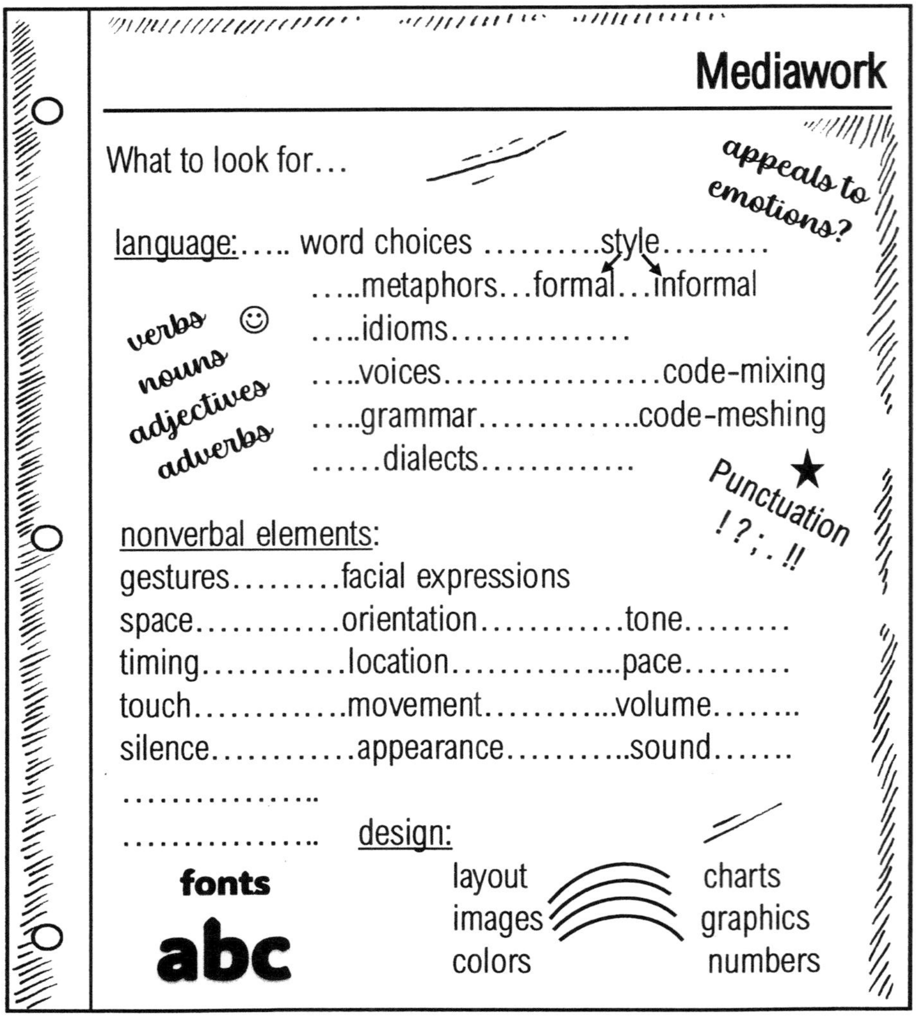

**Figure 9**

*Why Look Closely at Media?*

Even though we are not passive consumers of media who are directly affected by everything we see and hear, we are crucial participants in mediated storytelling processes. We play many roles. We can be creators, disrupters, editors, victims, consumers, educators, learners, and performers. And these roles can often be blurred, much as the lines between entertainment and news, education, or advertising can be blurred. Whether we like it or not, we are part of these complex communication dynamics, and we need to understand the parts we play. There are numerous theories and lines of research that explore the effects of media on people's attitudes, behaviors, and interactions (see Oliver et al.'s 2019 *Media effects: Advances in theory and research* for an almost 500-page overview), but I will focus here on two ideas from media studies that continually remind me of why media literacy is important. The first—cultivation theory—has to do with the storytelling power of media, and the second—media ecology—explores how different media modalities shape interactions, perceptions of credibility, and the ways we relate to our environments. In language teaching contexts, these ideas relate to intercultural and pragmatic dimensions of language learning.

From time to time, I refer directly to cultivation theory in classes or workshops when I hear arguments that nobody really gets hurt by media stereotypes because "it's just entertainment," and more commonly the claim that "media might affect others, but not me." To address these challenges, I think of a place where most of the students have never been, and I ask them to quickly write down what comes to their minds when I name the place. I might say "Africa." As a class they share the words, ideas, and phrases on a board or screen. We compare the lists generated by those who have never been there to the lists of those who have been to, are from, or have lived in an African country. You can imagine how different the lists might be, but the fact that those who have never been there even have an image of "Africa" (often an essentialized, monolithic one) in their minds proves the point that we learn some things second hand from various media sources. Next, we code the items on the list for negative and positive connotations and the attitudes or evaluations they incite. It doesn't take long to see how media can cultivate ideas and attitudes of places, people, and events when first-hand experience or adequate research is lacking.

Cultivation theory dates back to the 1980s and the work of George Gerbner and his associates. They were interested in the effects of television and movies on audiences of heavy versus light viewers. Gerbner described television as a powerful storyteller that had superseded the family, community, schools, and other institutions as the dominant mode of transmitting cultural knowledge. Cultivation theory posits that the more we see certain ideas and representations on screens, the more these images indirectly cultivate attitudes about the way the world works. Gerbner et al. (1980) found that heavy viewers of television were more likely to believe that a woman could never be president, that poverty was not a big problem, and that more policing was needed to manage crime rates, which were actually declining at the time (Glassner, 2009). These attitudes, according to the theory, are cultivated by years of repeated, stable images of women in submissive roles, of underrepresentation of poor people on television, and of the overrepresentation of White women as victims of violent crimes. Though attributing little agency to viewers and sociocultural factors, cultivation theory has generated a wealth of studies about the power of

media representation; moreover, it reminds us that within our rapidly changing and unstable media environments, certain stories endure despite changes
in presentation (Morgan & Shanahan, 2010; Signorelli, Morgan, & Shanahan,
2019). For example, mainstream film and media productions rely on characters'
accents and dialects to reveal impressions of their authority, agency, and trust-
worthiness. The further away they are from a mythical "standard American
English," the less likable the character (Chamberlin-Quinlisk, 2003, 2012a,
2012b; Lippi-Green, 2012). Although the identities of the characters may have
changed over time, the connection between a non-standard American and/or
foreign accent and villainy has remained stable. Repeated images of "others" as
dangerous, exotic, lazy, or unambitious cultivate a climate of distrust and suspicion. We should ask why these portrayals endure, and how they have been
disrupted. Cultivation theory can be a catalyst for thinking about the possible
impacts of media on our lives and how we can respond to them.

Second, I draw on media ecology as a big idea that has influenced my
conceptualization of media work. Media ecology is the study of interactions
between humans and their media environments. Casey Man Kong Lum
(2006) describes it as an intellectual tradition that explores how modes of
communication impact social organization and thinking. Media ecologists
ask how different media shape information, patterns of interaction, conceptualizations of truth, and even a sense of the self (Strate, 2017). You may
have heard the phrase "the medium is the message" avowed by Marshall
McLuhan in the 1960s. This phrase became popular not only in academic
circles, but also in popular culture as many began to question how media
was being driven by commercial and corporate motives. In his seminal work,
*Understanding media: The extensions of man*, McLuhan (1964) was not concerned so much with the content of television, but with the symbolic form of
this mode of communication and its effects on culture. Two take-aways from
McLuhan are that media are part of a sensory environment that impacts how
we perceive information (visual, auditory, tactile), and that media are a part
of our symbolic environment that defines how we come to understand the
world. These sensory and symbolic processes work together to create human
experiences of communicating. Decades later, in our current world of sensory
experiences through multimodalities, there is a renewed interest the ways in
which format determines how information can be produced, conveyed, and
received.

Although I had heard the phrase "the medium is the message" and had seen
Marshall McLuhan's cameo in the movie "Annie Hall," I did not truly connect to the idea until 1987 when I picked up a copy of Neil Postman's *Amusing*

*ourselves to death: Public discourse in the age of show business* (1986).[4] I was living abroad then without a television for the first time in my life, and couldn't put the book down. In *Amusing ourselves to death,* Postman argues that television is a modality that *requires* information to be fragmented, simplified, and decontextualized. Television is conducive to entertainment and advertising, but not news, politics, or education. Postman asserts, in fact, that television can only do one thing—entertain. I got it! The medium is the message! This is why news programs have logos and theme music and present news in a matter of seconds rather than the minutes or hours needed to fully understand an issue or event. That epiphany was over 35 years ago, and it has only intensified throughout the years. Today we find ourselves surrounded by screens almost everywhere we go, with information presented to us in entertaining fragments. The impact of media formats on messages carries over to our professional lives.

When preparing for a conference presentation or classroom lesson, I am expected to arrange my ideas into slides that can be projected on a screen while I talk. Sometimes this works for me, but more often than not it's a struggle to organize my message in a linear format. In a classroom, following a linear set of slides can downplay the role of feedback and comments from students that often lead to spontaneous, relevant, and meaningful discussions. Even the slide presentations that allow for movement around a screen in a nonlinear order, zoom in and out, and show connections, still impose a format with limits (not to mention that it tends to make the audience dizzy).

Yet we always have a format to conform to, and each has benefits and constraints. Even in writing this book I have to constantly think about the "logical order" in which to present my ideas. In spoken discourse I have the opportunity to get off track a bit, loop around from idea to idea, and respond immediately to feedback. So, which is more logical? Which is more valid or credible? As we are presented with new modalities at such a rapid rate, we must question what each one has to offer and what their limits might be. Do the benefits outweigh the limitations? Does the form in which the message is conveyed change the message itself? How do different modalities allow for different ways of learning and responding?

---

4. Postman argues for the supremacy of print media over electronic and digital modalities but does not consider how many voices have been excluded from print modalities. I do not agree with his hierarchical classification of modalities and who they represent, but I do find persuasive his ideas about fragmented, decontextualized information and how "news," as well as politics, education, and other facets of our lives, has become entertainment.

What happens to an idea when it is conveyed through a social media platform versus the same idea conveyed in a long speech, article, video, conversation, text, or book? From a media ecology standpoint, most social media platforms do not allow for in-depth analysis. They reduce complex issues to consumable, bite-size utterances. Moreover, the brevity of posts encourages the use of rhetorical devices such as humor, emotional language, or sensationalism to capture attention. Similarly, newspaper and website headlines grab attention through deliberate word choices and images, although these are complemented by space for more detailed explanations. In short, questions of "fake news" and credibility are not only about the stories being told but also about the platforms used to tell the stories (more about this in Chapter 6).

Media ecology can also make us think about language classrooms in different ways. First, we need to reflect on the media we use every day for teaching. I have spent hours creating slides, liquid syllabi, modules, calendars, websites, only to be told by students that they don't look at them very often. They want classroom experiences, not more information on screens. The course management platforms we have at school are excellent for organization, record keeping, and accommodating diverse needs, but they don't teach. Remember the "ooohs" and "aaahs" I talked about in the introduction? These were reactions to modalities, not relevancy or meaning; those reactions reflect a society where ethos is driven by performance and entertainment, just as Postman warned. To be clear, I am not a technophobe, and I use digital resources for teaching every day. Media ecology reminds me, however, that just because I can, does not mean I should. We need to question the value of a format in relationship to meeting specific goals.

The same questioning holds true for what we assign to our students. Is the format in alignment with the learning outcomes? For example, I think of a middle school assignment I recently saw to create a "documentary" that incorporates research, an oral history interview, and images. Students were given options for how to do it, but no formal training. One student collected their required information but had no idea how to put it together in a coherent story for a documentary, or how to use the unfamiliar technology. They struggled with the organization of ideas, trying to figure out what was most important and how to show that in the documentary format. Maybe this was a good challenge for them—a way to be creative and think outside of the box. Or maybe they spent more time on the medium and not enough time on synthesizing ideas from their research. Did the required format force them to organize material because it had to "fit" a formula, or did they organize material in a way that made it meaningful? Did their teacher assume that all students were familiar with the technology? Just as we can look at a variety of resources and platforms for media work, we must also keep in mind how we ultimately want media work to be processed and shared. Will your media work assignment include material that is a meaningful part of students' lives as opposed to a media source that is fun, but less relevant? What options will students have for sharing their media work with you, the class, or a wider audience? And how might the audience be given a chance to respond?

Finally, one of the most influential ideas that media work draws from is the concept of linguistic landscapes (LLs). A discussion of LLs could fit under the questions of "what do we look at" and "how do we look," but I chose to place it under "why look closely at media" because as a whole, paying attention to our LLs can tell us a great deal about who we are, the communities we live in, and the communities that we imagine for ourselves. LLs as research and pedagogy can encourage teachers and students alike to notice more and potentially engage more. When I first heard this term, decades ago, it captured my attention and never let go. I was not alone. LLs took off as an approach to looking at meaning created in public spaces, mostly urban, through signage on billboards, vehicles, storefronts, traffic signs, etc. Think of walking down a busy street in a city you know and taking in all of the text, symbols, and imagery you see as you move through the space. This is an LL. Then, think about what all of it means. Which languages are being used to convey what information and to whom? Whose voices are authoritative or welcoming? Which languages are valued or seen as prestigious? Whose voices are missing or subordinated? How is language used to convey ideologies? The list of questions goes on and on. Indeed, LL research and writing addresses an enormous scope of inquiry about how LLs reflect linguistic hierarchies, post-colonial language policies, social changes, language discrimination, and political movements and ideologies (Blommaert, 2013; Gorter, 2006; Nambu, 2021).

A vast amount of scholarly work in LLs describes the power of semiotic choices used to convey messages about public services (health care, education, emergency services), tourism (museums, maps, historical markers), transportation (schedules, traffic signs, parking), and commercial enterprises (advertisements, store logos and signs, restaurant signage). LL work today looks at suburban, rural, as well as urban spaces and can be used as a pedagogical approach to developing language awareness in local spaces such as classrooms, schools, neighborhoods, and virtual spaces (Dubreil et al., 2023; Malinowski et al., 2020). I relate media work examples shared in chapters 4 and 5 to the idea of interpreting language within specific landscapes.

LL scholarship, moreover, is not simply focused on visual semiotics, written language, and direct messages. Work in LLs expands into soundscapes, or what we hear as we walk through a public space (Birnie, 2022) as well as "skinscapes," or how the body becomes a dynamic space in which tattoos, for example, convey meaning (Peck & Stroud, 2015). LL research also takes a deep dive into language policies and practices in multilingual societies. It explores how immigrant communities are civically engaged or empowered, how voices of protest are expressed in public spaces, and how language policies play out during times of crisis (Baranova, 2023, 2024; Blackwood & Dunlevy, 2021; Gorter, 2006; Gorter & Cenoz, 2015; Gorter et al., 2019; Rubdy & Ben-Said, 2016; Shohamy et al. 2010). The emphasis is not only on language and imagery, but on relational dynamics of multicultural spaces, and the interplay of political, historical, and economic agendas. In other words, LLs reveal much about multilingualism, language hierarchies, translanguaging, and language policies in the places we live and work (Melo-Pfeifer, 2023). The media work I present in Chapter 6 echoes LL research by addressing language discrimination and disinformation about issues that affect language learners and teachers.

## What's Next?

Whether we are using mandatory textbooks, prescribed lessons, our own curated collections of media, or student selections of popular culture, media literacy education can naturally work its way into our practice. Every medium we use holds the potential for observing, interrogating, interpreting, reflecting and responding. These processes can be applied to the modalities themselves, to the symbols used to convey meaning, and to the stories or social narratives revealed in the media. Media work can begin at various points in the model, and it can focus on whatever is most relevant and meaningful at a given place and time. This flexibility, however, does not preclude a theoretically grounded approach and systematic analyses. Interconnected theories, ideas, and analytical approaches are the cogs around which media work revolves.

The symbolic nature of language means that words, symbols, and meanings are malleable, interpretive, and powerful. Language can be creative, manipulative, inclusive, and exclusive. But media content is not only about words. Language, images, and nonverbal cues are the components of today's multimodal media, and the messages they convey must be seen through the lenses of semiotics and critical analyses. Meaning is generated as texts interact with social contexts. Meaning is also generated through media platforms themselves. Our patterns of communication, ways of participating in our local and global communities, relationships, and conceptualizations of truth, success, and value are in some ways shaped by the tools we use to convey meaning.

And in the classroom, we need to consider the affordances and constraints of the media we use to teach. In the next chapter, I will demonstrate how the big ideas discussed in this chapter can be applied to media work.

KEY IDEAS

    modality

    format

    platform

    symbols

    storyline

    content

    processes

    context

    observing

    interrogating

    interpreting

    reflecting

    responding

    systems

    resources

    referential meaning

    social meaning

    arbitrary

    conventional

    signifier

    signified

    semiotics

    discourse analysis

    critical discourse analysis

    intertextuality

ideational function

interpersonal function

content analysis

cultivation theory

media ecology

linguistic landscapes


QUESTION

1. How do you already use media in your teaching? What formats do you use? Who selected them? What do you do with them? How do students respond to them? What do your students learn from them? How do you know?

2. What effects do you think media have on their audiences? What are some of the factors that mediate the effects? How do you think media has affected you? What do the stories conveyed through media tell you about the way the world works?


EXPLORE

1. Keep a media usage diary for a few days. Keep track of the following information (see figure 10):
   - Bring your "diary" to class or workshop to share with your peers. Were you surprised by how much media you rely on every day?
   - How does the time you spend looking at media correlate with the value of the information you receive? Looking over your list, how would you describe the media you use in terms of "grammar" and "context?" Which media is most critical to your daily tasks? Which ones are less relevant?

2. Choose one public place to conduct an informal content analysis.
   - Examples include shopping centers or malls, schools, tourist sites, parks, community centers, train or metro stations, restaurants, coffee shops, libraries, stadiums, etc. Take notes and counts of all the media you see in this place (standing in one place if it is a large space) and the messages conveyed.
   - What are the general functions of the media (information, warnings, advice, rules, advertisements, entertainment, etc.)?
   - What modalities are used (screens, posters, flyers, bulletin boards, etc.)? Who is represented in the media? How would you describe

| Modality<br>Analog or digital, format, platform? | E-mail<br>*2 accounts* | Texts<br>*Digital* | Newspaper<br>*Online Daily* |
|---|---|---|---|
| Purpose<br>Why did you access this medium? | *For work and for personal communication* | | |
| Time<br>For how long did you accesss the medium? | *At least once per hour during the day* | | |
| Relevancy<br>Did you find what you needed? | *Only 3–4 messages were relevant; the rest were ads or junk* | | |
| Symbols<br>What symbols are used most in this medium? | *Work messages are mostly texts; adverts have a lot of visuals* | | |
| Credibility<br>Do you rely on this medium for information? | *Messages from certain addresses are credible, but others are not. Hard to tell the difference sometimes* | | |

**Figure 10**

the tone or register of the language used? How are images used to convey meaning? Do the messages refer directly or indirectly to other cultural stories (pop culture, historic events, politics, etc.)? How do the media contribute to this place and the way people relate to this place or with each other in this place?

3. What is "friendship"?

How is friendship conceptualized in different contexts and modalities? Use the following chart to think about how you define friendship in specific places and through different modalities (see figure 11).

   a. Who do you consider to be a friend?

   b. What do you talk about?

   c. How much personal information do you disclose?

   d. How would you describe your interactions?

| *Friendship* | Work/school | Social life/ community | Family |
|---|---|---|---|
| Face-to-face | | | |
| Texting | | | |
| Writing | | | |
| Telephone | | | |
| Video call | | | |
| Instagram/Facebook | | | |
| Email | | | |

**Figure 11**

LEARN MORE

If you want to learn more, these books offer theories about how media affects individuals, social relationships, language, and the way we participate in society.

Oliver, M. B., Raney, A. A., & J. Bryant, J. (2019) *Media effects: Advances in theory and research*. Routledge.

Lum, C. M. K (2006). *Perspectives on culture, technology, and communication: The media ecology tradition*. Hampton Press.

McCullough, G. (2019). *Because internet: Understanding how language is changing*. Penguin Random House.

Morgan, M. (2012). *George Gerbner: A critical introduction to media and communication theory*. Peter Lang.

Morozov, E. V. (2014). *To save everything, click here: The folly of technological solutionism*. PublicAffairs.

Postman, N. (1986). *Amusing ourselves to death: Public discourse in the age of show business*. Penguin.

Strate, L. (2014). *Amazing ourselves to death: Neil Postman's brave new world revisited*. Peter Lang.

Turkle, S. (2011). *Alone together: Why we expect more from technology and less from each other*. Basic Books.

To learn more about analytical approaches to media, see:

Berger, A. A. (2019) (6th ed.). *Media analysis techniques*. Sage.

Gee, J.P. (2014b). *How to do discourse analysis: A toolkit*. Routledge.

Kress, G. (2010). *Multimodality: A social semiotic approach to contemporary communication*. Routledge.

Fairclough, N. (2011). *Media discourse*. Bloomsbury Academic.

To learn more about critical approaches in applied linguistics, see:

Chun, C. (2019). Methodological issues in critical discourse studies. In McKinley, J. & H. Rose (Eds.). *The Routledge handbook of research methods in applied linguistics*, 199–210. Routledge.

Chun, C. (2015). *Power and meaning making in an EAP classroom: Engaging with the everyday*. Multilingual Matters.

Kubota, R., & Lin, A. (2009). *Race, culture, and identities in second language education: Exploring critically engaged practice*. Routledge. https://doi.org/10.4324/9780203876657

Lin, A. (2014). Critical discourse analysis in applied linguistics: A methodological review. *Annual Review of Applied Linguistics, 34*, 213–232. doi:10.1017/S0267190514000087

Morgan, B., & Ramanathan, V. (2005). Critical literacies and language education: Global and local perspectives. *Annual Review of Applied Linguistics, 25*, 151–169. doi:10.1017/S0267190505000085

In addition, browsing articles in the following journals (to name just a few) will show you the wide range of application of critical theories and methodologies in applied linguistics:

*Critical Issues in Language Studies*

*Discourse and Society*

*Journal of Language, Identity, and Education*

*Research in the Teaching of English*

*TESOL Quarterly*

*TESOL Journal*

# CHAPTER 3

# Media Work: The Process

It is tempting to present media work as a prescriptive step-by-step model only because that would be an easy and safe way to talk about teaching, but that is not how media work or teaching unfolds. The process does not happen in a linear fashion. There is no fixed order. Typically, some part of a medium catches my attention or is brought to my attention by a student. This could be a visual element, a word, or a phrase, or a feeling invoked through sounds. What happens next can best be described as a messy process in which we zoom in and out, guided by the components of the media work model. In Chapter 2, I presented the model as layers (content, processes, and contexts), each with dimensions that interact with one another. In this chapter, I provide more detailed definitions of what makes up the layers of media work, offer examples of questions that can guide the processes, and illustrate an application of media work from a class in a second language teacher education program.

Let's talk about the model again. At the core are the processes that apply to layers of content and context. The processes of observing, interrogating, interpreting, reflecting, and responding can be applied to modalities, to symbols, to storylines, and to any relevant contextual variables. Media work typically starts with observations, but it is also possible to begin at other points in the process. What captures your attention? You may be listening to a popular song or looking at colorful images of an advertisement in a magazine. You might be watching a movie or program on television and take note of camera angles, accents of characters, and trajectories of storylines. You might be looking at a piece of junk mail that just arrived at your home announcing that you have won a vacation to a warm tropical island. You might be standing in an aisle of a grocery store trying to make sense of labels and ingredients. Or, you might be reviewing a textbook that you are considering adopting for a class next semester. When observing, you should ask: What do you think you see? What do you really see? This stage of media work might include a formal or informal content analysis. Media work could also begin with processes of interrogating and responding. For example, some people in my neighborhood responded to incidents of racial violence and media reports of protests in the United States by posting Black Lives Matter signs in their yards (see figures 12 and 13).

I bought materials, hand painted a sign, and hung it on my porch. It was only after I responded in this way to the events and media coverage that I began to reflect on and interrogate my response. I ended up walking through different neighborhoods to observe signage (see figures 14 and 15) and try to interpret anti-racist messages in my local communities, which led to a study of anti-racist discourse (Chamberlin, 2021).

**Figure 12**

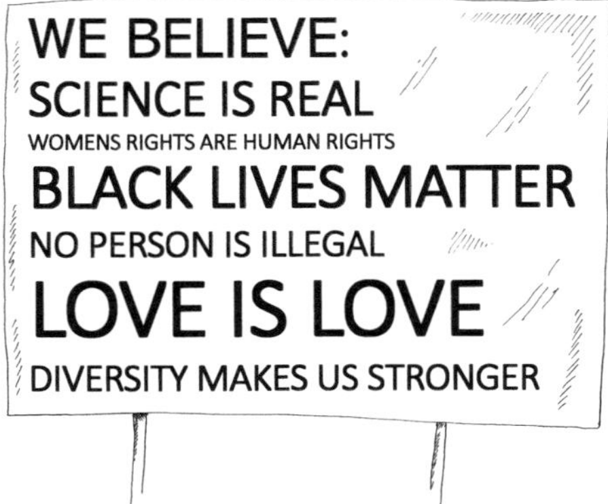


**Figure 13**

However, the process did not end with that study. I continued to interrogate, interpret, and reflect on my own contribution to this mediascape and how the processes of media work apply to all aspects of this specific context. For example, yard signs (figures 12–15) became a popular modality during the COVID-19 pandemic. In some cases they are interpreted as performance, in other cases as sincere displays of solidarity. What

**Figure 14**

**Figure 15**

story did I want to tell? My intent was a sincere show of solidarity, so is that why I made it myself? And what else did I do to back up my intent with action? What about the symbols? Words, colors, font, size? Is the message of those three words the same when it is displayed alongside other messages, or in colors other than black and white? And what does the Black Lives Matter message mean in my neighborhood, my community, nation, and internationally? The questions can go on and on, but the point I am trying to convey is that the processes, content, and context of media work are neither static nor sequential, and their boundaries are overlapping and fluid.

## Defining the Terms of Media Work

Let's begin with the medium itself. You remember from Chapter 1 that media includes analog and digital platforms. In the media work model, this is the *content*, which includes modalities, symbols, and stories (see figure 16).

Media include formats and platforms that convey meaning through various modalities. Media are not limited to books and digital resources but include maps, music, artwork, tattoos, graffiti, shopping lists, food wrappers, billboards, etc. Information is conveyed through certain channels (linguistic and non-linguistic) that are circumscribed by the medium. Videos can rely on visual and audio (speech, sounds, music) elements to convey meaning. Spoken word poetry relies on a mixture of language, voice, gestures, facial expressions, rhythm, pace, tone. Media and their associated modalities are also linked to credibility, accessibility, and participation.

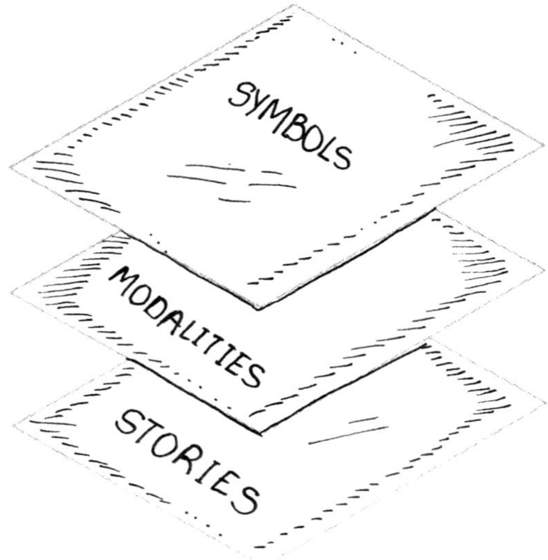


**Figure 16**

Symbols are the linguistic elements, imagery, layout, sounds, movement, and other nonverbal dimensions that contribute to the message of the media. As a language teacher, the linguistic elements will certainly stand out to you, but as you know, language works with other symbolic dimensions of communication to create meaning. This is where you can thoroughly enjoy the adaptable, creative, and arbitrary nature of language at any proficiency level. Look at the words, speech acts, and visual presentation of text. In general, you should ask some questions such as: What kinds of words are used (nouns, adjectives, adverbs, verbs, pronouns)? How is punctuation used? What varieties of language are used (formal, informal, prestige, non-prestige, etc.)? How are images used in this medium (photos, drawing, combinations of form)? How is language presented alongside visual elements (font, layout and design)? How are linguistic, auditory and visual elements used and juxtaposed? Depending on your class level, you can integrate lessons on vocabulary, grammar, genre, pragmatics, dialects, slang, etc.

Media also have explicit and implicit storylines in their content. These stories will vary according to purpose and intent, such as advertisements, entertainment, education, information. We should consider the explicit stories that tell us what happens, who is involved, when and where something takes place, and the implicit storylines that define what is normal, expected, and rewarded in a culture. Every medium tells a story, some more directly than others. You may listen to or read a story with a clear introduction of characters and an evolving plot, denouement, and resolution. Many media stories, however, are more subtle. They might appear to be educational, but they are persuading you to buy something. They might appear to be selling a product, but they are selling an idea. And many media contain mixtures of stories. On the surface we might think that we see something new and daring that breaks away from common stereotypes in a television show, but on closer investigation we see that traditional stories are being retold, only in different ways.

Next is the *context*. This includes an indefinite list of sociocultural variables that may affect how we see media in any situation. The media work model identifies a number of general categories that are not meant to be exhaustive, but instead serve as a guide to what we need to think about: place, time, people, identities, systems, resources, relationships (see figure 17.)

Place can be specific (room, virtual room, building, private digital platform, city, or town) or more general (region, public or private space, country, social media, local or global). Time includes the past, present, and future, and as mediated contexts these can be real or imagined (or a mixture of the two). People and identities refer to the desires (real and perceived) and motivation of your students, your school, or anyone consuming media. How we

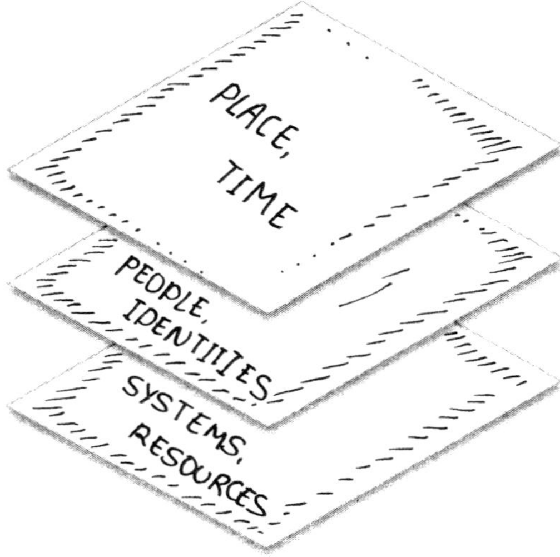



**Figure 17**

interpret media will depend on what we expect or need to get out of it. Desires for quick, emotional, and easily digestible information encourage media to reinforce stereotypes and essentialize identities. Identities also encompass language varieties, as well as gender, ethnicity, profession, sexual orientation, age, ability, religion, social class, and myriad other categories that shape our identities through ascription (how others see us) or avowal (how we choose to perform our identities). Systems refers to the lenses through which we see the world. These lenses are complex fusions of identities, culture, values, ideologies, histories, geographies. I use the term systems rather than "world views" or "cultural lens" because systems are dynamic, made up of many moving parts, and can simultaneously affect and adapt to different situations. The terms "cultural lens" or "world views" tend to convey the notion that cultural identities are monolithic, static, and inextricable from certain ways of seeing the world. An example of this would be the assumption that students from a particular cultural group are better at certain things because of traditional values that are associated with their culture. Systems undoubtedly filter our realities and can be resistant to change, but they are changeable, interconnected, and impacted by learning. Systems tell us what is valuable, how to act in different situations, what to wish for, and how to see ourselves in relation to others. Systems affect every part of media work.

Resources can be symbolic or concrete. Concrete resources are the tangible tools and technologies to which we have access in our daily lives for work, services, and entertainment. Resources relate to distribution as well as access. Symbolic resources include the unquantifiable things such as family members who know how to fill out forms online, the number of books in our homes, trips to libraries, museums, supportive communities, and exposure to diverse forms of media. Relationships are complicated and multilayered. In the larger sense relationships refer to the dynamics and boundaries between those who produce and consume media, noting how much power each has in controlling messages and representations. At another level, relationships can refer to one's status in a community, hierarchies within an organization, student/teacher or teacher/family relationships, professional status, identity roles and expectations, etc. Considering relationships as part of media contexts is a vital part of understanding the nuances of messages.

The processes, as introduced at the beginning of this chapter, are overlapping and can be related to any part of the content and context (see figure 18). To illustrate these processes, let's go back to my exploration of anti-racist media in local communities (Chamberlin, 2021).

Observing involves noticing media in all forms and taking a closer look to see what is really there in terms of content and context. You can think of observation as data collection. In media work, this is where you objectively describe what you see in terms of content as well as context. When I began

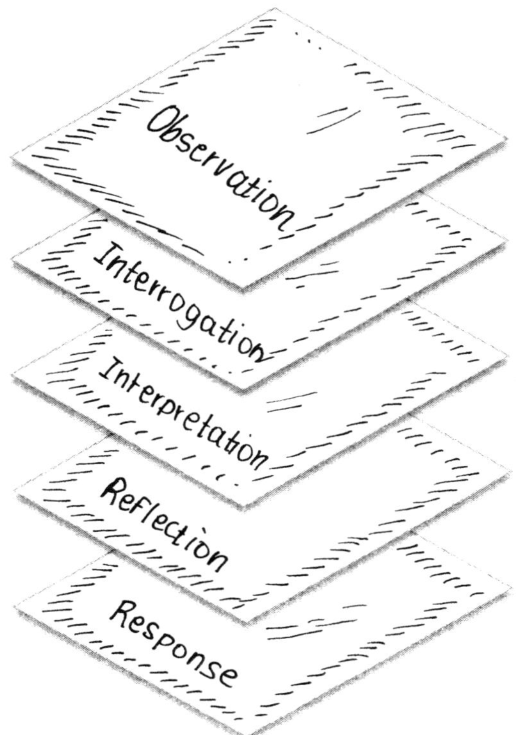


**Figure 18**

to notice certain yard signs with anti-racist messages, I had to make sure that I wasn't seeing only the ones I agreed with. For my study I delineated sections of neighborhoods and compared areas of similar density and then gathered demographic information. I then walked up and down all the streets and took photos of all the yard signs. Next, I interrogated the content and context of these media by problematizing the assumptions and intentions of the community members. Interrogating is about pushing ourselves to ask questions from different perspectives. This was not always easy because of the ideological and emotional messages that certain symbols in these yard signs tapped into. This interrogation forced me to think about myriad circumstances and personal experiences as well as language and aesthetic features that determine the way we interpret messages.

Reflecting includes introspection on all components of media work. In the examination of anti-racist media I reflected on motivations, sincerity, risk-taking, and the conceptualization of anti-racism as action. With my students, we reflected on these yard signs and their ability to reach audiences, convey messages, and symbolize moral positions. We discussed the resources, values, and needs of different communities, especially during times of social tension. Reflection is continual.

Responses are similarly ongoing and multilayered. Responses may be focused on students' media analyses to share with the class, on creation of new mediated messages that respond to content and contexts of the observed media, or on finding ways to participate in communities through effective media. Discussions with students about anti-racist media led to productive conversations about local organizations, civic responsibility, performance of anti-racism on social media, and individual involvement and commitment. Responses may include direct reactions to media work itself, and this can certainly fulfill pedagogical goals. However, responses might also include possibilities for future engagement if students want to explore different modalities and messages and create media that respond to specific issues.


## Guiding Questions for Media Work

The questions presented on the following pages can help you to get started processing the content and thinking about how it connects to contextual variables. These lists are in no way meant to be comprehensive, nor will all questions apply to every media source. Use these questions as catalysts for media work you want to do with your students. Be aware of the fact that you can do "media work" and "media literacy education" without ever having to

**Who** produced this media and for **whom**?

**Who** has the easiest access to this media?

**Who** might not have easy access or access at all to this media?

Does this media offer opportunity for **feedback or responses**? Are responses encouraged or discouraged?

Are there clear boundaries between the **producers and consumers** of this media?

How do the media platforms or formats make use of different **modes** of communication (oral, aural, visual, gestural, touch, movement)?

Do these different **modes** highlight information in different ways?

Do different **modes** of communication convey differnt levels of credibility, authority, and urgency?

Are certain **modes** of communication better suited to different topics?

What **platform** is used?

What modes of communication are tapped into by using this **platform**?

What are the **advantages** of using this media to convey the intended messages?

What are the **constraints** of using this media in terms of accessibility?

What are the **limits** of this media in terms of the type of information that can be conveyed accurately?

Is this medium the best **choice** for conveying the intended messages?

How would the messages be **changed** (or unchanged) if this information were conveyed through different media?

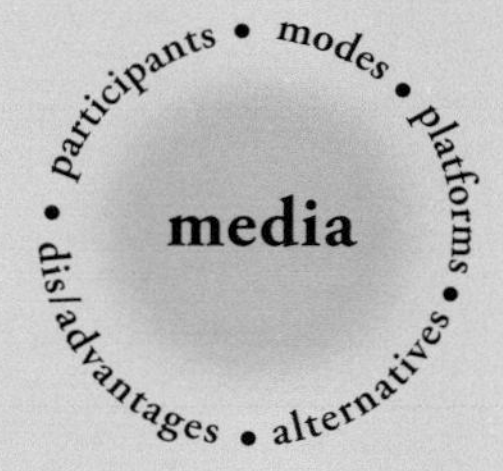


**Figure 19**

mention those words to your students. With a class of visiting 9-year-olds on my college campus, we explored maps and labels used to describe people, nations, and languages. These young students interrogated symbols, identities, and representations, but I did not need to say "let's work on media literacy skills." With a group of visiting international university students, we collected images of signs in commercial, historic, and tourist spaces, comparing mediated messages in urban and suburban areas. These students were able to talk about modalities, symbols, and contexts in intentional ways, and the term "media literacy" naturally came up in our discussions. A key element of media work is for the educator to guide students by asking questions and using accessible vocabulary that is meaningful to their experiences. Figures 19 to 21 provide guidelines, or lists of questions to use as prompts for media work.

What do you notice about the **layout or positioning** of text and images?

What takes up the most **space** and why?

How are **color and font** choices used to enhance messages?

Does this media convey a certain **style** (modern, pop, vintage)?

Are images and objects presented from particular **perspectives**?

Do the **visual elements or layout** convey movement, stability, change, urgency, relaxation, etc.?

How are **sound and movement** used in this media sample?

What do **music and sound** contribute?

How does the **presence and placement** of people, places, and objects convey messages about status and relationships?

What is conveyed through **vocal qualities** such as accent, tone, volume, rate, vocal fry, and range?

How do **nonverbal cues** replace, support, or contradict spoken or written messages?

What do you notice first about the **language**?

Document **word choices** and divide your list into nouns, adjectives, adverbs, verbs, pronouns, modals, conjections, puncuation marks, etc.

Do you see any **patterns** in word choices or punctuation?

Are any **words, phrases, or idioms** unfamiliar to you?

How would you describe the **linguistic style**? (formal, informal, slang, dialect, serious, light?) What signals this style?

How would you describe the **tone** of this media example? (conversational, satirical, ironic, humorous, serious, academic, colloqial?)

What **rhetorical devices** do you observe, such as metaphors, anecdotes, repetition, alliteration, rhyme, emotional appeals?

How is **credibility** established through language and nonverbal cues??

Whose **voices** are represented, directly or indirectly?

How do language and nonverbal cues define the **relationship** between the message creators and receivers?



**Figure 20**

Examples of Media Work

In the remainder of this chapter, I share two media work activities from my courses in second language teacher education. These examples illustrate how the process can unfold in both a casual and a structured lesson. My first example is a loosely structured media work activity that focuses on the types of media that school districts use to reach out to students who are learning English and their families. This activity is particularly relevant for students in a teacher preparation program. The overall goal is to see how schools make

Who are the main and supporting **characters**? Who has the most power or status?

How do the **characters** talk (dialect, accent, rate, volume, etc.), dress, gesture, move?

Where do the **characters** live and what do they own?

Are **identities** defined or open for interpretation?

How do the **characters** evolve over the course of the story?

How, when, and where do the **characters** interact with one another? How would you describe their relationships?

What is the **setting** of this story?

How would you describe the **physical space or time period** of the setting?

What **artifacts and details** are included and highlighted as markers of place and time?

Are **time and place** meant to be specific or more universal? How do you know?

Are the **physical spaces and artifacts** associated with particular groups of people and values?

What does **context** add to the possible interpretations of this story? How would meaning change if taken out of context?

Who are the intended **audiences** for this media?

How do each of the other elements of the story (time, place, characters, social narratives) relate to the intended **audiences**?

What parts of the story are likely to be familiar to the **audience members**, and what effect might this familiarity have (e.g. comfort, pride, likeability, boredom, nostalgia, anger, annoyance)?

What parts of the story are likely to be unfamiliar to the **audience members**, and what effect might this have (e.g. unease, suspiscion, curiousity, nervousness, ambivilence, dislike)?

What is the **main story or plot**? Are there any **subplots**?

How does the plot relate directly or indirectly to current **social issues**?

How to these stories relate to stories about the same **topic** told in other media?

What **social values** are validated or challenged by these stories?

What **lifestyles and identities** are challenged by these stories?

**Who is telling** these stories and for what purposes?



**Figure 21**

use of media to convey information about language learning and to reach out to immigrant students and families about important information. First, I ask students to look at the website, newsletters, and other accessible media of a school that they are visiting or working at as part of their teacher preparation program. The observations are typically encouraging, pointing out translations of information on websites, multilingual letters that go home to families, and bilingual resources in classrooms and common areas. These are welcome changes from the monolingual norm.

Next, I ask the students to collect media (or images of it) over a week or two that document the schools' public communication with families. This is an opportunity to take a closer look at the media of schools: websites, posters, classroom decor, newsletters, flyers, and announcements. In their observations, I encourage students to think quantitatively about exactly what content they see and then interrogate with qualitative inquiry. Note in figure 22 that the questions focus on OBSERVATION, INTERROGATION, and INTERPRETATION of the content (symbols, modalities, stories) and the context (place, time, people, systems, and resources).

Questions for REFLECTION might include:

- Is enough information (quality and quantity) available in languages other than English?

- How well do the languages available match the needs of the community?

- Are electronic or analog forms of communication the best way to show people how to participate?

- What alternative methods of communication are available, and what are the benefits and limits of those?

Knowing both the quantity and quality of messages in school media is a necessary step toward advocating for English language learners and understanding the social climate of a community. Examining school messages through media work illuminates what is being done well and what needs to be improved. RESPONSES for students already working in classrooms might include making changes in the way that information is conveyed to families and guardians and incorporating information about school activities into lessons. For students who are pre-service teachers, responses may take the form of working with parents in a community resource center.

The second example is a more formal analysis of media about language teaching. I have examined a local newspaper article with pre-service and in-service teachers as well as with classes of multilingual college students who attended ESL courses in their earlier schooling. The article tells stories about teaching ESL in some suburban communities. The article dates back to 2006, but I also maintain an updated list of articles from this newspaper database and that shows little change in coverage, except for the fact that no feature

# Let's observe:

When you look at the school website, how many clicks does it take to find information about classes for language learners?

What results do you get if you search for information about language learning classes and programs?

Is translation provided for the entire site? Which languages are included and what content is available in translation?

Do teacher websites have information in various languages?

How many posters, flyers, newsletters, yearbooks, announcements, and displays are multilingual?

Is information that is sent home or communicated though social media or other media offered in various languages? Which languages and what content?

# Let's ask questions:

Would it be easy for someone who is not fluent in the dominant language to learn about academic opportunities, to contact teachers and other staff, and to find out about events and activities by looking at the website?

What do students and their families and guardians need to know to participate in school and classroom activities? How are they expected to get information (formally or informally)?

Do the various languages represented in the school's media reflect the languages and dialects of the students' communities?

If information is conveyed in multiple languages, what is the nature of that information? Is it about academics, curricula, or assessments? Is it about health issues, safety procedures, or learning resources? After school activities, clubs, and sports?

**Figure 22**

articles about ESL have since been published in this local newspaper. The shorter and more recent articles refer mostly to charities that help immigrants, events that showcase a particular learner or teacher as a model for others, and funding issues. I still use this 2006 example as a starting point with students because it contains easily identifiable examples for analysis and because students are not reluctant to critique these "old" ways of thinking. When I later ask them to find current articles for comparison, they find that ways of thinking about immigration and language learning have not changed as much as they had thought.

The article we begin with was part of a week-long series about immigration in one county just outside of Philadelphia. This choice of a local newspaper story is deliberate; it is meant to inspire conversations about communities in which most of the students intend to work. Whether intentional or not, the article conveys community members' attitudes toward immigration and teaching English as both blatantly xenophobic and subtly complex. Because I want students to process this article for themselves, I lead them through media work by posing questions, giving them time to read individually, talk in small groups, and discuss as a class.

In the following description of the media work on this article, you will see how processes of observation, interrogation, interpretation, reflection, and response can weave in and out of analyses of modality, content, and context. The order in which topics emerge will depend on students' reactions. Figure 23 is a replica of a text box set off from other stories on the front page of the newspaper (Series at a glance, September 6, 2006) to preview a special week-long

## The Series at a Glance:

**TODAY**: An overall look at immigration's impact on Bucks County.
**Monday**: Churches, other service agencies are immigrants' lifelines.
**Tuesday**: A look at the lives of two immigrants– one legal, one illegal.
**Wednesday**: Are illegal immigrants responsible for a large percentage of crimes?
**Thursday**: Growing population of non-English-speaking children straining the schools.
**Friday**: Is an immigrant going to take your job?
**Saturday**: The foreign-born population might be pushing up your healthcare costs.

**Figure 23**

series. By itself, this preview is enough to inspire deep discussions about the framing of immigration in local media.

The article from the Thursday edition about ESL instruction in local schools is particularly relevant to teacher education, and it became the center of media work in several of my classes. The full article began as the top story on the front page of the newspaper with the headline in large bold font: "English instruction strains school budgets," followed by the subheading, "But school officials know that ESL courses give immigrant students the tools they need to succeed in America" (Canelli, 2006). Under the headline is a photograph of two children leaning over a table writing or drawing with thick markers in their hands. The caption reads: "The Latino Leadership Alliance offers English as a second language courses, easing some of the burden on local school districts." Already this headline, subheading, and caption contain semiotic choices, namely metaphors that frame ESL as a burden and as a key to success. The full article takes up about a third of the front page and continues for two full page columns on another page. The opening paragraphs, cited verbatim below, conjure up many attitudes and misconceptions toward language learners, the costs of public education, and the language teaching profession:

> A tan-skinned little boy walks nervously into a classroom, his hands shyly in his pockets and his head hanging low.
>
> "What's your name?" a teacher asks. But the boy just stares at her.
>
> "How old are you?" He doesn't reply. Tears brim his eyes because he doesn't understand what she is saying.
>
> So, the teacher picks up a yellow pencil and holds it in front of the child.
>
> "Pencil . . . peenncciill," she says, repeating the word.
>
> Finally, the boy smiles with relief. "Pencil!" he nods.
>
> This type of interaction is an everyday occurrence in many Lower Bucks schools. And since the school districts are responsible for educating all children—English speaking or not—they tolerate the costs for instructing immigrant students.
>
> (Canelli, 2006, 1A)

In this short passage, language learners are racialized and their presence is *tolerated*. English teachers' expertise is reduced to speaking slowly and repeating. The remainder of the article includes interviews with teachers, administrators, and non-immigrant English-speaking students, and focuses on the costs of educating ESL students and the negative effect of language learners on a school's test scores. Administrators are quoted as the voices of authority, and a few ESL teachers' comments are included, but the only student voices represented are native speakers telling a story about an immigrant student who succeeded aca-demically. As a success story, the immigrant student was positioned as a threat to the non-immigrant students, as he reportedly said to them, "someday you will be working for me." To guide students through this discourse, a sample activity might include the following three stages:

1. _Before reading:_

*This can be an in-class discussion or personal reflection.*

- How do you think English language classes are regarded where you live now or have lived in the past?

- Is/was language instruction supported by teachers in all of your classes?

2. _While reading:_

Use colored pencils or markers to highlight text as you encounter the following:

- words to describe language learners;

- words used to describe teachers;

- words used to describe ESL classes in public schools;

- metaphors used to characterize students, teachers, families, or programs;

- direct or indirect quotations from students, teachers, administrators, and other stakeholders.

3. _After reading:_

- What patterns do you see in the ways that students, classes and learning are described?

- Whose voices are presented as experts? How do you know that?

- What were the author's intentions? What messages were conveyed to readers?

- Write a response to this article for a "Reader Feedback" section of the newspaper.

Students recognize that the newspaper format necessitates an attention-grabbing headline, and that the author was trying to create a human-interest angle with emotional appeal in the opening paragraph. We could say that it's simply a marketing or journalistic technique to sell the newspaper, or we could go deeper and think about *why* this appeal works. The subheading that refers to giving "immigrant students the tools they need to succeed in America" appeals to American Dream mythology in which success depends on assimilating to the expected norms of White, middle-class, English-speaking cultures. Why do readers *need* assimilationist ideologies to appeal to their sensitivities? What is going on in the social climate that positions language learners as threatening? How well would this article be received if the voices of language learners were represented and if they were somehow portrayed as having their own agency or own visions of success? My students realize quickly that the voices of language learners are completely left out of this article, and their identities are constructed as "saboteurs" or "burdens." Only language learners are positioned as costing the schools money; presumably other students do not?

I wish I could report that this analysis represents out-of-date attitudes, but updates over the years revealed repetition of the same themes (Chamberlin-Quinlisk & Torigoe, 2016). The metaphors uncovered in this article, the series as a whole, and other studies of immigration or bilingual education in news media outlets make bold statements about language learners. For example, war imagery is used to describe immigrants and English language learners as invaders and saboteurs (Johnson, 2005), and newspapers make editorial choices that marginalize and disenfranchise immigrant students (González-Carriedo, 2014). Chamberlin & Torigoe (2016) report that immigrants in the United States and Japan were characterized in local newspapers as "lost puppies" who are vulnerable and dependent on others. Such word choices and metaphors shape readers' perceptions. They tell very powerful stories about identity.

These stories, in turn, support certain ideologies. Immigrants are constructed as part of an economic marketplace and are mostly welcomed at the lower levels (labor) of this hierarchy. Many articles also convey the idea that immigrants are given help by charitable organizations, so if they do not succeed, it is due to a lack of individual willpower. A more recent study of newspaper articles from small rural towns in Norway offers a slightly different perspective. The discourse about immigrants expressed appreciation for them as workers and as participants in civic life. However, those labeled as Muslim, refugees, or asylum seekers were discursively positioned as security threats and economic burdens (Berg-Nordlie, 2018). No matter where you teach, critically examining local stories about immigration or language teaching can be useful. Even if students are not old enough to conduct this kind of media work, teachers themselves need to be aware of the stories that are being told within their communities.

Responses to this article and others like it can take different forms. A class discussion might be the most appropriate response, or students can work individually or in groups to dig deeper into this issue. They might produce:

1. WRITTEN: a 500- to 600-word letter to the editor; a journal response to the article; posts to an online class discussion.
2. SPOKEN: a presentation of the resources available today for language teaching and learning in this school district; a podcast in which three or four students discuss their reactions to the article.
3. MIXED: an infographic displaying the common metaphors used to talk about language learning and immigration in media and offering alternative metaphors.

## Media Work in Your Teaching

As you prepare to do media work with your students, remember that there is not just one way to do it. It requires (as all teaching does) intentional and continual decision-making on your part. Only you will know what materials your students can handle and when. If it's too hard, you will know to pull back; if it's too easy, you will challenge them with more. Although you can use the model to guide your work, you must be open to deviations and spontaneous opportunities for exploration. Embrace the messiness of the process. I might share a media sample with a class and get some predictable interpretations that I am ready to discuss, but then someone says "That's not what I see . . ." and the fun begins. Be a model of inquisitiveness and openness. Teaching is not a neutral activity. It is value-laden, and we all come to it with our own values and points of view. It would be naïve of me to say that I completely suppress my values and beliefs in the classroom. The fact that I choose to teach about language reflects what I value. And, I am passionate about what I teach. I am just as passionate, however, about wanting my students to learn how to back up their claims with evidence and understand how language and images convey emotional messages that are not always connected to facts. We can use media to explore differences between opinion and fact and teach students to be curious about what they see in media, rather than just accepting it without challenge.

## Consider Your Local Needs and Contexts

In teacher education programs I ask students to find media that highlights stories of language learners, educational policy issues, or reactions to immigration in local communities. My purpose is to talk about these controversial issues within the context of advocacy for ESL in local schools. In my courses about language and culture, we cover a broader range of topics, and I choose examples that present a wide range of viewpoints when I model media work for the students. I also make sure to ask students for their interpretations during each step of the process. They should investigate language, images, modalities, semiotics, and social contexts without feeling an imposition of my perspectives as the only interpretation. As often as possible, ask students to select media for analysis. It should come from them and reflect their interests and their surroundings.

Student-generated data can also include texts in languages other than the target language of the classroom. A large number of my students are multilingual, but not enough of them have been taught to recognize this as an asset. Whether students want to use media produced in various languages because they are language learners, because their surroundings are replete with media that mixes languages and dialects, or because they have not had opportunities to use and legitimize their multilingualism in school, we should encourage them to seek out these resources for media work. Media work is a site where translanguaging can be a norm, and students can draw on their full linguistic repertoires throughout the process (García 2009; García & Kleifgen, 2020; García & Li W., 2014; Li W., 2018; 2020; Li W. & Garcia, 2022). Analyzing and discussing modalities, texts, and social narratives that span cultures and languages yet draw on the media of shared local spaces can be an eye-opening experience for all.

## What's Next?

In the coming chapters I share examples of media work that concentrate on media that we encounter in our daily lives and demonstrate a range of levels of analysis, from a focus on vocabulary to explorations of identity and cultural values. Media work might be a 10-minute discussion of a meme that a student shares with the class or a multiweek exploration of identities within a community. In any case, you and your students will create variations of media work that will inspire new ways of thinking about the familiar.

KEY IDEAS

symbols

identities

place

time

needs

systems

resources

relationships

processing modalities

processing symbols

processing stories

observation

interrogation

interpretation

reflection

response


OBSERVE

1.  Think about media work as a process. Start by observing and reflecting on your teaching environment using the worksheet in figure 24 as a guide. Look at:

    • school websites;

    • posters and other media displayed in common areas;

    • the media in your classroom (e.g., posters, books, magazines, computers, signs);

    • communication sent home to parents (e.g., emails, letters);

    • school newsletters and flyers;

    • morning announcements;

    • flyers, pamphlets, screens, etc.

| What media do you see? | Who made it and for whom? | What stands out? language-sound-images | What messages are conveyed? directly/indirectly |
|---|---|---|---|
|  |  |  |  |
|  |  |  |  |
|  |  |  |  |
|  |  |  |  |

Figure 24

2. In groups with your classmates, compare your charts and interrogate your media by asking more detailed questions about each media example. Refer to the guiding questions for media work presented in this chapter for a place to start.

3. Interpret/reflect/respond: What are some of the prevalent messages being conveyed in schools today? What makes these messages effective/ineffective? How do students respond to them? Are there symbolic features of the messages that require background knowledge? Are the messages accessible to everyone? Do the messages give attention to a range of needs, values, and abilities? Is there anything you would change about the modalities, symbols, or stories?

EXPLORE

1. Repeat the observation process in the activity above, but this time step out to the wider community. Document media that tell stories about immigration or language learning in the communities where you live. Look at:

   • local newspapers and magazines;

   • websites for local organizations and local government offices;

   • signs and billboards along streets;

   • displays and signs in shop windows;

   • signs and decorations in yards;

   • bumper stickers on cars or elsewhere;

   • social media posts about local events and issues.

Are any stories told about immigration or learning English? Are certain stories related to certain modalities? What range of voices, experiences, and attitudes are represented? How can one respond to these mediated messages?

LEARN MORE

Many teacher-scholars have used CDA, semiotic analysis, and content analysis to examine rhetoric about language teaching, immigration, and culture. These analyses often reveal ideologies that reflect social attitudes and expectations about language learning, particularly as it intersects with politics, policies, and identities. I list below a few articles to illustrate the scope of topics, but I recommend browsing journals such as *Critical Inquiry in Language Studies, Critical Discourse Studies, Language and Discrimination, Linguistic Landscapes, and World Englishes,* to name just a few.

Bhatia, T. K., & Kathpalia, S. S. (2019). World Englishes and cross-cultural advertising. *World Englishes, 38,* 348–35. DOI: 10.1111/weng.12419. (Introduction to a special issue on multilingualism in advertising.)

Bori, P. (2021). Neoliberalism and global textbooks: a critical ethnography of English language classrooms in Serbia. *Language, Culture and Curriculum, 34*(2) 183–198. DOI: 10.1080/07908318.2020.1797082

González-Carriedo, R. (2014). Ideologies of the press in regard to English language learners: A case study of two newspapers in Arizona. *Critical Inquiry in Language Studies, 11*(2) 121–149. DOI 10.1080/ 15427587.2014.906808

Lee. J. S (2014). English on Korean television. *World Englishes, 33*(1) 33–49.

Lorenz, E. P., & Frisby, C. M. (2022) Disability on drama TV: How attitudes about disability in the US relate to viewing frequency and identification with a character with a disability on "Glee." *Media Education 13*(1), 81–91. DOI: 10.36253/me-12641

Risager, K. (2021). Language textbooks: windows to the world. *Language, Culture and Curriculum, 34*(2), 119–132, DOI:10.1080/ 07908318.2020.1797767

Wang, G., & Ma, X. (2021). Representations of LGBTQ+ issues in China in its official English-language media: A corpus-assisted critical discourse study. *Critical Discourse Studies, 18, 2,* 188–206. DOI: 10.1080/ 17405904.2020.1738251

# CHAPTER 4

# Exploring the Language of Our Daily Lives

Every day we are bombarded by messages that compete for our attention. These messages are amusing, inflammatory, persuasive, informative, and emotional. We see them on billboards, in clickbait on screens, public signage on the streets, news headlines, memes, bumper stickers on cars, shop windows, magazine covers, menus, junk mail, and even food labels and wrappers. These seemingly mundane examples of media can be rich resources for language teaching and learning. In this chapter I focus on the language and imagery of everyday media as a way for teachers to introduce students to media work. Although everyday media can engage students at any level, the focus on the "here and now" of media that we encounter in our daily routines is particularly appropriate for beginner language learners. I look for language of the everyday as I walk through campus and local communities. I have my own collection of media to draw on to get media work started, but I ask students to collect samples of their own or take photos of interesting things that they see. For those who are new to the area, these explorations of local media highlight what captures their attention and perhaps does not make sense to them. Student-selected media from everyday settings may reveal linguistic structures and cultural norms that are unfamiliar to newcomers or taken for granted or unexamined by longtime residents. In any case, working with media that is drawn from students' experiences connects media work to meaningful language learning.

## Content, Contexts, and Processes: Where to Start?

If the goal of your lesson is to unravel language and linguistic structures, then start with the language, modality, and message. You can share a sample of almost anything:

- What words in (media sample) do you know? What words do you not understand?

- Identify nouns, adjectives, verbs, pronouns, articles, modals, etc. in these media.

- Is any of the vocabulary unfamiliar? Does the language conform to grammar rules that you know? Does the language include dialects or patterns that you do not know?

- What is the main message? Is there anything confusing about the message?

- Where would you see this message? Who is it written for?

These questions can get students thinking about language and explicit messages. The goal here is to focus on how the language of public media uses grammar, voice, intertextuality, conversational style, metaphors, and other features of discourse to convey meaning. Whether or not you use the vocabulary of discourse analysis with your students is a pedagogical choice. With an advanced group, I might introduce Fairclough's (2010) term "intertextuality" as a way to develop their overall language awareness. For younger and/or less advanced students, we might discuss the connections in the text to presumed cultural knowledge without using the term "intertextuality." Your choices will match the needs and abilities of your students.

Next ask students to observe and gather samples of linguistic structures that you are working on in class, or start with your own collection. You might ask them to find examples of imperatives, of subjects and objects, of verb tenses, proper nouns, and punctuation marks. In addition, images and other semiotic features (font, size, layout, etc.) can reinforce the meaning conveyed through linguistic structures. Semiotic analysis can be conducted in varying degrees. Questions can range from why certain colors and fonts are used to how design and layout choices impact the effectiveness of the message (see figures 19, 20 and 21 in Chapter 3). Interrogation can take place on various levels. Interrogation of language specifically will look for semantic choices, grammar, metaphors, punctuation, voice, tone and register, connections to different genres and other texts (intertextuality). Some students might only be ready to closely examine referential meanings and individual interpretations, and others will be ready to interrogate symbolic meanings, modalities, and ideologies.

Media work affords a wide variety of approaches. Students can work in pairs or small groups to talk about how they each interpret the messages and why. They can complete worksheets that lead them through a series of questions, or they can compare the media with something similar in other languages that they know. This is an opportunity to engage students with their surroundings and discover how interpretations vary. Reflective activities might ask students to think about different ways that public information is presented in different places or how interpretations are affected by assumptions of cultural knowledge. What does the message mean to you? Responses can range from oral or written comments to creative multimodal activities or projects. Create and conduct a survey about the topic addressed in the media. Create your own sign that conveys the same or similar message using different language and symbolic tools. Create media that conveys your own message about the topic. Create a new piece of media that exemplifies specific linguistic features. Search for examples of the same media message you examined in different modalities.

The following examples come from my students' and my personal collections of media that we have observed while moving through our local urban and suburban environments. As we sit in heavy traffic, rides buses and trains, shop for clothing or food, visit parks, go out to eat, or walk in deserted streets during quarantine, we see all kinds of media. In the examples here, the three basic components of media work (processes, content, and context) are combined and recombined to adapt to the media, students' reactions to them, and the pedagogical needs of the class. The samples I present below are connected to the context in which I teach. The content is not meant to be universal, but the processes of observing, interrogating, interpretating, reflecting, and responding to local media are applicable to all contexts.

You will notice that most of the examples shared in this chapter are analog. There are several reasons for this. First, much of the media we see in analog form is relevant to the "here and now" and connected to tasks at hand or current issues in our communities. Second, looking for analog media takes students away from screens for a while and makes them more cognizant of the physical world around them. When teaching takes place in online environments, in particular, looking for common artifacts adds variety by changing the visual field, pacing, and scope of a learning activity. Moreover, asking students to find examples of something online can often result in last minute searches in which several students end up with the same results. This being said, online media such as school and community websites are meaningful to students' lives and are excellent resources for media work. Both analog and digital media are part of everyday media. Figure 25 provides a guiding structure that you can modify to make worksheets or online modules for media work.

The following pages describe examples of media my students and I have collected for class discussions. For each example I will share some of the key ideas that emerged as we moved through media work exercises. In addition to the general questions listed in the previous figure, each medium generates its own set of questions based on context, so I have included these extended inquires in the examples. These examples come from years of classes that focus on language and intercultural communication, and they represent artifacts that can be seen every day in our local environments.

<table>
<tr><td colspan="2" align="center">     Observing the World Around Us     </td></tr>
<tr><td colspan="2">Identify a theme of interest with your class (such as pets, bumper stickers, store front signs, school bulletin boards, food labels) to explore. Ask students to collect 3–4 examples in the selected category. Show them how to document the examples (photo, notes, or drawings).

Create a worksheet or lesson based on the questions below. After discussing answers, students can create their own media in the selected category or sort the class collection into different categories (funny, serious, interesting, boring, etc.)</td></tr>
<tr><td align="center">For older students...</td><td align="center">For younger students...</td></tr>
<tr><td>What examples did you find and where?</td><td>What did you find?</td></tr>
<tr><td>Why was this (media) created?</td><td>Where did you see it? Who is it for?</td></tr>
<tr><td>Who will see this (media)?</td><td>What does is mean?</td></tr>
<tr><td>What interesting vocabulary (idioms, slang, abbreviations, acronyms, dialect markers...) do you see or hear?</td><td>Did you learn any new words?</td></tr>
<tr><td>What grammatical features do you notice in this media?</td><td></td></tr>
<tr><td>What do the images, colors, and fonts add to the meaning of this media?</td><td>What do you like or dislike about it?</td></tr>
<tr><td>Are there any words or cultural references that you do not understand?</td><td></td></tr>
<tr><td>Do you think that everyone will understand this media in the same way that you do?</td><td>Make your own version of this media.</td></tr>
<tr><td>Is there anything that you would like to change about it? Why?</td><td></td></tr>
<tr><td>Learning outcomes:</td><td>Learning outcomes:</td></tr>
</table>

**Figure 25**

## Example 1: Pets are people too?

At first glance, posted signs that remind pet owners to clean up after their pets are not very exciting. And unless you are a dog owner, you might not even notice them. If you look closely at the signs represented in figures 26a–d, however, they use language, imagery, and layout to create different messages about the same action. These signs provide a good starting point for media work because they ask students to identify how semiotic choices change the tone but not the general meaning of the signs.

Share signs such as those presented here to lead a class activity. Of course, the signs you see may be about other issues such as littering or loitering.

**Figure 26a**

**Figure 26b**

**Figure 26c**

**Figure 26d**

Encourage students to think about where these signs are posted and make note of the word choices, the amount of information, the shape of the signs, the fonts and colors, and the images, or lack of images. You may ask students to address the following questions:

- Whose voices are represented on these signs?

- How do all of these features (text and imagery) convey a tone for this message?

- How does the tone differ from sign to sign?

- What kinds of emotional appeal does each sign make?

Students are quick to discern differences in vocabulary and obligations to be a "good neighbor," to maintain safety and hygiene, or follow the law. The sign on the right even threatens a fine. Moreover, the only punctuation used is the exclamation point! Signs such as these (including other topics such as privacy, warnings about a danger) might be commonplace and seemingly straightforward, but they often contain layers of sociolinguistic coding that can be interesting to unravel.

In our everyday media work, we also come across stickers, decals, and other ephemera that refer to pets. Students have wondered about pets that are considered to be a part of the family, organizations that support rescuing and adopting pets who need homes, or those who are fond of particular breeds. The role of a family pet, of course, varies from culture to culture and family to family. This topic can be a catalyst for conversations in many age groups, ranging from favorite animals or pets to the ethical treatment of animals.

We see in Figure 27a and b drawings of bones to represent dogs, and hearts to replace the word "love." Then, of course, we have the idea that a person could think about pets as people and as endearing members of the family,

**Figure 27a**

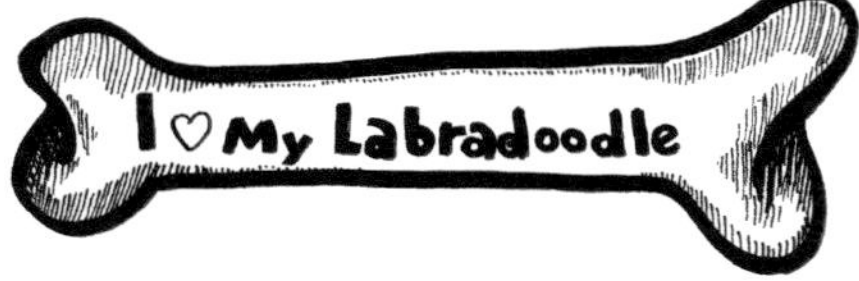


**Figure 27b**

even combining the prefix "grand" with dogs. (The word "labradoodle" is a mix of Labrador and poodle and refers to a recently popular mixture of breeds.) Linguistically we can have fun with these compound words, and this can inspire interesting sociocultural discussions about humans' relationships to animals, the role of pets in a culture, and even the stereotypes associated with dog owners versus cat owners. A student brought to class a photo of a bumper sticker that reads "My Boston Terrier Is Smarter Than Your Honor Student," a message that draws on the passion of pet ownership as it sarcastically challenges the proud parents who display stickers on their cars that read "My child is an honor student." You can use such examples to talk about comparatives ("smarter than") and discuss the meaning of "honor" in educational contexts, how parents show their pride, and whether or not students want to have their accomplishments displayed on cars.

Bumper stickers are a public display of private life—a kind of social media post on your car. Interrogation of this modality brings up many good discussion points. Are people so used to the idea of publicly sharing personal information that they feel the need to do so all the time? What are the boundaries between private and personal information? How do these boundaries change from culture to culture (and any sub-groups of culture)? You can start with these larger questions and then discuss the modality and text. It is interesting to note how closely tied decals and bumper stickers are to local knowledge and specific social narratives. When you are selecting media to use in your classrooms, you can certainly choose items that are more global, but even global symbols take on more local meanings as they are interpreted through the eyes of individuals in smaller communities.

## Example 2: Follow the rules!

Other signs convey messages about how to act. These messages tell us to be careful, to stay off private property, and how to behave during a pandemic. Understanding the language and basic messages (especially for safety) is of course important, but unpacking modalities, imagery, layout, design, voices of authority, and emotional appeals can be a fascinating study of language and culture. Classrooms and school buildings are a good source of signage that reminds students how to behave, and taking photos in neighborhoods and cities while walking or using public transportation reveals directives for safety as well as expectations for social codes of behavior. The signs in figure 28a–f offer advice for driving, parking, shopping, eating in a café, and going to the beach. In addition to linguistic features, the messages in each sign are part of larger stories that presuppose, but do not fully require, contextual knowledge.

Prescriptive grammar would call for the first sign (figure 28a) to say "Drive *as if* your kids live here," but students argue that that sounds awkward, so then we talk about the difference between prescriptive and descriptive grammar. If you are working with students who learned prescriptive rules for one variety of a language, they may have many examples to share of the differences between the language they actually hear in comparison to the language they studied. In addition, this sign was put up in a yard, not as an official sign (although the original seems to be professionally printed), but most likely in reaction to people driving too fast in a neighborhood where children play. Does everyone feel as if they have the right to post a sign like this?

The traffic signs in figure 28d—"No Stopping Any Time" and "Deer Jawn Crossing"—are posted on a road that runs through a busy urban park. The

Figure 28a

Figure 28b

Figure 28c

Figure 28d

Figure 28e

Figure 28f

top sign is an official street sign aimed at keeping the road clear of vehicles, but the interesting component is the yellow sign beneath it. It mixes the style of an official road sign that warns drivers to look out for deer (very common in some regions of North America) with signs that say watch for children playing, and with a popular word from the local dialect. "Jawn" is used informally in Philadelphia as a flexible catchall to replace any noun when the speaker and listener both know what it signifies, as in "thing" or "whatchamacallit." ("Hand me that jawn.") The bottom sign was made of metal and securely posted like the sign above it, but it is not clear who posted it. Nevertheless, it is a meaningful display of cultural identity and language.

Other signs refer to the COVID-19 pandemic. "Mask Up" (figure 28b) at the entrance to the beach reflected an official mandate in the state where it was located; people visiting the beach, however, represented different viewpoints about mask mandates. How does the sign assert authority and try to persuade people to wear masks in a gentler tone? The handwritten sign in a local coffee shop (figure 28c) appeals to a sense of mutual respect for "neighbors" and also draws attention to the need for limited occupancy. "At least a cart apart helps keep us safe" (figure 28f) also appeals to a sense of community with "we" and uses a suggestive tone with the phrase "at least." Signs about "Classroom rules" (figure 28e) may also come in a wide variety. Some are direct and authoritative; others are more informal and light-hearted. How would you interpret this one? These are just a few of the signs we encounter daily that tell us what to do.

One day, while on a long, leisurely bike ride, I encountered the sign in figure 29 in front of a house in a very affluent neighborhood. I was surprised to see the warning message in two languages in such a monolingual area. The illustration below shows the front yard in this neighborhood where 97% of the population is White.

An ostensibly direct sign about trespassing becomes much more than that when considering the language choices and the demographics. This sign begs for media work that looks beyond the direct message. In an area where Spanish speakers are few, why did the homeowners feel compelled to include Spanish on the sign? Do they feel that Spanish speakers are somehow a threat to their property and privacy? "No trespassing" signs can reflect a wide range of ideas about safety, privacy, respect for others, but also about insecurities and suspicion. The scene invokes discussion for students who are mature enough to understand the discriminatory nature of this message. What caption would you provide for the text bubble?

**Figure 29**

Example 3: Where's the bathroom?

Although signage for toilets (figure 30a–c) might seem to be straightforward and a topic reserved for pages of a travel guide, the tendency for stores and restaurants to post interesting signage can make this basic need confusing in an unfamiliar language or culture. This is an opportunity to talk about vocabulary, symbolic images, and distinctions between male and female in different cultures. From a linguistic point of view, asking for the "toilet" will in most cases elicit an adequate response. Yet when we enter public spaces, we do not always see the word "toilet" or familiar icons. Comparing the different words such as *men, women, boys, girls, guys, gals, ladies, gents, gentlemen, gender neutral,* and all the other labels associated with binary and nonbinary representations of gender constitutes a lesson in semantics, lexical choices, and use (correct and incorrect) of the possessive "s."

Obvious social and cultural definitions of gender identities can also lead to engaging discussions. In the local communities where I work and

**Figure 30a**

**Figure 30b**

**Figure 30c**

live, the different signage for toilets seems to be associated with different neighborhoods, assumed ideological perspectives, age of customers, and the type of public space. Each has a lot to say about labels we use to classify gender, general public expectations for restrooms to be separated or unisex, and the range (or lack thereof) of vocabulary that signifies toilets in different contexts: Bathroom, water closet, toilet, little girls' room, little boys' room, etc. This signage also presents opportunities for discussions about transgender and nonbinary identities, though these discussions may not be allowed in all teaching contexts.

Example 4: What's happening at school?

School websites can be a place to start media work. The information and language will be relevant to students (and they might be compelled to look more closely into resources and opportunities.) Media work on school websites can focus on vocabulary, ways in which information is categorized and presented, and comparisons among different platforms (websites, TikTok, Instagram, YouTube, etc.). Look at the words used to describe categories of information on home pages. You can see that labels are used to organize information and that the layout and language choices create a hierarchy of topics. What information would students expect to find included under each category? What meaning do the images add to the site? Figure 31 illustrates a screenshot from a local school website during a particular time period. The tab labels reflect what was important to schools during the COVID-19 pandemic.

Other media from schools, such as daily announcements, letters to parents, newsletters, posters in hallways, newspapers, yearbooks, etc., are filled with meaning. These everyday messages include essential vocabulary that may be unfamiliar to some students and their families. Many school events

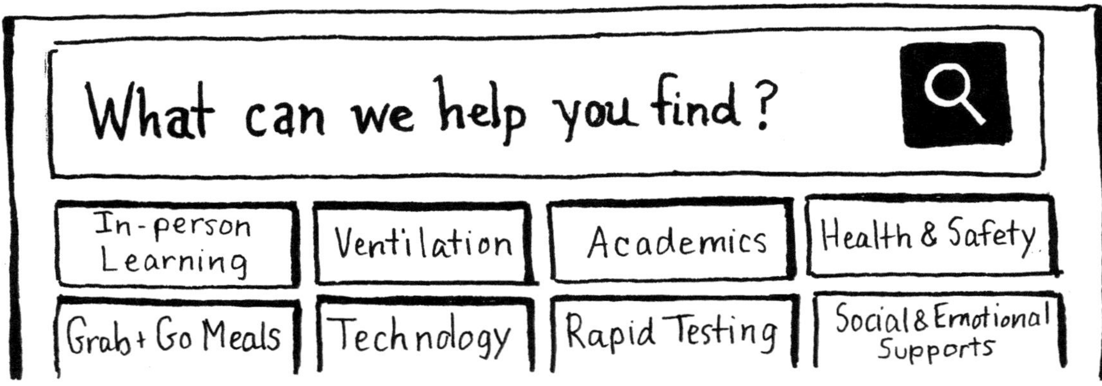


**Figure 31**

and activities are referred to by proper nouns and nicknames and assume prior knowledge of how students and families are expected to participate. Deciphering the language and grammar of these messages with language learners may also serve as a way to familiarize them with school culture. Look at the names of student clubs, take note of what information is translated to languages other than English, look at promotional materials for annual school events. The messages of everyday media in schools are easily taken for granted by those who are familiar with the language and traditions of the community, but these messages may be cryptic to newcomers. Media work can help bridge this information gap.

## Example 5: What do you meme?

A search for current popular memes online yields more than 400 million items. Clearly memes are part of our everyday mediascapes, and the vast number of them is daunting. You can ask students to share one of their favorite memes in general, or one that is associated with a particular location or event. Ask them to observe, interrogate, interpret, reflect, and respond:

Observe:

How many versions of the meme, with different text, have you seen?

In what ways does the language and imagery stay the same and how does it change in each version?

Interrogate:

How are references to popular culture embedded within this meme?

What parts of the text can change, what parts need to remain unchanged to preserve meaning?

Are the cultural references well-known, contemporary, or decades old?

What are the emotional appeals of this meme?

How is humor or satire conveyed?

Interpret:

What is the main social commentary that this meme is making?

Can this message be interpreted in different ways?

Reflect:

> What do you think about the social commentary?
>
> What do you find to be most interesting about the language, grammar, and images?

Respond:

> Did you pass this meme on to others? How could you change the meme to reflect your point of view?
>
> Can you find this meme in different languages?

In 2019, a meme about Philadelphia circulated on social media that was based on the image of an iceberg that is often used to talk about culture (see figure 32 for a general impression but not the original version of the meme).

The iceberg metaphor shows that certain aspects of culture are visible, but more are below the surface. There are well-known facts about Philadelphia, for example, that appear at the top of this meme above the surface: Ben Franklin, Independence Hall, Liberty Bell, Rocky, "Jawn," etc. The creator, Cameron Jones, filled in three layers, with the deepest representing facts about the city that are less well known. As the meme evolved, four layers were added below the surface. This particular meme eventually included over a hundred historical events, places, slang, food, people, and current events that are all associated with the city (some material may not be appropriate for a general audience, so the original meme is not reproduced here) (Tanenbaum, 2021). As an object of media work, students can create their own iceberg meme of their school, community, or city.

**Figure 32**

Individually or in groups, students can sequentially add to the meme, paying attention to repeating language patterns (vocabulary, idioms), local dialects, slang, and cultural knowledge. Begin with an empty iceberg (see figure 33) and fill it in together as a class or pass it around the room, having each student contribute one item at a time.

## Example 6: Cars and identity

In places where cars seem to be an expression of identity, many people profess something about themselves on the stickers that they place in windows or on bumpers (figure 34a–d).

The oval shaped sticker has become popular in the past few years. These stickers are modeled after the registration stickers that used to appear on cars in Europe, designating the country in which the automobile was registered. In the United States, these have become symbols of places or ideas, and rely on abbreviations and knowledge of local places to convey their meanings. Typically, the text consists of two to three

**Figure 33**

**Figure 34a**

**Figure 34b**

**Figure 34c**

**Figure 34d**

letters centered in a large font for high visibility and the full name of the place in smaller font that is only legible from close up. In this case, the "NYC" (figure 34c) stands for New York City. Students can discuss why someone would put that on their car. The cultural infatuation with these stickers may not cover every region, but they all rely on the use of abbreviations that refer to local knowledge. Some are familiar in certain communities, and others require the viewer to get closer and read the accompanying fine-print text. It is possible, from these decals, to launch a discussion of abbreviations that are widely used in public spaces. What are we expected to know in a certain city, college campus, or social environment?

Another example of the oval decal includes those with visual elements, such as figure 34b with the numbers "26.2." Like the initials for local places, this one too requires specialized knowledge to understand its intended meaning. Does this convey a sense of inclusion and exclusion in a certain group? The number refers to the length, in miles, of a marathon running event. Should we assume that the only ones who display such a decal have earned the right by actually completing the endurance event? Take a close look at the font. What does the rough-edged font symbolize? How does this decal reflect the importance of sports in US society? Do you think that everyone who runs a marathon has one of these on their car? Is it a source of pride, of showing off, or a bit of both? Would you display one of these if you competed successfully in a marathon? How does this reflect a competitive nature in an individual, or of a group? The "I don't run" oval sticker (figure 34d) is clearly a response to those who post their achievement on their cars. I have heard various interpretations of this sticker including that it is a sarcastic statement about showing off or that it is a representation of those who are proud that they do not run. Car decals are appropriate to use with beginner and intermediate level learners, as you can focus the discussions on places, such as tourist attractions, shops, and schools, or on sports and fitness.

Next are some of the "family" decals that became a trend to place on the back windows of cars. These come in interesting configurations. Each family member can be represented by a cartoon figure that is usually performing some kind of activity (see figure 34a). Some people even include figures of their pets. On a surface level, these decals could be used to talk about vocabulary associated with family members. But these can take us much further into discussions of what family and even marriage means. As a language teacher you will have to decide on the direction to take this conversation. If you are working with a mature class, then you may be able to venture into discussions of gender roles, the meaning of marriage, and the "ideal" family. In the decal in figure 34a, the man is wearing a tie and carrying a briefcase because he is going to work. The female is baking a cake. The boy is playing football and the girl is dancing. Even if these gendered roles are a reality for some families, they do not represent most families in the United States where females work outside the home. These represent a specific group. Next is the concept of "family" itself and the idea that it is supposed to consist of two parents—one male, one female—and more than one child (rarely do I see a display of just one child). The "perfect" family can be an interesting topic for discussion. Like the artist's interpretation of the "family" car decals shown in figure 35, students can share their opinions. They can make their own decals and describe what they represent.

There also seems to be an interest in challenging the family decals. A recently spotted sticker states; "I Think, Therefore I'm Single." This correlation of intelligence with marital status gets a few chuckles from students, but it also opens up some serious conversations about marital status and how unmarried people are perceived. An interesting question to ask is who would have this sticker displayed on their car? Would their gender make a difference in the way in which it is perceived? In addition, the discourse itself is a play on Descartes' "I

**Figure 35**

think, therefore I am," a good example of intertextuality that presumes preexisting cultural knowledge.

## Example 7: Food for thought

A popular topic in class is, not surprisingly, food. For newcomers, the language associated with the variety and offerings of food in public markets, food trucks, cafeterias, supermarkets, convenience stores, and restaurants can be overwhelming and almost indecipherable. Even for local residents, decoding menu items and food labels can present a challenge. Names of menu items can reflect local knowledge or popular culture. In many of my classes, discussions about the language of food have led to deeper conversations about meal time, sources and availability of food, variations in diets, local culture, and cooking. We should all realize, however, that having choices in where and how we get our food is a privilege. We cannot take for granted that all of our students share this privilege and have access to sufficient healthful foods. You must consider the possibility of food insecurity among your students before focusing on this issue, or you might decide to focus only on foods in the cafeteria that are accessible to all students. If this is an appropriate topic you can ask students to identify:

1. The actual food or ingredients
2. Adjectives used to describe its flavor or quality
3. Adjectives used that are not typically associated with food
4. Adjectives, verbs, nouns used to describe how one might feel when eating this food
5. Language varieties and translations used to convey something about the food
6. Places or people referred to in the description of the food.

Much can be said about the modalities in which menus are displayed, their size, fonts, colors, and whether they are printed or handwritten (legible or not?). Menus may change every day or rarely, some require a glossary, knowledge of different languages, or familiarity with local people, places, and events. The texts of menus often include mixtures of familiar and unfamiliar language, idioms, word play, and references to local knowledge. Socially, each sign or menu reflects different expectations for what a meal or snack should be, how many choices should be offered, how and where it should be consumed, with whom, and how much one might expect to pay. More mature classes can talk about the origins of ingredients, where they are sourced, how they are distributed, and who has access to healthful choices. Conversations about food do not need to be superficial or essentializing.

In figure 36 we see a handwritten sign. The handwriting is not easy to decipher, but this example can elicit many questions: What words do you see that refer to a specific food? What words might hint at the type of restaurant or cafeteria this is? What words are unfamiliar? What kinds of meals (breakfast, lunch, dinners, snacks, desserts) are represented?

**Figure 36**

The sign depicted in figure 37 is a more typical sight to students who eat in a university cafeteria. Notice the colloquial language and wordplay on the idiom "to put your best foot forward."

This also displays current vocabulary and trends with "meal deals" and "vegan bowls." Why are these ideas relevant to the targeted audience? What does "National Nutrition Month" mean, and why does it exist? The vocabulary is interesting, but the potential for conversations about cultural expectations for meals (both as rituals and sources of nutrition) is even more enticing. Students who spend time in Philadelphia might be familiar with this sign in

**Figure 37**

figure 38a about "Fancy Donuts" and need to explain to others what they are, what some of the descriptions refer to, and how they were able to recognize the establishment that sells them from a simple sign. The sign for gluten-free water in Figure 38b is an example of the availability of foods for special diets, which is a positive thing. And it is also an example of advertising and marketing strategies. Some students say that this is an example of sarcasm; others say that it is meant to inform consumers that the product never entered an environment where gluten was processed.

Collecting menus from local restaurants offers another way to tap into vocabulary that reflects both practical and creative language. Most menus are available online today, some can be photographed if they are posted on walls, and some businesses may give you a menu to keep for teaching purposes. It is obvious to students that descriptions of cheap food use simple, straightforward language, and that as the prices go up, the descriptions become more mysterious. Consider how and why a single food item can be referred to in multiple ways. This artist's interpretation of a "page" from a chain restaurant's menu in figure 39 reflects the type of language used to describe "combos" through catchy phrases and idioms.

Some menus use familiar terms from popular culture, such as "Eggs 101." Menus from national restaurant chains often include language that is idiomatic in the names of a dish but then describe the components or ingredients underneath the name.

**Figure 38a**

**Figure 38b**

Combos
HEART ATTACK ON A PLATE.
5K WALK BEFORE HOLIDAY DINNER
THE HEART HEALTHY
CHICKEN PARM SCRAM
THE 1 OF EACH
ONLINE ORDERING AVAILABLE
THE CLASSIC
Eggs 101
Get your eggs
how you like them.
Scrambled
Over Easy
Over Medium
Over Hard

Figure 39

Menus can also present an opportunity to study vocabulary related to nutrition, specialized foods, herbs, and spices, as well as cooking techniques. Beyond the food itself, however, menus can indirectly point to cultural information about how and when we eat, what the experience of dining out with friends entails, how certain dishes represent specific communities, and how we expect food servers to attend to our needs. Students can look for information about serving times and different categories of choices (starters, main dishes, desserts, etc.). How long should it take for food to arrive? How quickly are people expected to eat? In addition, restaurants that advertise as offering specialized cuisines can be a springboard for discussions about fusion, authenticity, and appropriation. Linguistically, these places may code-mesh, incorporate borrowed words, or exemplify language and cultural contact in the dishes they offer.

**Figure 40**

Menus and ephemera from local restaurants use a wide range of colorful and interesting vocabulary. Many places also refer to their menu items with names that include local places, events, or famous people, and regional dishes are highlighted through dialects. This creates a sense of nostalgia for place and established family-owned businesses in the community. Among many Philadelphia culinary traditions, cheesesteaks are the most closely associated with the city. (There is, in fact, a ritualized pattern and vocabulary for ordering cheesesteaks.)

The text on a beverage cup (represented in figure 40) from Pat's Steaks reads, "Pat's King of Steaks, in business since 1930. ORIGINATORS OF THE STEAK SANDWICH. Where 9th St, crosses Passyunk and Wharton Sts." Those familiar with South Philadelphia would know exactly where those three streets intersect, and they would also know that directly across the street from Pat's is another famous cheesesteak establishment, Geno's, also with a history in the community. The public signage at both take-out shops provides local references to places, rituals for ordering, and symbolizes the cheesesteak rivalry in the city.

Media associated with food is not, of course, limited to restaurants and public venues. Some descriptions, labels, and advertisements refer explicitly to social narratives about nutrition, sources of food, and support of progressive or traditional values. The label on milk sold in glass containers at a grocery store, for example, reads "Rediscover the wonderful flavor of truly farm fresh milk" from "grass fed cows on family farms." This is an interesting lesson in vocabulary and marketing associated with products that appeal to our sense of sustainable practices. Younger students might learn new vocabulary, and older students can be challenged to investigate what "organic," "natural," "non-GMO" mean in terms of farming, labeling, and distributing.

## Connecting Local Media to a Larger World

As I mentioned earlier, the examples I shared in this chapter are relevant to my students and their daily routines. Students should explore the world immediately around them, but they should also be encouraged to connect the local to the global. For example, in an introductory sociolinguistics class consisting of an equal number of domestic and international students, the final project of the semester included an analysis of media in a public space (linguistic landscape project). Students who are gaining confidence in their English and are unsure about their ability to interpret popular American media can bring a global perspective to the class by working with media in their heritage languages. Students can select media in languages other than English (or other target languages), talk about different connotations and cultural meanings, and compare and contrast media from two or more speech communities. This comparative component could be built into any class where students are multilingual, but comparison is not always necessary. In some of my classes, students analyze media in a variety of languages and describe their interrogations and interpretations to the class in English. Students also work in groups where they call upon their shared linguistic repertoires to find and interpret media that involves a mixture of languages.

Most importantly, local issues are part of larger national or global discussions. In the early 2020s, most of us were dealing with the consequences of a global pandemic that highlighted social inequities, exacerbated divisive politics, and profoundly changed the way we teach. Gathering media from our local communities is one way to engage students in their immediate worlds, perhaps even helping them to navigate their daily lives. Media in the public spaces where we live can increase awareness of how global issues and national and state policies are connected to local communities. For example, a sign in a shop that says "Speak English Only" (see figure 41) can lead to discussions

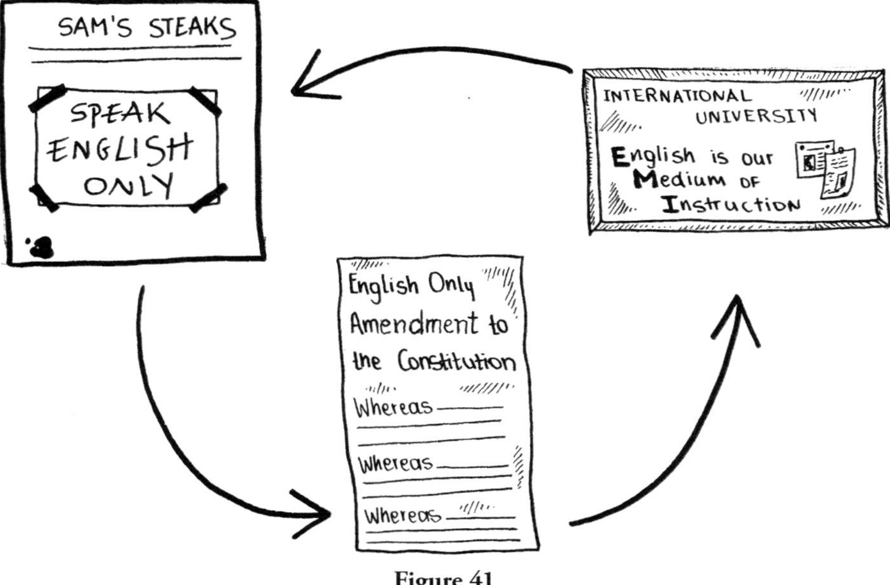


**Figure 41**

of national language policy (e.g., the proposal of an English Only amendment to the Constitution) and the globalization of English as a lingua franca or medium of instruction.

## What's Next?

In this chapter you have seen how you can draw on media of the everyday to explore language, meaning-making, and local knowledge. The seemingly mundane objects that we encounter every day consist of creative uses of text and interesting combinations of language and imagery. In the language learning classroom, media work using analog and digitial resources that are tied to the "here and now" and the current needs of students provides opportunities for meaningful language learning and may also introduce students to useful resources and practical information. Look at vocabulary, verb tenses, language varieties, metaphors. Uncover references to local popular culture, to historical events, to other media, and to places that are meaningful to members of a community.

I encourage you to curate your own collection of objects, photos, and screenshots to use in class as an introduction to media work. You can keep this collection at hand and reach for an example at any time. One week, you may only have time for a quick look at a flyer from a school bulletin board; another time you might incorporate a multiweek media work project into your calendar. In both cases, the media work model can be your guide to approaching this work in a theory-driven, adaptable, and purposeful way.

In the following chapter, the emphasis shifts from looking at media messages of selected modalities in local spaces, to exploring selected themes that can be found across modalities in local and global spaces. The symbols, modalities, and plots are still central to media work but are more closely examined as "storytellers" as a way to talk about the intersection of language and culture.

## KEY IDEAS

local mediascapes

anlaog versus digital

bumper stickers and window decals

public signage

memes

menus and food advertisements

local to global connections

## REFLECT

1. What are authentic materials for language teaching? What is "inauthentic"?
2. Think about the media you encounter everyday. When is analog more important, when is digital more important? What is the role of each?
3. Take notes over a two-to-three-day period of key vocabulary in the mundane media that you encounter (advertisements, announcements, signage on public transportation, signs in shop windows, etc.). How much of this vocabulary is idiomatic, formal, informal, local, high frequency, or low frequency? Do certain languages or dialects dominate?

## EXPLORE

1. Select a familiar setting where you can see media around you, such as a market, local shop, classroom, or school hallway. Online, a setting might be a website devoted to one topic such as an activity you like or organization you belong to. Use the example worksheet in figure 42 to help you explore these settings.

| What setting did you choose? | *Explore a familiar place* |
|---|---|
| **What is the purpose of the media you see there?** (information, persuasion) | |
| **What kinds of specific platforms are used and why?** | |
| **Interesting vocabulary** (idioms, slang, abbreviations, acronyms, dialect markers) | |
| **Grammatical structures** (rules followed and rules broken) | |
| **Cultural Content** What background knowledge does the viewer need to know to understand these messages? | |
| **How might some of these media messages be interpreted through different points of view?** | |
| **How does my background influence my interpretations of these media?** | |
| **How could I use some of this media with my students?** (e.g. as examples, model for an activity…) | |

**Figure 42**

Discuss your responses with a classmate or colleague. What kinds of everyday media are part of your students' experiences? What media would be appropriate for media work in your classroom? Are there media messages that you would like to avoid? Why?

LEARN MORE

Teacher-scholars in education, healthcare, history, and many other fields look at messages in local mediascapes. The few examples I share here include an examination of signage and menus in coffee shops in South Korea, how the use of English functions as a demonstration of cosmopolitanism, and a study of how signage in a Hispanic-serving college in the United States is dominated by English. In addition, you can read about how LLs can be combined with a narrated walking method to engage with contested discourses of local place, and how the Anne Frank House in Amsterdam developed a "memory walk" method in which learners walk through a town and film or photograph monuments and memorials to learn about local history. These approaches can be combined in various combinations with media work.

Boerhout, L., & van Driel, B. (2013). Memory walk: an interaction-oriented project to interrogate contested histories. *Intercultural Education, 24*(3), 211–221. doi.org/10.1080/14675986.2013.799804

Curran, N. M., & Chesnut, A. (2022). English fever and coffee: Transient cosmopolitanism and the rising cost of distinction. *Journal of Consumer Culture, 22*(2), 551–570. DOI: 10.1177/1469540521990869

Hallett, R. W., & Quiñones, F. M. (2023). The linguistic landscape of an urban Hispanic-serving institution in the United States. *Social Semiotics, 33*(3), 645–659. doi: https://doi.org/10.1080/10350 330.2021.1916391

Stroud, C. & Jegels, D. (2014). Semiotic landscapes and mobile narrations of place: performing the local. International Journal of the Sociology of Language. 228, 179–199. DOI 10.1515/ijsl-2014-0010

In addition, looking at every day media relates to studies of popular culture and artifacts. You may find ideas and inspiration by looking at objects and other media from local art and cultural organizations, museums, popular shops and hang-outs, local festivals, town newspapers and newsletters, and markets. Adult language learners may benefit from exploring the media distributed by local services and organizations that they encounter in their daily activities.

# CHAPTER 5

# Media Work and Storytelling

Chapter 4 illustrated how signs and symbols we see every day are language-rich media that illustrate the creative use and power of language. In this chapter, language and images are further explored as storytellers. First, I describe what I mean by "storytelling" and its relationship to teaching about culture and language. Then I position storytelling within the media work model, including guiding questions for exploring mediated stories about people, places, and ideas. I share examples of mediated stories about language and culture that are inspired by decades of teaching experience.

You are probably already familiar with stereotypes and misrepresentations that inundate screens today. It is not difficult to see the over-used formulas and tropes in advertisements, video games, movies, series, news, labels, and so on, but sometimes these well-worn stories are less obvious, disguised by updated themes and images. Old stories in new packaging. Uncovering such stereotyped and often harmful portrayals of people, places, and ideas is the focus of media work in this chapter. Media work can interrogate and critique narrow or negative representations, but it can also reveal how these stories are disrupted, challenged, and replaced by new perspectives and portrayals. I present media work here as not simply a defense against harmful media content, but as a process of understanding how media create multiple realities and what these realities mean to those who consume them.

## What Is Storytelling?

We are surrounded by storytelling. Stories entertain, inform, and educate. Stories inspire us, challenge us, and help us to navigate our paths in the world. Most people think of stories as narrative structures with defined parts: beginning, middle, and end. Some stories such as full-length films, books, documentaries, myths, or often-told family stories may follow this pattern. Some stories even begin with "Once upon a time . . ." Most of the stories told by media, however, are more fragmented and decontextualized, yet they are nevertheless powerful because of their repetition and pervasiveness. For example, the article about ESL in schools that I shared in Chapter 3 contains not one coherent story but several fragmented (yet related) stories about immigrants and language learners: immigrants are a burden to schools; they are motivated, hard workers; they are in need of help from others, and they are both a boost and a threat to the economy. Storylines like these become powerful because they are reinforced through repetition over time and through multiple modalities—movies, memes, campaign speeches, social media, TV shows, and so on. The storytellers in our lives include families, friends, institutions, communities, governments, and, of course, media.

Let's look at figure 43 and revisit cultivation theory, one of the big ideas from Chapter 2. Gerbner asserted decades ago that television had replaced schools, families, and other institutions as the primary storyteller in our lives. In the Media Education Foundation video "The Electronic Storyteller" (2014), Gerbner, Jhally, and Morgan describe how some common and constantly

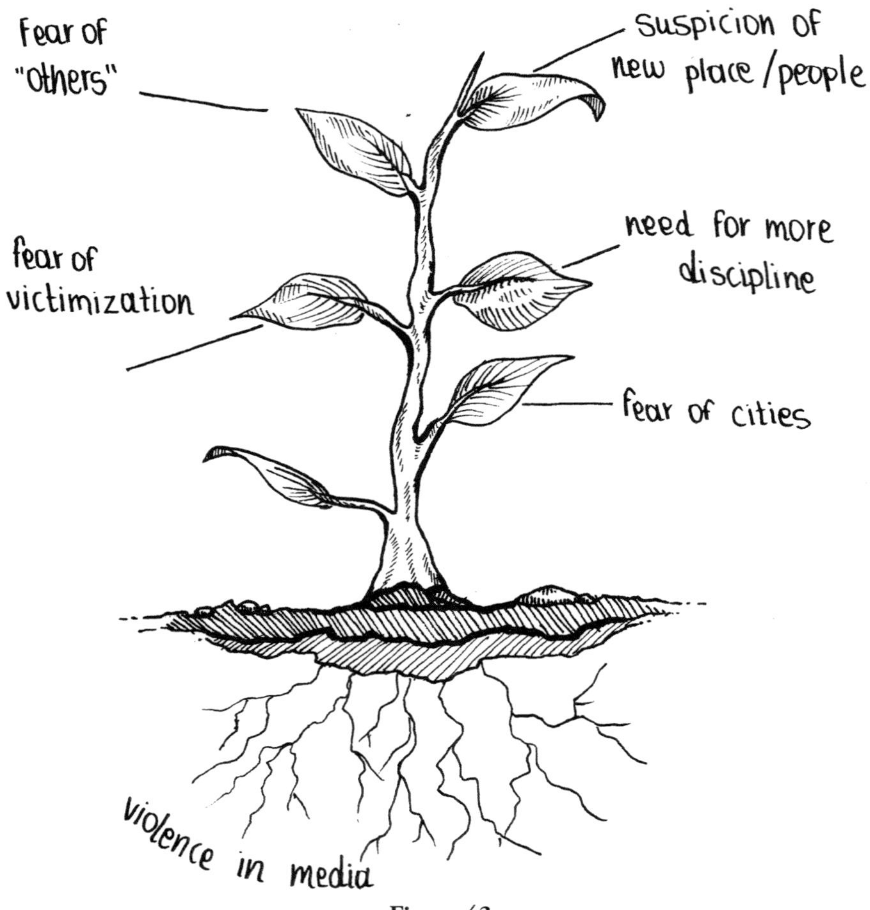


**Figure 43**

repeated behaviors on screen tell us powerful stories about race, class, gender, and violence. Gerbner believes, in fact, that the stories are so powerful that television (or today, all screens) actually structures our social narratives. He offers the example of driving cars. In reality, driving in an automobile is statistically one of the most dangerous activities in which we can engage. Yet on screen, driving is portrayed as a low-risk and exciting activity, whereas using public transportation such as subways is portrayed as dangerous. After viewing years of such images, we begin to fear things that are not particularly dangerous. We prefer driving over public transportation and may not support funding for buses, trains, and metros. Powerful storylines such as this one about cars cultivate beliefs and values and shape our cultural realities.

Storytelling and culture are deeply intertwined. Culture is created and transmitted through stories that teach us how the world works, our place in the world, how to act, and how to evaluate the world around us (Hall et al., 2022). Obviously, media are not the only sources of storytelling, but the amount of time we spend in front of screens is on the rise. Census data from Common Sense Media (CSM) reveals that 8- to 12-year-olds in the United States averaged 5 hours 33 minutes on screens for entertainment (not schooling) per day and 13- to 18-year-olds averaged 8 hours 39 minutes per day (Rideout et al., 2022). CSM's most recent survey of children of 8 years and younger shows that 5- to 8-year-olds spend just over 3 hours per day in front of screens, 2- to 4-year-olds, 2 hours 30 minutes, and those under 2 years average 49 minutes per day. All the CSM studies indicate a strong rise in the domination of videos (YouTube, TikTok, etc.) in terms of time spent with screens and heavier usage by Black and Hispanic/Latinx populations. Moreover, most parents believe that screens mostly help their children to learn (72%) and be creative (60%). With this much usage and confidence in screens, we must take their storytelling function and cultural content seriously (Rideout et al., 2022).

Language teaching is not separate from teaching about culture, yet this relationship has not always been recognized in curricula. I learned French in high school and had to wait until the third year of study to learn about "culture." At the time, culture was viewed as traditions, customs, artistic endeavors, foods, and historical events that could be talked about through language, but was otherwise treated as a separate subject. Teaching about culture in the language learning classroom has changed dramatically since that time, now shifting our thoughts from culture as a fixed, objective set of knowledge to culture as a fluid process that is interwoven with language. Language scholar Ingrid Piller asks us to think about culture as a verb. She argues that culture as a noun is narrowly defined as national assets, as obstacles or challenges, or as a mark of citizenship—all of which can serve to include and exclude people

(2017, pp. 7–8). To reframe culture as a verb, Piller quotes Brian Street who writes that "culture is an active process of meaning-making and contest over definition, including its own definition" (Street, 1993, p. 25). I also refer to a definition of culture from the communication scholar B. J. Hall who defines culture as "a historically shared system of symbolic resources through which we make our world meaningful" (Hall, 2022, p. 4). Both definitions highlight culture as meaning-making. Piller and Street emphasize culture as an active process, and Hall reminds us of its ties to community. The symbolic resources that Hall mentions are particularly relevant to media work because they refer to language and other symbols that carry shared meaning, evoke responses, and provide us with tools to interact in the world. As we decipher and respond to the messages encoded in symbolic resources such as media, we participate in a continual process of storytelling that transmits and transforms culture.

## Processing Storytelling Through Media Work

Let's refresh our memories and take another look at the basic components of media work. You recall that there is no prescribed order for talking about the relationships among all of the components, but it does help to have guidelines. In Chapter 4, looking at everyday media included examination of a full range of content, processes, and contexts, with particular emphasis on the modalities and symbols of media. In media work about storytelling, the entire model must likewise be considered, but the processes of observation, interrogation, interpretation, reflection, and response are centered on the specific stories that teachers and students identify.

The stories told through media—whether hours, minutes, or seconds long—rely on building characters, (re)creating events, and conveying ideas in relatively short periods of time. Digital media, in particular, competes for our immediate and often distracted attention. A great deal of information is conveyed in a matter of seconds through imagery, language, and nonverbal communication that rely heavily on representations that resonate with viewers. You can show students a very short excerpt from the beginning of a program or film or a short YouTube video (or commercial) and ask:

1.  What did you know about the people, products, places, or activities in the scene before you saw it? What information was new to you?
2.  What language, images, and other nonverbal aspects conveyed information to you about the people, products, places, or activities represented?

3. What stories are being told about the people, products, places, or activities?
4. Are these stories already familiar to you? Are they conveyed in other media?

As your students answer these questions, they will quickly realize that interpretations are based on both explicit and subtle linguistic and nonverbal cues. Varieties of speech, pacing, colors, sounds, movement, close-up shots, panoramic frames, lighting, and much more contribute to how stories are read. Sometimes it is advantageous to make a complete transcription of spoken discourse and corresponding nonverbal behaviors. It is also important to note details that might be in the background, the ways in which characters relate to one another, and the order in which ideas or characters are introduced. Content analysis (e.g., making a list of precisely what is seen and heard and how often), can be very useful for these observations in order to capture details. Go back to the video excerpt, discuss whether or not all of the students noticed the same details. Chances are, they will notice different things about the content and will see the importance of collecting objective data.

As you engage with media work about storytelling, students may need guiding questions to spark their interrogations and interpretations, to help them make connections to contextual variables, and to encourage reflection and response. In addition to the lists of questions offered in Chapter 3, you can create more extensive lists of guiding questions with your students. Adapt the questions to align with students' proficiency levels, and arrange them creatively to focus on language structures. For example, tap into vocabulary by asking students to describe physical characteristics and behaviors in detail. Focus on tenses with questions about what students think happened before the story was told or what might happen in the future. Work on expressing opinions, agreement, and disagreement while interpreting, reflecting, and responding to stories.

Like all media work, exploring stories can be integrated into class discussions, short group work assignments, or longer projects. Allow time for students to explore stories. Observation and documentation of media samples can take place over a period of weeks outside of class, and you can periodically ask students to share what they have found in class. I have incorporated this form of media work into journal assignments in which international students were asked to document signage and other media that fit into themes they had identified as a class. As newcomers to the area, they were intrigued by the language and signage of grocery stores, displays of identities through flags, and references to local sports teams, to name a few. One group of students on a short-term visit to Philadelphia kept journals in which they wrote anything they wanted and included at least one photo each day of a sign or other text that was unfamiliar or confusing to them. Photos ranged from signs in their hotel rooms about fire safety and other policies, to information about public transit, to menus that barely mentioned food directly. After interrogating the language and interpreting stories from multiple viewpoints together in class, the students worked in groups to collect more data, reflect on meaning, and create multimodal presentations for the class. I have also included journal assignments as individual projects in intercultural communication classes and as the basis for ongoing informal discussions in response to current events and media representations.

To illustrate this process, I share examples of stories that students in language (ESL and EFL), intercultural communication, sociolinguistics, and second language teacher education classes have selected to examine over the past decade. Students propose themes that are fairly broad (climate change, health, fashion, multilingualism) or more specific (transgender policies in a school district, urban versus suburban real estate descriptions, historical markers and plaques in Philadelphia). Those who begin with broader topics typically narrow their focus once they are immersed in media work processes.

Although these stories can be categorized by general themes, such as people, places, events and ideas, the truth is that no story is self-contained or static. They intersect, overlap, shift, and change. Nevertheless, I want to provide you with examples of three categories of media work about stories that illustrate the adaptability of the processes. For each of the three categories (people, places, ideas) I offer guiding questions that build off the "starting points" introduced in Chapter 3. I then include highlights of students' media work to illustrate how they processed stories.

## Stories About People

Stories about people cover an immense range of intersecting identities—ethnicity, neighborhoods, regions, gender, age, social class. Sometimes depictions of people in media can be expansive, thought-provoking, and multidimensional. Too often, however, portrayals of people rely heavily on stereotypes and images that are simplified and comfortable for mass audiences to digest. Such stories can serve us pedagogically. First of all, thorough observations of characters evoke linguistic structures used to talk about physical and emotional qualities, behaviors, professions, communication styles, living environments, activities, and patterns of interaction among characters. Lessons in vocabulary, pragmatics, and nonverbal communication can be extracted from such observations. Second, stories about people in media tap into the cultural knowledge that viewers bring with them to interpret meaning. This cultural knowledge itself can be the focus of discussions and assignments. For example, the use of various American English dialects are powerful triggers of stereotypes to those who *know* the stereotypes, but they might go unnoticed by those unfamiliar with these associations. Third, misrepresentations and essentialized portrayals of people in media can be examined through cultivation theory to discuss social attitudes and discrimination. My classes are made up of diverse students who sometimes encounter negative social attitudes and may not be ready or willing to talk about their personal experiences. Talking about mediated images and fictional characters, however, provides a way for students to interrogate, interpret, reflect, and respond without feeling pressured to disclose personal stories. I find that most students become comfortable with their peers and voluntarily share their own stories as they participate in media work.

Figure 44 provides guiding questions for storytelling about people that you can add to and adapt as necessary. The "X" in the list refers to any individuals or groups of people that are portrayed in media. Depending on the modality and scope of the sources, some questions will be more relevant than others.

Next, I share how some of these questions can be applied to stories related to two topics: gender and accent. Gender is a popular topic for media storytelling because conceptualizations of gender are culturally defined, easy prey to stereotypes (i.e., they provide easy explanations for behaviors), and are experienced by everyone. As a subject for interrogation and interpretation, gender can be related to discussions of social roles, expectations, and communication styles, or we can take a deeper dive into gender equity, nonbinary identity, queerness, sexual or gender-based harassment, and other topics. Likewise, accent is applicable to everyone but is used almost exclusively to evoke stereotyped characterizations. Discussions of accent can range from the use of language varieties (dialects, slang, code-switching) in popular culture to linguistic hierarchies, discrimination, and language policy. The context of your teaching and the needs of your students will dictate the level of interrogation.

Let's look at gender first. You can begin with traditionally oversimplified labels that are easy to find in media and then expand to more current and inclusive examples of language about gender. Examples that the students share are catalysts for discussions about gendered caretaking roles, professional roles, and all the obligations and expectations that are associated with gender. Stories range from the representation of gender in familial roles (breadwinner, authority figure, nurturer) to how gender is depicted

# Guiding Questions: Storytelling and People

## Observations

How is this character (X) represented physically and symbolically (e.g. clothing, accessories, phone, vehicle, hairstyle, glasses, tatoos, piercings)?
How long and how often does X appear on screen (or other format)?
To what social class, lifestyle, profession, level of education, etc., is X affiliated?
What information about X is highlighted (given most attention)?
How does X communicate with others (face-to-face, in groups, one on one)?
What topics does X talk about with others?
What adjectives are used to describe X?
In what contexts or settings does X appear?
What accents, dialects, and languages are associated with X?
What emotions does X display? When, where, and to whom?
What is the audience initially presumed to know about X?
How does X live? What does X own?

## Interrogations and Interpretations

How does X behave in ways that conform to common stereotypes?
How does X behave in ways that disrupt common stereotypes?
What is the status of people and places associated with X? What is X's status in this story?
What will X's future be? (and how do we know this?)
What traits are associated with X (e.g. intelligence, compassion, ambition, greed, complacency)?
What kind of emotional response does X evoke from the audience?
What are X's values and beliefs?
What kinds of attitudes toward X might be cultivated by these media portrayals?
What impact might these attitudes indirectly have on social narratives about X?

## Reflections and Responses

How do these representations of X challenge or align with your own experiences and knowledge of diverse people?
How do these stories about X reflect mythologies and/or facts?
What surprised you the most about the representations of X?
Do you think the representations you examined are common or uncommon?
If you were to produce a story about X, how would you portray them?

**Figure 44**

in relation to jobs and careers, to the cultivation of attitudes toward non-binary and transgender people through media representations. If students choose to look at stories about gender for group or individual assignments, I encourage them to focus on specific stories where gender intersects with other aspects of identity, place, and events.

Over the years, students have shared their collections of stories about gender from all kinds of media. They look at television programs, streaming videos, printed advertisements, commercials, pop-ups, children's books, parenting magazines, music lyrics, clothing, book covers, greeting cards, coffee mugs and other gift shop artifacts, to name just a few. They find stories that align with traditional stereotypes, stories that blatantly challenge these stereotypes, and stories that manage to do both. Here are some of the ways students have explored stories about gender in various mediated environments:

- Arcades and bars: students collected photos of signage, menus, drink lists, arcade games, and decorations in different establishments geared toward young adults; they found that colors and language on the displays of arcade games reflected stereotypical masculine and feminine characteristics (competition and collaboration, respectively) in some places, while one arcade seemed to be more gender neutral.

- Personal care products: students have looked at items displayed in stores, advertisements on screens and in print. They found similar products (lotions, soaps, shampoos) to be marketed differently for males or females through the choice of language, colors, and images. The language in products for men is about strength and power, while the same product for women uses language related to confidence and beauty.

- Sporting events: students examined media outlets' (digital and analog) coverage of women's and men's events. They saw differences in semantic choices such as "gracefulness" versus "powerful," and they noticed patterns in which female athletes are photographed at home in sexy clothing while men are more often seen in team uniforms in action. One student who was a teacher of martial arts took a close look at an article about a highly respected female martial arts champion. He was pleased to see such in-depth coverage of the athlete and her accomplishments, but discovered that a great deal of the article was devoted to talking about her father (a former champion) and her husband (her coach) as being responsible for her success.

- Health and fitness: many students are interested in looking at media about health and fitness. In several classes, groups of students have identified this broad topic then broken it down into subtopics for group members to explore. Although they are not surprised to find gender differences, they are surprised at the extent to which gender stereotypes are used as marketing tools. Different colors, font, images, and language are used for gendered audiences for products such as sports drinks and supplements, even when the products are exactly the same. Students also gather media from gyms (actual physical spaces and their websites), dance studios, yoga studios, and magazines about health and fitness.

The results of these media work activities are not surprising, but the work should not stop with observations and interrogations. Next, students have to think about their own interpretations. Some feel that emphases of gender differences are necessary to make people comfortable, while others feel that they are unnecessary or harmful. Students need to reflect on their own expectations for gender roles and how they feel when these roles are redefined. Because the stereotypes are fairly easy to find, I often ask students to respond by finding examples of media that transgress traditional gender roles and expectations. What are the new stories that are being told today?

Figure 45a–c illustrates traditional stories about gender that can be found in various media. The three illustrations depict two mugs and a t-shirt that are printed with expressions that confirm traditional ideas about femininity and marriage. These items were found in local gift shops.

Figure 46a–c, also based on signs from local shops, tell us that all men like to drink beer, that a married man is nagged by his wife and not allowed to have fun, and that a father's role is to fix everything. These stories are conveyed through interesting colloquial language choices. Encourage students to talk about idioms such as "said no one, ever." The second example uses the word "superpower" as well as the phrase "to shut something down." All of these

**Figure 45a**

**Figure 45b**

**Figure 45c**

| | | |
|:---:|:---:|:---:|
| **Figure 46a** | **Figure 46b** | **Figure 46c** |

choices convey degrees of sarcasm, nostalgia, and humor as they overtly reinforce stereotypes of masculinity and femininity. Some argue that these artifacts should not be taken seriously, that they are just for fun (I will come back to this idea later in the chapter).

Stories about masculinity and femininity still abound, but they are challenged by messages that dissolve these binaries and expand ideas about gender. Traditionally, fitting rooms and restrooms in the United States have been separated for males and females. The use of all-gender or unisex spaces can be seen in some public places, but the practice is not widespread. Advocacy for LGBTQ+ communities is displayed through signage and representations, but this varies from place to place. In a large city such as Philadelphia, certain neighborhoods and businesses are known as spaces that are welcoming to all expressions of gender. A sandwich shop re-named a menu item during Pride Week (advocacy, marketing—or both?). On a shelf underneath the mugs that portray patriarchal traditions, we can find a "they/them" mug. The pronoun shift to the singular "they" is not new, but not everyone has embraced it. Overall, the stories told about gender in Figure 47a–c reflect diverse perspectives.

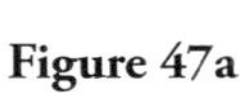

| | | |
|:---:|:---:|:---:|
| **Figure 47a** | **Figure 47b** | **Figure 47c** |

If you or your students decide to explore stories about gender, you do not need to limit your discussions to gender identity alone. Gender intersects with other identities such as race, age, social class, sexual orientation, and religion, as well as with relationships, athletics, healthcare, harassment, social justice, and human rights. From the photos above students have interrogated and reflected on the ideas of what marriage is supposed to mean to heterosexual and homosexual couples, why the institution of marriage exists as it does, how girls today are encouraged to be athletes but still have to conform to beauty standards, how boys and men are pressured to like sports, and how respect toward nonbinary and trans identities is growing but is still limited to certain social spaces. The stories that media tell about gender are powerful. Sometimes they reflect fixed ideas, sometimes fluid. For example, the advertisement for the LGBTQ sandwich elicits a range of interpretations and responses: outrage at the commodification and trivialization of queer identity, lack of surprise at the opportunistic marketing, pleasure that queer identity is openly expressed. All are legitimate responses, and open up good discussions about context. The location of this sign in the Philadelphia neighborhood known as the "Gayborhood" matters, and Pride Week is a popular and very visible event. Students question the shop ownership (local, queer, or corporate) and customer base. Is this an appropriation used to increase sales to tourists, or is it an authentic show of support for the local community? Is it possible and acceptable to be both?

The second topic for stories told about people has to do with accent. I have been interested in how different accents are used on screen to portray characters for several years now, especially how the use of accent creates a character with undefined, but clearly "foreign" identity (Chamberlin-Quinlisk, 2012; Lippi-Green, 2012). Some of the stories that are told and retold on television, film, videos, and streaming platforms include:

- Characters with certain accents are romantic or charming.

- Characters with certain accents are criminal or nefarious.

- Characters with certain accents are less successful or ambitious.

- Characters with certain accents are less intelligent or competent.

Far too many examples exist in which characters who speak in non-prestige varieties of languages are qualitatively and quantitatively different from those who speak with a prestige-variety accent. As a place to start, I ask students a simple question: "Who in this classroom speaks with an accent?" For a few seconds, they look around and hesitantly raise their hands. If some students are native speakers of English, they often do not raise their hands at all—until I or someone else points out that we ALL speak with accents. This leads into discussions of attitudes, prestige, status, and discrimination associated with different socially marked accents and the word "accent." This is a good time to emphasize the fact that all languages are inherently equal but that they are judged unequally in societies. When students begin to make their own observations of the media they select, their content analyses often reveal that marked accents define characters and their actions, sometimes in positive terms but most often in negative. They then ask questions such as why are these images acceptable or popular? For example, would mass audiences be comfortable if the main hero or heroine of a Hollywood film spoke with a non-American accent, and the supporting roles were filled by prestige-variety speakers? If not, what does this say about accent being used to mark a character's ability to be a hero? Under what circumstances can a "foreigner" be the most powerful figure on screen? Do certain conditions need to be met to make this acceptable? Although a character's accent might seem random to viewers, or appear as simply natural to that role, there is nothing natural or arbitrary about it. At some point during the writing and production process, someone made a decision that a character should speak in a certain way, and that decision was based on the emotional response that the accent would evoke from the audience.

Without much searching, students find representation of various accents, regional dialects, and "foreign" languages in their favorite programs, movies, music, games, videos, and social media platforms. They also find attitudes toward different languages, monolingualism, and multilingualism in signage in public places, neighborhoods, and schools. The following examples of media work from various classes (intensive English, sociolinguistics, and second language teacher education) attest to the myriad opportunities to talk about linguistic features as well as stories about language. Below are some take-aways of individual student, group, or whole class activities in which students examined accents.

Students are quick to realize that animated and live action movies, programs, and videos have characters with a wide variety of accents. Cartoons on TV make use of German, Russian, and other Eastern European accents to enhance characteristics of villainy. British accents can be used to convey charm and sophistication or pretension. Typically, students are surprised by the quantity and scope of examples. Particularly poignant stories connect characters who speak with non-prestigious, or non-American accents to lower paying jobs, lack of ambition, and complacency. If a character with a non-prestigious accent does succeed, they often have to go against the grain and learn to behave differently, sometimes rejecting or making fun of the "traditional" ways of their heritage. In the movie *Pocahontas* (Gabriel & Goldberg, 1995), for example, why does Pocahontas speak with a prestige-variety American accent, but all the other people in her family and community speak with an accent meant to represent their Native American identity? Why doesn't she sound like them? Why is their uncertainty toward White colonizers portrayed as a traditional and narrow-minded point of view? A similar positioning of young, sophisticated people against the traditional ways of older generations is often exaggerated by the use of accent in portrayals of immigrant families.

In my own study of non-American accents in Hollywood movies that I discussed in an earlier chapter, I followed up my content analysis with interrogations and interpretations of a character who is almost wholly defined by his status as a non-native speaker of English. He is constantly made fun of for his perceived lack of proficiency, despite the fact that he makes fewer grammatical errors than the main protagonist native speaker. Although this character plays a big role in the film, his actions are inconsequential to the plot, he is never seen as being in control of his own destiny, and while all the other characters develop and become more successful, he does not change (Chamberlin-Quinlisk, 2012a). When I shared clips of this film with my students, we all tried to identify the character's accent but could not pinpoint it. We were struck by the fact that this artificial accent did not even have to be realistic to be powerful. The fact that it deviated from the accents of the native speakers in the film was enough to mark it as foreign, and being foreign was enough to render this character's lack of power as acceptable, comical, and comfortable for a mass audience. Lippi-Green (2012) thoroughly describes social attitudes and discrimination toward accents, highlighting how media representations and language ideologies impact education, work, housing, and rationalization of prejudice. Unfortunately, too many of these stories about accent resonate with our students' experiences. The more we develop awareness of how attitudes toward accent are cultivated through media, however, the more we encourage others to reflect on the impact of stories and seek out or create counter-stories.

If you want to talk about dialects in the United States as well as other accents, an easily accessible source of stereotypes is the old Looney Tunes productions of Bugs Bunny and friends that began in the late 1930s and are still produced today by Warner Brothers. In the Looney Tunes that were on television when I was watching as a child, Bugs Bunny was the street-wise clever rabbit who speaks Brooklynese. Foghorn Leghorn was a slow-witted chicken with a Southern accent. Yosemite Sam was a gun-wielding wild man with a Texan accent. Speedy Gonzalez was a clever, somewhat sneaky mouse with a Spanish accent who often had to cover for his lazy, drunken mouse friends (also with Spanish accents). Pépé LePew was the overly romantic and unsuccessful-in-love skunk with a French accent. Such outrageous stereotyping would be unacceptable today, but went unquestioned decades ago. Students are often surprised by the blatant stereotypes of cartoon and other characters in older media. I ask them to find out how much things have changed. This is an interesting challenge. Without much effort, students can find representations of characters who speak with various accents and regional dialects, as well as global varieties of English, and although some of the stereotypes have diminished, accents still carry meaning. The foreign exchange student in *That 70's Show* (1998–2006) nicknamed "Fez" (for f̲oreign e̲xchange s̲tudent) provides comic relief with his accent and linguistic errors (that do not at all align with his high level of proficiency!). He is never taken seriously, and he believes that everything American is superior to his own culture. Moreover, his real name is never revealed. His identity as "foreign" supersedes everything else about him.

Another character who comes up in class discussions is the Colombian actress and comedian Sophia Vergara who plays a Colombian character Gloria in the wildly successful American sit-com *Modern Family* (Levitan, et al., 2009–2020). Her accent and semantic choices define her character, and her cultural background is consistently represented as corrupt, violent, shady, and extremely dangerous. Students like to talk about this character. She is funny, strong, endearing, and an interesting mixture of naïveté and cleverness. However, the overt sexual objectification of her character and use of language "deficiencies" (her accent, mixing up idioms, incorrect word choices) for humor lead to serious questions about comedy. How do jokes perpetuate or rebel against damaging stereotypes of sexism, racism, or linguicism? Media work that explores comedy often leads to extended class conversations about the process of interpretation. Students become aware of colorblindness, erasure, and other social lenses that filter perceptions of jokes about and representations of "others" (Billig, 2005; Drakett et al., 2018; Horisk, 2024; Yoon, 2016; Yosso, 2002, 2006, 2020).

Stories about people in media cover a vast array of representations. The few examples of gender and accent described here barely scratch the surface. In some ways, media are more careful today about misrepresenting or essentializing people for fear of being canceled, but the fast-paced nature of current media technologies encourages simplification as screens and other modalities compete for the attention of a global audience. And depending on the social climate, some misrepresentations are more accepted than others. Students still find stories that tell us that lawyers are unethical, teachers are either buffoons or martyrs, scientists are socially awkward and unsociable, certain groups are untrustworthy, others are terrorists, some are arrogant, and on and on. Students also interrogate "new" portrayals such as representations of disability, political affiliations, age, neurodiversity, immigration status, mental illness, sports fandom, transgender identities, substance use disorder, and so on. Intriguing questions arise when students find that some of these current representations might be more accurate or positive than in the past but they are portrayed by actors who do not share an identity with the characters. This is a good conversation prompt. Should only (trans, gay, disabled . . .) actors portray (trans, gay, disabled . . .) characters? It is easy to brush many mediated representations off as entertainment, but we have to remember that "entertainment" has become one of the most powerful storytellers in our society. To be sure, the heroes on screens today represent a wide range of identities, and we should encourage students to conduct media work on positive images. In reflecting on these images, students should think about what "positive" representations look like and sound like. Understanding a wide range of stories empowers us to notice and support portrayals that include deeper, complex, and more accurate representations.

## Stories About Places and Belonging

Media tell powerful stories about what it means to be a part of a group, to come from or live in a certain place, and to have strong emotional ties with that place. Think about where you live or where you grew up and what that community means to you. When you see your familiar places and communities in media, how are they represented? Is the life you experience represented as a common reality, a norm? Do you feel nostalgic? Do you connect to familiar images and feel comfortable? Do the media representations of places you know evoke fear or safety? In general, stories about place, affiliation, and belonging convey messages about where we live (or where we are from), what we believe, and who we are. It is neither easy nor desirable to separate these intersecting stories, and students often find that an exploration of one theme cannot be disentangled from others. Interrogation of the intersection of place, values, and identity, in fact, is a critical part of thought-provoking and transformative media work. The guiding questions in figure 48 direct students to focus on places but encourage them to think about the convergence of place and identities.

# **Guiding Questions: Storytelling about Places and Belonging**

## Observations

How is this place (Y) represented physically and symbolically (e.g. space, architecture, cleanliness, order, chaos, attractiveness, crowded, desolate)?
Who lives in Y? Who visits Y?
What kinds of businesses, activities, institutions, and shops are found in Y?
How is Y positioned in relation to other communities and the larger world?
Which social classes are represented in Y?
What adjectives are used to describe Y?
How do people move around in Y (e.g. walking, driving, trollies, buses, subways, taxis, bikes)?
Who belongs in Y, and who are outsiders?

## Interrogations and Interpretations

How do images of Y conform to common stereotypes?
How do images of Y disrupt common stereotypes?
How expensive is it to live in or visit Y?
Is Y a desirable place to be? For whom?
What is the past, present, and future of Y?
What emotional responses does Y evoke from the audience?
Are there values and beliefs associated with Y?
How strongly do audiences associate social class, ethnicity, and other identities with Y?
What does it mean to come from or live in Y (advantages, and disadvantages)?

## Reflections and Responses

How do these representations of Y challenge or align with your own experiences and knowledge of diverse places?
How do these stories about Y reflect mythologies and/or facts?
What surprised you the most about the representations of Y?
Do you think the representations you examined are common or uncommon?
If you were to produce a story about Y, what would you highlight?

**Figure 48**

*Stories About Where We Live*

Looking at stories about local communities encourages students to explore their surroundings, take a closer look at the language around them (such as the examples in Chapter 4), become more familiar with local dialects and place names, and perhaps even discover new opportunities and resources. I began using media work about place with international students who were unfamiliar with their surroundings. Over the years I have discovered that students who were born and raised in the local area also gain a great deal from the activities. In linguistically and culturally diverse classrooms, students hear multiple interpretations of stories that they originally saw through a narrow lens, and in some cases, they discover communities that they knew little about and were perhaps even afraid of.

One of my most poignant teaching memories was about stories of place. We had been talking about cities and suburbs in class, and a student from a suburb shared the fears she had about the city because of news media coverage. We looked at this coverage as a class and interrogated its content, emotional appeal (i.e., fear), and connections to other stories about race and social class. At some point, the student also admitted that she had never taken public transportation because she was taught to be afraid of it and therefore never used it. This connected directly to cultivation theory and the perception that public transportation is dangerous, while driving cars is not (Gerbner et al., 2014). The class conversation was engaging and inspiring, but that wasn't the best part. The following week in class I learned that a group of students had talked after class and made arrangements to go to Philadelphia together on the weekend with the student who was afraid. They used public transportation and spent the day together in the city. Students from the city wanted to show off their communities and dispel the misrepresentations and fear. Students from the city shouldn't have to defend their communities, but the fact that they took the initiative to teach and learn from each other rather than avoid and/or argue was inspiring. Since then, students have continued to do media work that unveils stories about the city, the suburbs, and rural areas. There are many misconceptions about all of these places that typically come from media rather than first-hand experiences. When students bring photos of their own places to class this showcases not only their analyses of media but also their diverse experiences.

I could fill an entire book with images that students and I have collected of signage and other media about our local communities. You have seen some already in the previous chapter, and others appear in stories about people and

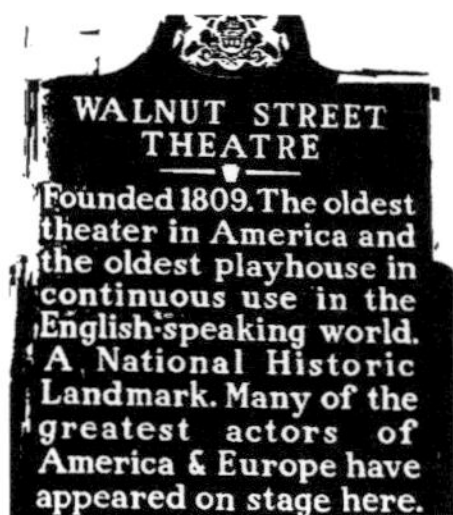

Figure 49a

Figure 49b

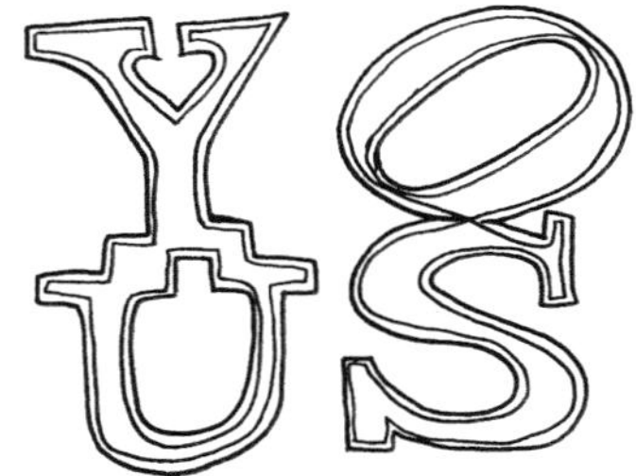


Figure 49c

ideas. The images in figure 49a–c represent just a few of the themes that students explore. Philadelphia has many historic sites that are marked by dark blue plaques with gold-colored writing (see figure 49a). Students interpret the format and language as formal in order to convey a sense of seriousness and historic importance. This particular sign for the Walnut Street Theater interestingly notes that it is "the oldest playhouse in continuous use in the English-speaking world." We can interrogate the intended meaning of "the English-speaking world" and why that phrase was chosen. Students can collaborate to collect images of these markers and locate them on a map and create their own tour of the city as a podcast, web page, or printed brochure. Students can rewrite the text in a different style or research a site more thoroughly and rewrite the content. Through the whole process they can reflect on the how the history of a place is told and can be retold through different modalities and voices.

The "YOUS" in figure 49c is printed on a t-shirt and refers to a plural "you" in a local dialect. Though not completely inaccurate, the use of "yous" has been exaggerated in media such as movies and television to represent a Philadelphia dialect. Students can interrogate several ideas associated with this local speech as well as the reference to the Robert Indiana "LOVE" sculpture in which the letters are stacked two by two and the O is tilted. The LOVE statue is an iconic marker of Philadelphia. Students can research the features of a local dialect, ask themselves where it is seen or heard, and what it means that examples of the dialect are now found on t-shirts, bumper stickers, and other media. Is this connected to commercialization, tourism, gentrification? What specific places within the city (neighborhoods) are associated with the dialect and other iconic images? Encourage students to survey their peers' attitudes toward local dialects. Because the Philadelphia dialect is not typically associated with high-prestige neighborhoods or communities in popular media, this opens the

**Figure 50**

door to conversations about social evaluations of language and place and takes us back to one of the big ideas from Chapter 1: all languages are equal linguistically—but not socially. The photo in figure 49b is another example of "jawn," this time being used to keep people at a safe social distance while waiting in line while shopping during the COVID-19 pandemic. How does the use of a familiar word, in particular one that has an affiliation with a specific identity, make an appeal to community membership without mentioning people?

Finally, in figure 50 you see an illustration of a handmade sign outside of a local shop that says "BIRD WATCHING SEASON! GO IGGLES!" A lot of information is packed into these five words.

Philadelphians would know that "iggles" is a reference to the local pronunciation of "Eagles" and that the Eagles are the city's professional American football team. "Bird watching season," of course, is a play on words to refer to the imminent football season and the implied obligation to observe and be interested in it. To whom is this message directed, and what does it mean to understand the intertextuality or presupposed knowledge? Moreover, what does it mean to be a football fan in this city? To an outsider, such as the tourist driving a camping vehicle in the illustration, what could that sign mean? Fill in the blank speech bubble. Students can discuss how visitors or newcomers might interpret local identities. As you can see, stories about where we live can range from serious discussions of social class and fear of the unknown to more light-hearted discussions of the language of fandom.

*Encouraging Discussions of the Local Mediascapes in Your Classes*

When given the opportunity to select a place to do their own media work, students choose places that are meaningful to them. Examples include:

- Neighborhoods in Philadelphia have strong identities, accents, ethnicities, foods, events, and stereotypes associated with each. For example, for students Chinatown evokes a range of interpretations. Some see it as marketing and tourism while others describe the sights and sounds as "feeling like home." Both interpretations, and everything in between are legitimate reflections of identity and belonging.

- Regions of the United States, such as the South, are seen through images of warmth, hospitality, and charm as well as poverty, racism, and lack of education. Students from the South are acutely aware of the stereotypes in all kinds of media that put them in the position of having to defend where they come from.

- Representations of African students' families' home countries, whether they are recent immigrants or their families migrated generations ago, tell stories about Africa that frame the continent as homogeneously poor, at war, and underdeveloped.

Media work on place also opens up discussions of how one place can be portrayed through different lenses. For example, I can ask students to provide examples of images and text that portray their hometowns in both positive and negative lights. For each of these perspectives they must analyze the modalities, language choices, and contextual elements that frame different stories of one place. Simplistic portrayals of places are rampant in movies, music, literature, social media, news, and all media platforms. One place, as depicted in figure 51, can be portrayed through different stereotypes as paradise, poverty-stricken, dangerous, or safe.

At the same time, images that disrupt stereotypes and present more realistic, multidimensional realities do exist in some modalities, and students can be encouraged to find these alternative stories or create ones of their own.

**Figure 51**

## Stories About Ideas

Media tell many stories about what we should believe, value, and desire. Because media is an industry, many of these stories are overtly connected to consumerism and marketing. Still, they should not be dismissed as only commercial endeavors because of their pervasiveness, consistency, and attractiveness. Even if the ultimate goal is to sell us something, media's impact goes beyond selling products to selling us ideas about how to live and evaluate the world. Moreover, non-commercial media produced for public service, education and activism also contribute to stories told in every culture. For media work, we do not have to look far to collect both analog and digital content. You are most likely already familiar with various terms that refer to the processes of media storytelling—framing, spin, ideologies, narratives, discourse, world views: even these word choices carry certain social connotations but are nevertheless useful for media work.

Media can *frame* an event as extraordinary or typical, news outlets put a *spin* on political stories, *ideologies* underlie the construction of media messages, *narratives* are created through *discourse*, and *world views* can be presented as implicit norms or explicit aberrations. If we revisit the discourse in the article about ESL in local schools (Chapter 2) in detail, we can see that the story frames ESL as a "problem," as racially marked, and as a challenge to school systems with an implicit spin toward individual student achievement over more funding for resources. This reflects an ideology of meritocracy and maintains social narratives that claim immigrants who do not succeed are just not working hard enough. The description of a "tan-skinned little boy" reflects another story in which "foreignness" is defined by physical traits and language proficiency, assuming that readers will not question this offensive characterization (at least at the place and time when the article was published). The stories told about ESL, immigrants, language policies, and bilingual education in media around the world are especially relevant to educators who need to understand the sociopolitical contexts of their work.

In my classes, I approach stories about language from a wider angle: I focus on stories about multilingualism and monolingualism, which I will share in detail in the following sections. I will also share topics that students have selected to explore. In both cases, the guiding questions in figure 52 help elicit various interrogations and interpretations.

### Stories About Multilingualism

Early in the semester I ask my students "are we a multilingual or monolingual nation?" Group and whole class discussions never end up with definitive conclusions, but instead spark conversations about when and where the use of diverse languages and dialects is accepted or looked down upon. As a warm-up to media work, I ask students to look around them, and post a photo and comment on an online platform (such as Padlet) that they think exemplifies "monolingualism," "multilingualism," and "language mix." We look at their postings together in class and talk about the different modalities that use multilingual texts and the different places they can be found. I anticipate and hope for some examples to be difficult to categorize. The "language mix" category in figure 53 is a space for students to offer examples of code-mixing, meshing, and any variations they find.

As students go out to explore the concept of multilingualism in different places, they look at their own college campus, schools, libraries, community centers, and other public places. Relevant questions for media work include: What languages are positioned as valuable, prestigious, or worthwhile to learn? Is bilingualism or multilingualism seen as a positive attribute? What kinds of messages (content) are presented in multiple languages, using which modalities, targeting which audiences? Students are typically aware of linguistic diversity in their own communities, but taking a closer look at media leads them to think about what linguistic diversity means in different places to different people. What stories do the flyers shown in figure 54 convey about multilingualism in local communities? Each of these flyers is promoting multilingualism, but in different ways.

# Guiding Questions: Storytelling and Ideas

## Observations

What modalities are used to convey stories about specific ideas (Z)?
How is Z positioned in relation to other ideas, events, and beliefs?
How much does Z appear in this media?
With what social class, lifestyle, profession, level of education, etc., is Z associated?
What information about Z is highlighted (given most attention)?
How are word choices, grammar, layout, font, color, etc. used to communicate Z?
What metaphors and euphemisms are used to talk about Z?
To what contexts or settings is Z typically connected?
What kinds of images in this media are linked to Z?
What kinds of attributes are associated with Z? (intelligence, independence, ambition, caring, empathy, etc.)
What is the audience presumed to know about Z?

## Interrogations and Interpretations

How are representations of Z linked to other stories or cultural references?
How does this portrayal of Z fit into or disrupt common stereotypes?
What is the status of people and places associated with Z? And why does this matter?
What will Z's future be? (and how do we know this?)
Whose voices are telling stories about Z? Whose voices are left out?
What emotional responses does Z evoke from the audience?
What values does Z exemplify?
What kinds of attitudes toward Z might be cultivated by these media portrayals?
What impact might these attitudes indirectly have on social policies, intercultural relations, education, politics, etc.?

## Reflections and Responses

How do these representations of Z challenge or align with your own experiences and knowledge of this idea?
How do these stories about Z reflect mythologies and/or facts?
What surprised you the most about the representations of Z?
Do you think the representations you examined are common or uncommon?
What is an appropriate response to these stories?

**Figure 52**

Multiligual signs are in the subway and train stations. I go from Philly to NYC a lot. They are in at least 5 different languages.

There are many signs like this on campus to guide students to different events. The ones on this board are all in English. Maybe these could be multilingual to reach more students?

I go to this Indian restaurant in the weekends and I see this sign in French. In an INDIAN restaurant! They could use an Indian saying.

**Figure 53**

**Bucks County Free Library**

# CUENTO BILINGUE

## BILINGUAL STORYTIME

**MARTES/TUESDAYS**
Octubre/October 8, 15, 22 1:00pm

**JUEVES/THURSDAYS**
Octubre/October 3, 10, 18 6:30pm

Acompános para leer, cantar, y jugar juntos en inglés y español. 30 minutos. Para niños de todas edades. Gratis!

Join us to read, sing, and play together in English and Spanish. 30 minutes. For children of all ages. Free!

# Spanish Development

Fun Spanish classes for preschoolers ages 2-5!!!

**FREE TRIAL!**
register at
xxxxx@xxx.com

singing, dancing, stories, games, puppetry, activities for home, and more!

**Location:**
Community School
Philadelphia

**When:**
Saturdays
9:15 and 10:30

**Figure 54**

Students observe, interrogate, interpret, reflect and respond to these flyers for language learning activities on all three levels: modalities, symbols, and context. These two flyers were hanging in public areas (a library and a park bulletin board) in small communities near Philadelphia. Who is the intended audience, and why was this modality chosen to reach them? What information is highlighted, who has access to it, and how are language varieties used? The language and design also elicit several areas of exploration. How do layout and font choices direct attention to specific information? What is communicated to the audience by the inclusion or exclusion of multiple languages? The context should also be considered. Both of these flyers were posted in English-dominant communities. Do these flyers disrupt or maintain assimilationist mindsets? How is Spanish positioned in relationship to English or other languages? Some interpretations point out that the flyer on the right positions Spanish as a resource for speakers of other languages. Some students have felt that this reinforces the idea of Spanish as a commodity for non-Spanish speakers but not for native speakers. Others say that it reflects social acceptance of Spanish as an increasingly powerful language in the United States and the need for more people to learn it. Both interpretations are valid.

Media that tells stories about language learning and multilingualism covers a wide array of modalities, places, and content. Too often, the messages convey an attitude of English superiority and insistence on assimilation as a requirement of acceptance or competency. In the advertisement for a house cleaning agency in figure 55, "We speak English!" is the most prominent item emphasized by a larger font size and placement above the bulleted list of the business' attributes.

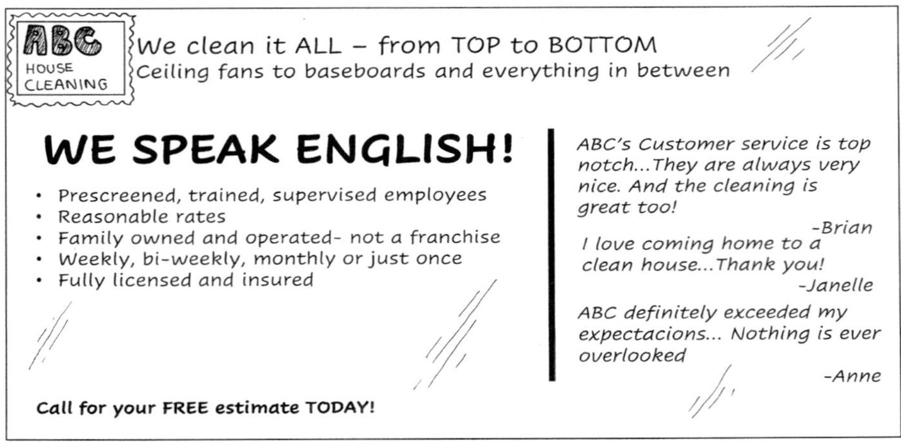


**Figure 55**

The other side of the mailing includes a full image of a smiling White female in a maid's uniform. The decision to highlight English-speaking and Whiteness is an obvious marketing choice deemed to be an effective way to gain clients' trust. Unfortunately, I have a collection of signs and bumper stickers that convey such explicit, derogatory messages about language learners. A restaurant in the city posted signs some years ago (since removed) that read "Speak English Only" and "Press 1 for English; 2 for deportation." The owner proudly espoused these views through local media outlets and received responses of support or outrage. In reaction to messages of linguistic discrimination, you can ask students to create responses by writing op-eds, creating their own signs and bumper stickers, and producing podcasts.

Media work can also uncover positive depictions of linguistic diversity in certain settings such as schools, health care settings, grocery stores, museums and cultural organizations, as well as increased inclusion of different languages in mainstream media outlets. Part of this media work also includes interrogations of the simultaneous use of two or more languages by multilingual speakers (code-switching, translanguaging) and the mixture of languages in social media such as memes and advertisements. An international student examined code-switching in popular music lyrics involving English and her heritage language and discovered that musicians from different genres of music used code-switching differently. The student reflected on her own use of code-switching within her family and community, and she reflected on how musicians might assert part of their identity by using more than one language.

Often the stories are more complex or mixed. In a language teacher education class, I asked in-service teachers to take notes of the multilingual media in their schools for a few days. They came back with an impressive list of materials and resources that disrupt stereotypes and position language learners and their families as positive contributors to the school community. The teachers pointed out school magazines, web resources, and programs designed to engage immigrant families in school activities. Veteran teachers especially were able to provide historical context and reflect on the shift away from the view of bilingualism as a deficiency. Nevertheless, a closer look at all of the content revealed that the information for program and engagement opportunities at their schools was presented almost exclusively in English. One teacher discovered that a highly-acclaimed program for families included free ESL classes for caregivers, but all of the information about these classes was conveyed exclusively in English. This teacher responded by contacting the right people in the district and proposing change. Deeper dives into all the social media posts, mailings, and websites of local schools interrogate content that is multilingual or English only, the modalities chosen to deliver different content, and the strengths and weaknesses of schools' outreach efforts. Pre-service teachers and other students can look at the media of their former schools to see how multilingualism and diversity are conceptualized, communicated, institutionalized, and practiced (Chamberlin & Khan, 2022).

*More stories*

Media stories about ideas, events, beliefs, and values cover an immense variety of topics. As your students examine mediated stories, emotions and deeply held beliefs have strong potential to emerge. Rather than avoiding these conversations, guide the processes and model productive dialogue, listening, turn-taking, and critical thinking. Give students the space to make connections, negotiate meaning in context, and communicate effectively (more is provided on this in Chapter 6). These are summaries of some of the stories that students have selected to explore:

- Education: Observations include advertisements all over the city (billboards, buses, street signs, and signs in train stations) for local universities and private schools. Collections of media, mostly photos of billboards and advertisements, revealed common themes of making classes convenient, accelerated programs, upward mobility, and economic empowerment. Interrogations, interpretations, and reflections brought up various issues associated with education: Is a college degree enough to improve opportunities for all? Are certain majors associated with ethnicity, culture, gender, etc.? How is diversity is represented on school websites and how do these representations come across as inclusive or exclusive to different audiences?

- Success: Stories about what it means to be successful can be found in a wide array of media, particularly in movies, videos, and programs that highlight material possessions and wealth as a sign of success. Counter-stories also exist in which success in equated with happiness and fulfillment. Students find examples of these extremes, but reflect on their visions of success as being somewhere in the middle of these two stories. In addition to films and videos, students have looked at board and video games and motivational decor. Games by their nature are competitive, but students interrogated the language and imagery that defines success and the pathways to achieve it. How do you reach your goals? Work hard, cheat, catch a lucky break? Defend and defeat? Work against each other or collaborate? Motivational decor refers to posters, stationery items, and decorative plaques that have sayings such as "We are in this together," "Be kind," "Be the change you want to see," "Believe." These well-marketed items define success in terms of how we choose to live our lives, treat others, and ourselves. I have had students examine these motivational media with varied responses. Some find them to be inspirational and others find them to be kitschy and trite. In either case, reflections on why such positive messages are attractive or desired can be connected to larger social narratives of our current times.

- Ability: Representations of people from a wide range of physical, emotional, and intellectual abilities have increased in mass media (television and movies) and through social media. Students have interrogated representations of visually-impaired characters in movies, physically challenged characters in video games, and neurodiversity on television. In each case they compared the media representations to reality in order to dispel myths and stereotypes. A student surveyed campus for signage and information about ways to navigate the space without using stairs. Another looked at bulletin board flyers, pamphlets, posters, and social media posts relating to counseling and mental health issues for students to see how support programs and initiatives could be framed to encourage student participation.

- Family and relationships: Sitcoms and rom-coms tell formulaic stories as well as new, alternative stories about what it means to be a family, or what relationships are supposed to look like. Students observe more frequent representations of LGBTQ+ characters over the past decades, but closer interrogations reveal the tendency for these characters to still be buffoons, overly dramatic, and essentialized. A wider range of representations can be found, but acceptable mainstream images still tend to be narrow. Stories of marriage and relationships are intertwined with stories of people, of course, and involve plot lines of partners tricking each other, hiding information, and so on. Typically, men are portrayed as not expressing their feelings well, and women are experts at it. Family members in media also play certain roles in terms of providing and caring for material and emotional needs. Many students like to compare these representations to reality and focus media work on the more realistic and complex portrayals of family and relationships they encounter. These stories are, not surprisingly, circumscribed by the limitations of modalities and genres. To take a local perspective, students walk through local business districts or school campuses and take notes or photos of the text and images they see that refer to relationships.

- Environment: Stories about the environment are framed as issues of political policy, human rights and social justice, science, and responsibility. Students easily observe language choices such as "climate change" versus "climate crisis" and uncover a great deal of metaphors used to talk about necessary actions and imminent consequences. Local media include signage in public spaces from the city's campaign for recycling as well as public relation materials from local business, museums, and organizations. A story that emerges frequently is one of responsibility. How do language, metaphors, and images create a sense of individual responsibility for and impact on the environment? How do language, metaphors, and images create a sense of corporate, institutional, or governmental responsibility and impact? Who, what, and which places are positioned as victims, as perpetrators, or as bystanders? How is environmental activism framed in news media outlets? How is "green" used as a marketing tool?

As you can see from the stories about education, success, relationships, and the environment, the possibilities for media work are unbounded. More importantly, you can see that the stories told about any one of these topics are not only complex within themselves, but are also inextricably intertwined with other stories. Students should always be encouraged to recognize these intersections in order to provide more context for interpretations.

## What's Next?

Embracing the interrelationships among stories, in fact, is an essential part of media work. The goal is not a definitive analysis or evaluation of media, but an ongoing commitment to the processes of observation, interrogation, interpretation, reflection, and response. These processes of media work provide opportunities to dig into the complexities of stories, rather than trying to simplify and decontextualize them. The multitude of platforms and stories that surround us constitutes an endless supply of pedagogical material. Assignments can be tailored to the specific needs and interests of students. I have elaborated in this chapter on stories told about accents, linguistic hierarchies, and language discrimination because I see media work as a way to develop awareness of relationships among language, race, social status, power, and educational opportunities. It is also a way to explore social narratives and counternarratives about gender, history, social movements, environment, health care, poverty, technology, and so on. The next chapter addresses the inevitable connections among these social issues and political climates.

## KEY IDEAS

storytelling

narratives

stereotypes

accent

language discrimination

framing

ideologies

discourse

world views

## REFLECT

1. Who/what have been the most important storytellers in your life? What did you learn from them? Who/what are the most important storytellers in your life today?
2. What media stories about people/ places/events/ ideas dominate the communities where you live and work? What are the stories that are told, who is telling them, and how accurate/inaccurate do they seem to be?

EXPLORE

1.  Choose a public space (school, library, market, community center, neighborhood, museum, etc.) and take notes or photos of all the signs, symbols, and sensory information that you see, hear, taste, smell. What do all of these things tell you about the place? Who is expected to be there? What roles do people play in that space? What does this place signify to the community? Does it mean the same thing to visitors? How is the public image of this place created through media?

2.  Watch or listen to one of your favorite films, songs, podcasts, or television programs. Take note of the different characters and the way they talk, with whom they interact, what they talk about. How do their communication styles contribute to their character or personalities? How much agency do they have? Are their actions ever intended to represent specific identities? If so, how?

3.  Make a list of five stereotypes that you feel are the most common in media today. Are they positive or negative representations? Are they wide in their scope, or narrow? For each of the negative ones, describe media representations that counter these stereotypes. Was it easy to find counternarratives? Are they widely accessible?

4.  Refer to the prompts in figure 56 as a guide for creating a lesson plan for your students. Add relevant questions from the guides in this chapter to each component. Notice that this exercise focuses on content, but the roles of processes and contexts are not to be dismissed.

LEARN MORE

You can find a plethora of books, articles, podcasts, videos, and other media sources that take a detailed and critical look at representations of people, places, and ideas. I cannot begin to do justice to the creative and scholarly work in this area. Many universities and educational organizations around the world have websites affiliated with various departments that address media representations. I will offer a few ideas to get you started, and I suggest that you avoid resources that are connected to commercial or partisan interests. Educational resources might have their biases, of course, but their primary interest is educating people to make informed decisions about media consumption and the stories told through media.

# Prompts for Lesson Planning

When you find examples of media that you might want
to use for teaching, ask these basic questions to assess their
potential for your students' learning.

**Modalities**

How does this platform
shape the information that
it is being used to convey?

Who produced this media
and for what audiences?

**Stories**

What are the main
stories being told about
people, places, and
ideas?

How do these stories
relate to students other
school work or outside
of school experiences?

**media**

**Symbols**

How are text,
sound, imagery, and
other nonverbal symbols
used to convey stories?

**Processes**

What do you objectively
observe in this media?

What should be
questioned?

How might interpretations
vary?

What aspects of this media
are worth reflecting on and
responding to?

**Context**

How do the stories relate to
specific times and places that
are important to my
students?

How does the time and place
in which this media is
produced affect the way it is
interpreted?

What processes of media work do you want to focus on?
What learning outcomes do you want to achieve?

**Figure 56**

The Representation Project (https://therepproject.org/) focuses on ending harmful gender stereotypes. The Project has produced films such as "Miss Representation" and "The Mask You Live In" about negative impacts of media representation on gender.

The Media Education Foundation (MEF) produces educational videos to encourage critical thinking and discussion about social issues and how they are represented to the public though media. MEF films are often available through public, school, and university libraries on the Kanopy streaming platform. If you have access, browse through their titles about gender, the environment, violence, racism, ethnicity, class, commercialism, health and media studies, to name just a few. For a short and concise introduction to cultivation theory, watch MEF's film *The Electronic Storyteller*. Although dated in terms of media examples and technology, discussion of who serves as storytellers in today's societies continues to be poignant and relevant. Through this link to the MEF website, https://www.mediaed.org, you can browse film titles, including *The Electronic Storyteller*.

Canada's Center for Digital Media Literacy hosts the website Media Smarts (https://mediasmarts.ca/) where you can find resources about representations of diverse populations in the media, including Indigenous people, people with disabilities, 2SLGBTQ+. Media Smarts focuses on digital media literacy and provides some tips, guidelines, and tutorials for teachers and parents.

Books and journals that interrogate media representations can be found across a wide domain of subject areas from language teaching and learning to psychology, sociology, communication studies, climate change, marketing, etc. As a language teacher you might be interested in the following:

Rodriguez, C. E. (2018), *America, as seen on TV: How television shapes immigrant expectations around the globe.* NYU Press.

Berg-Nordlie, M. (2018). New in town. Small-town media discourses on immigrants and immigration. *Journal of Rural Studies, 64*, 210–219. https://doi.org/10.1016/j.jrurstud.2018.05.007

# CHAPTER 6

# Challenges in Media Work

Learning language through media and popular culture occurs organically in language classes as we teach students to navigate their environments. Media work homes in on this convergence, and would not be complete without addressing the darker side of media literacy—that is, the divisive discourse fueled by fake news and images, misinformation, disinformation, and propaganda. When media work confronts this these challenges, the goal is not only to identify disinformation but to discuss how and why it circulates and how to respond to it. This may require delving into political topics and admitting vulnerability to propaganda and disinformation. In this chapter, I discuss these challenges and hesitations that may arise when we bring media literacy in to our classrooms. Although the subject matter of media work in this chapter lends itself to a more mature audience (high school and college students), younger students are also exposed to the darker side of media. Growing concern for young people's socio-emotional health has brought more attention to the disinformation and propaganda that floods many social media platforms. Students of all ages need guidance as they navigate an unprecedented volume of media messages.

## Defining Terms

Let's start by defining some of the terms we hear in discussions of media: misinformation, disinformation, fake news, propaganda. How do they differ? *Misinformation* refers to inaccurate or incorrect information that is not necessarily shared with intent to deceive. You might ask me when a particular event is going to take place and I tell you the wrong day because I confused it with another event. I misinformed you, and hopefully I have the chance to correct this. However, if I intentionally give the wrong information or leave out important information in an effort to mislead you, then I am spreading *disinformation*. In casual conversations, misinformation and disinformation are often used interchangeably, but the underlying intentions are different. Both are disseminated alarmingly fast through today's media, which leaves little time for attention to accuracy and context, easily blurring the boundaries between the two. A piece of misinformation, for example, may quickly become disinformation when shared by people with ulterior motives or bad intentions.

*Fake news* items and images are false stories that are intentionally created to spread inaccurate narratives through media outlets. Although the term "fake news" has become popular in recent years, Nolan Higdon's book *The Anatomy of Fake News: A Critical News Literacy Education* (2020) begins with a historical overview that dates fake news back to the 15th century and traces its evolution to current times. Higdon argues that political motivations to lie have increased public distrust in news media today, leading to the belief that there is "no universally trusted source to determine falsehood from fact" (Higdon, 2020, p.5). This mistrust and skepticism does not encourage people to seek out ways to discern fact from fiction and reinforces the continual proliferation of fake information.

*Propaganda* can certainly contain disinformation and fake news in its pursuit of selling ideas and political ideologies. Propaganda embeds information in intriguing, compelling designs and formats that capture attention. Messages are crafted through rhetorical strategies that create or amplify emotions such as discontent, pride, and fear, and sometimes in ways that are difficult to detect. Propaganda appeals to strong emotions, decontextualizes and simplifies issues, attacks opposing points of view, and builds arguments on logical fallacies. Not all propaganda, however, is harmful. Some is used to help people find resources for health care, education, housing, and other issues. Beneficial propaganda, such as public service announcements, typically appeals to emotions of caring, safety, wellness, and belonging. There are numerous educational resources that define and suggest ways to decipher propaganda. In the introduction to her book *Mind Over Media: Propaganda Education for a Digital Age* (2020), Renee Hobbs argues that:

> as people activate critical thinking skills in recognizing and responding to propaganda, they increase autonomy and personal freedom. As the emotional jolts and the promise of simple solutions and easy answers become easier to spot, people can use the power of inquiry, dialogue, and reflection to evaluate propaganda's explicit and implicit claims. They can appreciate how propaganda can be interpreted in different ways (Hobbs, 2020, p. xvi).

Developing this "power of inquiry" is a central component of all media work. Deep interrogations will help students identify misinformation, disinformation, fake news, and propaganda as they navigate their semiotic landscapes.

## Confronting Challenges

Demands for media literacy education are steadily increasing. Across the globe, harmful effects of disinformation and propaganda have sparked initiatives to mandate media literacy in formal education. This attention to media literacy has been driven by mis- and disinformation that spread about COVID-19 and by propaganda and fake news that promotes division, hatred, and violence. The threat of disinformation to safety, health, equality, democracy, and sustainability is real and recognized globally. The Media Literacy Index (Lessenski, 2023) evaluates and ranks 41 nations on several weighted indicators including freedom of the press (40%), media literacy education (45%), trust in others (10%) and use of communication technologies for civic participation (5%). Finland has ranked at the top for several years, followed closely by Denmark, Norway, Estonia, Sweden, Switzerland, and the Netherlands. An expanded version of the Index includes 47 countries outside of Europe, a few named here with their rankings: Canada 7, Australia 10, South Korea 17, United States 18, and Japan 22 (Lessenski, 2023). Perhaps even more important than the rankings themselves is the realization that media education and policy making need to be prioritized in order to maintain democratic processes. UNESCO (2023) has developed media literacy initiatives in multiple languages to reach countries in the Middle East and North Africa as well as European countries who ranked lowest on the Media Literacy Index. In the *International Encyclopedia of Media Literacy* (Hobbs & Mihailidis, 2019) you can find summaries of initiatives in India, Croatia, Australia, Singapore, Nigeria, China, South Korea, Russia, Israel, and many more. Organizations focused on media literacy and resources for education are more accessible than ever before (see Learn More at the end of the chapter for a list of media literacy organizations around the world).

In the United States, media literacy is gaining ground through educational policy. As of 2024, Illinois, Delaware, and New Jersey have adopted requirements for media literacy in K-12 classrooms. Eighteen other states are proposing or considering similar policies (Fromm, 2024). These initiatives may not happen quickly, but they are getting attention and pointing to the need to provide media literacy resources for teachers. Illinois is setting a strong example by creating professional development and curricular resources for teachers.

Still, policies and proposals are inconsistent, underfunded, and focused more on safety than equity and engagement (DiGiacomo et al., 2023). I do not expect to see dedicated courses in media literacy suddenly appear as core curriculum in K-12 settings, but I hope to see more and more teachers weaving it organically into their practices, much as technology has been integrated. In fact, many media literacy advocates and organizations provide lesson planning resources for identifying disinformation and propaganda (see Learn More at the end of this chapter).

Media work can be used to call out mis- and disinformation, fake news, and propaganda. But media work doesn't begin and end on the dark side. It is an extension of developing critical inquiry and thinking skills to respond to the multimodal world in which languages and all communication are embedded. As such, media work cannot ignore the challenges raised by contemporary social conditions, and it must confront them as opportunities for learning. The most common objections that I have encountered over the years from both teachers and students are summarized here:

1. Everything is biased, truth does not exist, so it's best to avoid media.
2. Young people are media savvy; they are not fooled by disinformation and propaganda.
3. Media literacy education is political and too risky to teach.

My goal is to unpack these assertions and the attitudes behind them. Reflections on these challenges open up opportunities for our students to participate as informed members of their communities. As I discuss each challenge, I will offer some related teaching tips and activities.

### *"Everything Is Biased, Truth Does Not Exist, so it's Best to Avoid Media"*

Not long after beginning to teach a course called "What is Information?" to undergraduate students, I realized that many students were extremely critical of all media sources, claiming that all are biased and therefore untrustworthy. In students' written reflections and classroom comments, I could see that they were positioning bias as the opposite of truth, instead of the opposite of impartial. Students wanted to completely discount a source because it was biased. Bias is not necessarily disinformation or fake news, though bias does determine how a story is presented. Most news sources are explicitly or implicitly biased. Language is biased. So, students should learn to recognize and interrogate the bias of a source before determining its credibility and worth. They should ask questions about the language and imagery used in storytelling, question whether information is omitted intentionally, and ask how specific word choices lead to powerful emotional responses. The point is not to avoid bias but to understand how it frames information and how we might respond to it. Bias must also be understood as playing a role in media at a hidden level. For example, students might come across a website that seems to promote environmental education and policies, but a deeper dig into the source finds that it is sponsored by a company that profits from non-renewable resources. Now the stories on this site need to be read in light of that understanding. Knowing about this bias should change the way students interrogate and interpret content.

To convince students that bias is not something to avoid but something to understand, I turn back to the symbolic nature of language (discussed in Chapter 2) and the idea that all language is biased. A thesaurus or synonym finder provides an easy example (and vocabulary lesson) of subtle and stark differences in connotations. Although a long list of synonyms may be available for one word, they are not completely interchangeable. For example, how many synonyms can we think of for "walk"? Saunter, stride, wander, trot, amble, hike, stroll, and so on. How are they different, and how does each word invoke qualities beyond the act of walking? "The teacher walked into the classroom" versus "The teacher sauntered into the classroom." Quick activities that ask students to list synonyms can be used with children, adolescents, or adults. For homework, you can ask students to find examples of as many words as possible that refer to one object. This activity can be based on vocabulary you are currently addressing in class, and you can ask students to look at specific modalities (their favorite anime, memes, books, shows) or find examples from across a wide range of formats and platforms.

To pull directly from media sources for an exercise on bias, I introduce my students to "Today's Front Pages" at the freedomforum.org (https://www.freedomforum.org/todaysfrontpages/#1). This website was associated with the Newseum in Washington DC, a museum dedicated to journalism and free speech issues. Although the museum closed in 2019, some of its initiatives continue virtually. On the site for "Today's Front Pages" you can find the daily (current only) front pages of hundreds of newspapers from around the world. This offers an overview of top stories in multiple languages, ranging from small-town papers to international publications. Although limited to the front pages of the current day only, this site is a semiotically rich source for media work; language choices, fonts, colors, images, layout, and context all contribute to the storytelling process. To explore linguistic bias, you can choose a story that appears repeatedly in many of the newspapers and look at the word choices in the headlines. Depending on the topic and your students, you may have to spend some time finding out what they know or don't know about the topic. Figure 57 shows how headlines from one day can be used in an exercise to talk about linguistic choices and their consequences.

This type of exercise can be the first stage of continued media work on a selected topic or serve as a vocabulary activity embedded in a writing or social studies lesson. As part of media work, it emphasizes subtle biases that can be found in all language.

If all language is biased, how can we know the truth? I have heard this question before! "Truth" may depend on subjectivities, but for media work it refers to facts that are backed up by empirical evidence verified by multiple sources and contextualized for accurate interpretation. The truth is often complex, and many media platforms do not support these complexities. This doesn't mean that a snippet of news is not truthful, but it may be incomplete and presented out of context. I remind students that when they see an issue reduced to a simple idea (sometimes a phrase or one sentence even) in media, this typically signals propaganda. Simple ideas with simple solutions are red flags. Divisiveness relies on the simplification or breakdown of ideas to digestible, emotional, and easily shared bits of information. In contrast, layered, nuanced, and complex understandings of social issues, theories, people, and places invite questioning, reflection, conversation, and learning.

Students must learn how to go beyond the simplified headlines that appear in a search or social media post (TikTok, Instagram, X) and practice "lateral reading" (McGrew, 2024; Wineburg et al., 2022). Rather than clicking on hyperlinks and moving deeper and deeper into one site, lateral reading refers to leaving a site to find out more about the story, author, owners, or sponsors. Content should be verified through other sites or sources that are not affiliated with the sample. I use the term *lateral research* in classes where students need to hone their research skills. Assignments should emphasize that before students share information or profess it as the truth, they need to verify their claims. They might not reach an ultimate truth, but they often find that the "truths" they started with are much more complex than they realized.

Let's go back to the headlines from Today's Front Pages to explore fact-checking resources and encourage lateral research. The cost of higher education in the United States today is a big problem, and many students are left with enormous student loans to repay after they graduate from college. The headlines represented in figure 57 refer to a proposed plan to relieve current and former students of some of their debts. This story was popular in the news for a while and directly affects most of the students I teach. They have opinions about it, but how much do they know about it? And how can they find

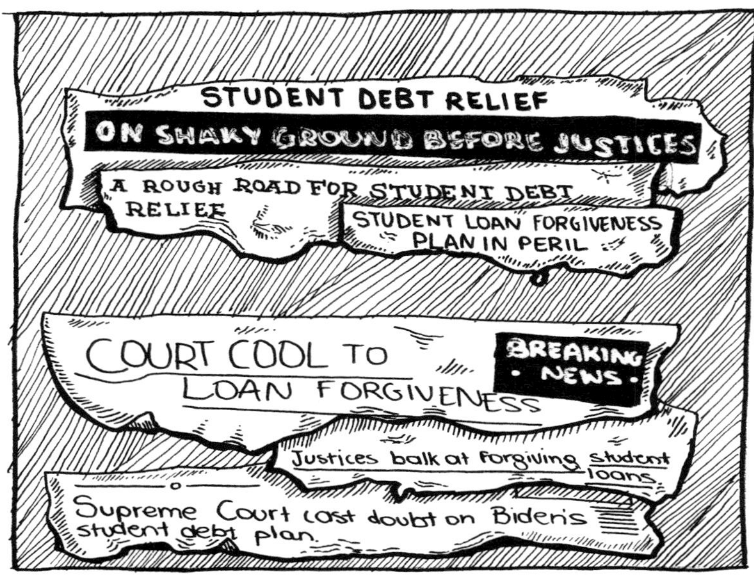



## Observe the language

Verb choices:
*question, balk at, casts*
Nouns (people and titles):
*Court, Supreme Court, Biden*
*student loan forgiveness plan, student debt relief,*
*loan forgiveness plan, loans, student loans, student debt plan*
Figurative language:
*In peril, rough road. cool to, balk at, casts doubt,*
*shaky ground, before justices*

## Question the language

What is the difference between *question, balk at,* and *casts doubt*?
How do these verbs reflect the perceived attitudes of the justices?
Does it matter how people are referred to?
How do the words *loan, debt, forgiveness,* and *relief* frame this issue?
What impressions do *in peril, shaky ground,* and *rough road* convey?

# Do linguistic choices convey biases in these headlines?

**Figure 57**

| Step 1: data collection options (observation) | Step 2: fact-checking lateral research (initial interrogation of content) |
|---|---|
| Compare stories about student loans from 3 different newspapers. Choose 3 papers that represent different biases. | Make a list of information that is presented as facts. You can focus on the key ideas if there is too much.<br><br>Categorize the information you have into these categories: factual (verified), commentary or opinion, incomplete, inaccurate. |
| Compare coverage of the student loan story in the past week on 3 different social media platforms. | Use resources such as factcheck.org or snopes.com to verify information.<br><br>Search through a library database for primary sources that confirm or challenge the information from your selected media. |
| Find 3–4 sources that explain the history of student loans in the U.S. Look for government reports, books, education policies, etc. | How is credibility established in the stories you observed?<br><br>Is it difficult to distinguish an author's commentary or opinion from facts?<br><br>Are you surprised by the accuracy/inaccuracy of your sources? |

**Figure 58**

out more? Pose general questions as an introduction then encourage lateral research and fact-checking. Consider the resources your students can access. The exercise in figure 58 shows a few options, using the student loan topic as an example.

Fact-checking exercises can be integrated into the observation and interrogation phases of media work and then built upon for longer assignments. Student loans might not be the most exciting topic, but media that relates to it is more pervasive than I had imagined. Young people are bombarded with emails, internet ads, and mailings for universities and financial programs to help them pay for their education. Even walking through the city offers no escape. Ads on trains, in stations, at bus stops and on buses themselves target a young audience (see figure 59). Media work on these types of advertisements can incorporate lateral research not only to lead students to a better understanding of language, but to also help them better comprehend an issue that affects them directly.

## *"Young People Are Media Savvy; They Are Not Fooled by Disinformation and Propaganda"*

My students impress me with their knowledge of popular culture and technology. They teach me some current regional slang when we talk about sociolinguistics, and they are motivated to talk about the platforms they use

**Figure 59**

to get information, socialize, and entertain themselves. They bring a lot of knowledge with them to the classroom. However, the confidence they have in their abilities to use technology and access information sometimes translates to inflated confidence in discerning fact from fiction. Students are certainly aware that their media environments are full of propaganda and clever marketing strategies, but that doesn't mean that they can always identify disinformation. Think of a common cultural myth and ask your students what they know about it. For example, as we approached a holiday, Halloween, during which children dressed in costumes knock on neighbor's doors and are given candy, I asked my students how many of them had heard about the dangers of children receiving poisoned candy. They all raised their hands without hesitation. I then asked if we need to be cautious and how to protect children from this threat. They offered their advice and warnings that they had heard growing up. I then asked them how many times children have been poisoned by Halloween candy. They were unsure but figured that it was a significant number. The truth is that contaminated Halloween candy is not a problem. The two documented cases of it turned out to be hoaxes by family members.[1] This urban legend began before the age of the internet and persists today. Although it is not too difficult to dispel urban legends such as this with some investigation, many students do not make the effort to confirm information.

---

1. Sociologist Joel Best at the University of Delaware has written about this topic and other social myths, fads, and fears for decades. See Best and Horiuchi (1985).

A study of 3,446 high school students across the United States (including a cross section of geographical areas, home languages, ethnicity, socioeconomic class, rural/suburban/urban) by Stanford University researchers (Breakstone et al., 2021) reveals fewer than 1% were able to accurately (or partially) discern fact from fiction on six tasks. For example, when asked about the credibility of a website about climate change, 96.8% were unable to accurately evaluate the site. They assumed that its .org domain ensured credibility and looked to the "about us" section to confirm reliability and unbiased perspectives. Less than 2% of the students left the website, googled the organization, and found that the site is funded by fossil fuel corporations. More than half agreed that a video posted on social media that showed people stuffing multiple ballots into boxes was "strong evidence" for voter fraud in the United States. The caption read "Have you ever noticed that the ONLY people caught committing voter fraud are Democrats?" Only three students out of over 3,000 actually used a search engine to quicky attribute the video to a story from the BBC on voter fraud in Russia. Students also struggled with discerning advertisements from news content and other tasks that questioned evidence on social media posts. Even if students are aware of variations in reliability of information they encounter online, very few seem willing to take an extra step to find the truth.

A big challenge to uncovering truth is to understand how boundaries between genres are expertly blurred in media. Memes, as discussed in Chapter 4, are one example of intentionally blurring boundaries by combining a clip or fragment of one media genre with sounds or text from another (or newly created) source. A serious news story can be transformed into entertainment, and the result is something that is easily shared and adapted. Satirical media also blur boundaries by adopting the style of a serious news format (written, audio, or video) to convey irony, make fun of modern life, and entertain. Examples of this in the United States are satirical papers such as *The Onion* and comedic television programs such as *Last Week Tonight* and *The Daily Show*. The entertainment outlets address current political and social issues and copy the format and delivery styles of traditional news media. At the same time, news media outlets often adopt features of entertainment media in order to capture and hold audience attention. The audience is not always aware of how the fluidity of these boundaries reshapes notions of credibility, expertise, and journalism.

Similar disruptions occur in the various mixtures of advertising, news, entertainment, and education that we find across media formats. The Stanford study (Breakstone et al., 2021) confirmed difficulties in distinguishing advertisements from news articles, even when the label "sponsored content" was clearly demarcated. Indeed, there are now entire publications of sponsored content and public relations articles that present themselves as local newspapers.

These publications offer event calendars and public service announcements, but feature articles are submitted by local business owners or public relations people; stories are not written by journalists. They are written in the style of a news article, but are linked to monetary gain rather than the democratic dissemination of relevant information. This is not to say that the information in any story is false, but it is not intended to give a fair or complete story. It is public relations and advertising disguised as journalism.

Likewise, videos and texts posted on social media confound propaganda with education. Students are invited to join honor societies or enroll in educational opportunities that mimic the formats of legitimate non-profit educational organizations but are profit-making companies. Websites sponsored by corporate interest groups pose as educational or non-profit resources. Hate groups create media that appear to be calls for participation in activities for community good rather than for planting seeds of hate and violence. Emails, telephone calls, and letters from scammers copy the styles of banks and government organizations in order to dupe people into sharing personal financial information. Even if some of this is easy to see, not all of it is, and the blurring of boundaries creates a media environment in which audience members lose track of what distinguishes one genre from another and fact from fiction. The ability to discriminate fact from fiction and to analyze media forms and content, however, can be taught. Media literacy education prepares students and teachers alike to navigate creatively (and sometimes deceptively) designed mediascapes. And part of learning to navigate our mediascapes requires addressing controversial, politicized issues.

### *"Media Literacy Education Is Political and Too Risky to Teach"*

Education is inescapably political. Policy makers mandate curricula, distribute resources, include or exclude participants, and define and reward achievement. They legitimize certain world views and disenfranchise others. Many local school boards in the United States have become battle grounds where political parties divide communities by focusing discourse on value-laden and emotional issues such as book banning and restrictions on free speech (PEN America, n.d.). Educators in the 2020s are being accused by parents and community members of indoctrinating students or creating a hostile learning environment if they have any putatively "political" symbols or signs (rainbow flags, Black Lives Matter, Science is Real) in their classrooms. Some states have taken measures to criminalize teachers for assigning banned books that are predominately about gender identity, race, and social justice (Meehan et al., 2023).

Some educators are resisting these bans and punishments through unions and organized efforts with their communities (Alvarez, 2023; Flannery, 2024; McArdle, 2023). But some teachers are self-censoring. Two-thirds of public-school teachers, in fact, report self-censorship for fear of losing their jobs, even in states where restrictive legislation has not been passed (Woo, Diliberti, & Steiner, 2024). You might be thinking at this point "This isn't what I signed up for when I became a language teacher. I want to leave politics out of the classroom." The reality is that we signed up for teaching students about communication, about the situated and negotiated nature of language, and about communication tools they can use to respond to the world around them. And the world around them is political. Unless it is part of the curriculum, we are discouraged from talking about politics in reference to specific political parties and politicians, but we can talk about the politics of the everyday: hierarchies and structures of organizations, language policies, allocation of school resources, and so on. Of course, the overlap between the two categories is enormous, yet we can focus on the everyday social and educational settings in which students find themselves. The media are out there, and we must give students the tools to navigate them.

For example, I asked undergraduate college students to find and read a proposal to the state legislature that seeks to ban the discussion of "divisive issues" in higher education classrooms in Pennsylvania (see figure 60).

Figure 60 shows the first page of a public document that is easy to access on the state government website. Students worked in groups to analyze semantic choices and how language can be interpreted in different ways. I asked them what the proposal entails? What problems would it solve? What problems would it cause? I didn't tell them what to think about it or who is supporting or opposed to it. They investigated and formed their own opinions, and our class discussions were a model for how to talk about opinions and listen to others. What surprised me and

PRINTER'S NO. 1679

**THE GENERAL ASSEMBLY OF PENNSYLVANIA**

## HOUSE BILL

No. **1532** Session of 2021

INTRODUCED BY DIAMOND, GLEIM, METCALFE, BOROWICZ, HAMM, KAUFFMAN, KEEFER, M. MACKENZIE, ROWE, RYAN, SMITH, STAATS, ZIMMERMAN, MOUL, COX, LEWIS, GROVE AND MUSTELLO, JUNE 7, 2021

REFERRED TO COMMITTEE ON EDUCATION, JUNE 7, 2021

AN ACT

1  Providing for restrictions on racist and sexist concepts, for
2    contracts, for penalty and for private cause of action.
3    The General Assembly of the Commonwealth of Pennsylvania
4  hereby enacts as follows:
5  Section 1.  Short title.
6    This act shall be known and may be cited as the Teaching
7  Racial and Universal Equality Act.
8  Section 2.  Definitions.
9    The following words and phrases when used in this act shall
10  have the meanings given to them in this section unless the
11  context clearly indicates otherwise:
12    "Contractor." An individual, organization, corporation or
13  business of any kind that enters into a contract, or a
14  subcontract pursuant to a contract, with a Commonwealth, county
15  or municipal agency, public school district entity or public
16  postsecondary educational institution.
17    "Postsecondary institution." As defined under section 2001-J

**Figure 60**

my students was the fact that none of them had heard about this proposed legislation. They told me that they avoid politics, or that they don't pay much attention to local or state politics. They have been so overwhelmed by the contempt, extremism, and self-promoting rhetoric of political media that they have chosen to shut it out. I understand that. It's difficult to consume. But if teachers and students avoid the political nature of communication, we are depriving future adults of the skills they need to have important conversations and solve complex problems.

Avoiding or banning politics from the classroom is often supported by the argument that the classroom must be a comfortable space at all times. Yes, students should be safe from discrimination, bullying, and threats! Yes, students should not be afraid to express their emerging and developing ideas! Students should feel comfortable to explore their opinions and those of others without fear of condemnation or retribution. Productive and respectful conversations that encourage critical thinking, active listening, and thoughtful responses are crucial to learning. Erasing all discomfort, however, need not be our goal. Learning takes place when we move outside of our comfort zones, question our assumptions, learn to build a solid argument, and discover how to talk about it constructively with those of opposing viewpoints. This is an *intellectual* discomfort, not a physical or affective discomfort based on hateful, ignorant, or insulting comments. If a student unintentionally makes an insensitive remark, this could be used as a teaching moment to point out why the remark can be interpreted as harmful and how the same intention could be expressed differently. If we avoid challenge and discomfort completely, what are we teaching young people? They need—perhaps now more than ever—to be equipped to solve problems, to work effectively with others who hold diverse values and beliefs, and to adapt to unpredictable futures.

Consequently, educators need to be able to create a new space in classrooms that allows students to interrogate, reflect on, and respond to difficult and controversial issues. Media work can contribute to the creation of this space. Essential points to remember are that media work does not position students as empty vessels waiting to be influenced by either media or teachers, nor is it about blame. Media work is about developing skills that allow students to purposefully question the world around them and choose how to respond. Media scholar Julian McDougall (2019) argues that some media literacy approaches are based on a false binary of "real" versus "fake" news. This sets up an antagonistic rather than inquisitive foundation. Instead, we need to treat all news as potentially "fake" in the sense that we question not only the facts, but how it is distributed, and what it means in larger contexts.

McDougall is also concerned that a binary approach positions the audience as being solely responsible for checking validity rather than holding those who produce the stories responsible.

Media scholar Elizaveta Friesem (2021, p. 21) also addresses the "us vs. them" misconception of media literacy as she discusses a human tendency to look for blame. She reminds us that media are typically conceptualized (through language) as something external to us but that "media is us, people, communicating with each other through technology." Friesem describes how easy it is to blame corporations, people, or institutions for false information while ignoring personal responsibility and empathy as part of a larger complex and interconnected system of communication. She says:

> I strongly believe that, no matter how unacceptable we find somebody's actions, it is always possible to find explanations that go beyond "they are just wrong/stupid/evil" kind of response. Holding people who hurt others accountable does not have to cancel out our ability to place their actions into a bigger picture, of which we are also a part. It might seem like a stretch because it naturally makes us very uncomfortable to look for connections between choices of somebody we resent and our own decisions (Friesem, 2021, p. 105).

Both McDougall and Friesem encourage media literacy approaches that do not focus on exacerbating binary oppositions. Together they remind us that producers of mass media are responsible for content, that media literacy is not a question of right versus wrong, and that individuals need to be better at listening to one another. This doesn't mean that truth does not exist and everyone is right; it means that the truth is complex and context-dependent.

## Media Work on Controversial Issues

Media work does not promote a political agenda, indoctrination, or blame, but it does recognize that politics and media are inextricably intertwined with our students' lives. Media work gives students the opportunity to see how language, culture, and media are interconnected in all formats and platforms. By working through processes of observation, interrogation, interpretation, reflection, and response, students will learn more about a topic, different per-spectives of it, and possible responses. Media work helps them develop their own positions on controversial issues based on research and contextualization. To illustrate this process, I will describe a few examples of using media work to look at controversial issues. First, I share how a class of pre-service teach-ers learned about critical race theory (CRT) by dissecting a social media text.

Second, I apply media work to a poster about police funding and third to ads concerning environmental issues.

### Example 1: Critical Race Theory in Our Schools

Let's begin with CRT because it is particularly relevant for language teacher education programs, adult language classes that explore community issues, and high school or college classes that examine the power of language and social media. My experience introducing CRT in a language education course for undergraduate pre-service teachers began when a local school board (an elected council with policy-making powers for the school district) began a heated debate over the role that CRT plays in K-12 education. This topic aligned with the course objectives of leadership and advocacy in language teaching.

**Figure 61**

I shared with my students a social media post (figure 61) that was circulating among parents in the school district.

I could have selected an article, poster, podcast, blog, or video that fully supported my point of view. However, even if (or especially if) all the students agreed with me, that would have provided less space for the students to deepen their understanding of the controversy. Instead, the social media post from an opponent of CRT (anonymous, personal communication, January 22, 2021) provided arguments that many people find compelling and convincing.

Observations can begin with students reading and marking up the text individually or in small groups. Encourage them to read the text then highlight, write, scribble, translate, list questions, and mark it up any way they prefer. Prompt them with questions: What are the advantages and limits of texting this information? Who is the intended audience? How much context is provided? What language choices stand out to you? At this stage, observations spawn many questions and naturally lead to interrogation of the media. Next, in small groups, the students probe deeper into the content and context of this post. I give them a hard copy of the post and ask them to note the specific questions they have. Their group comments might look something like figure 62.

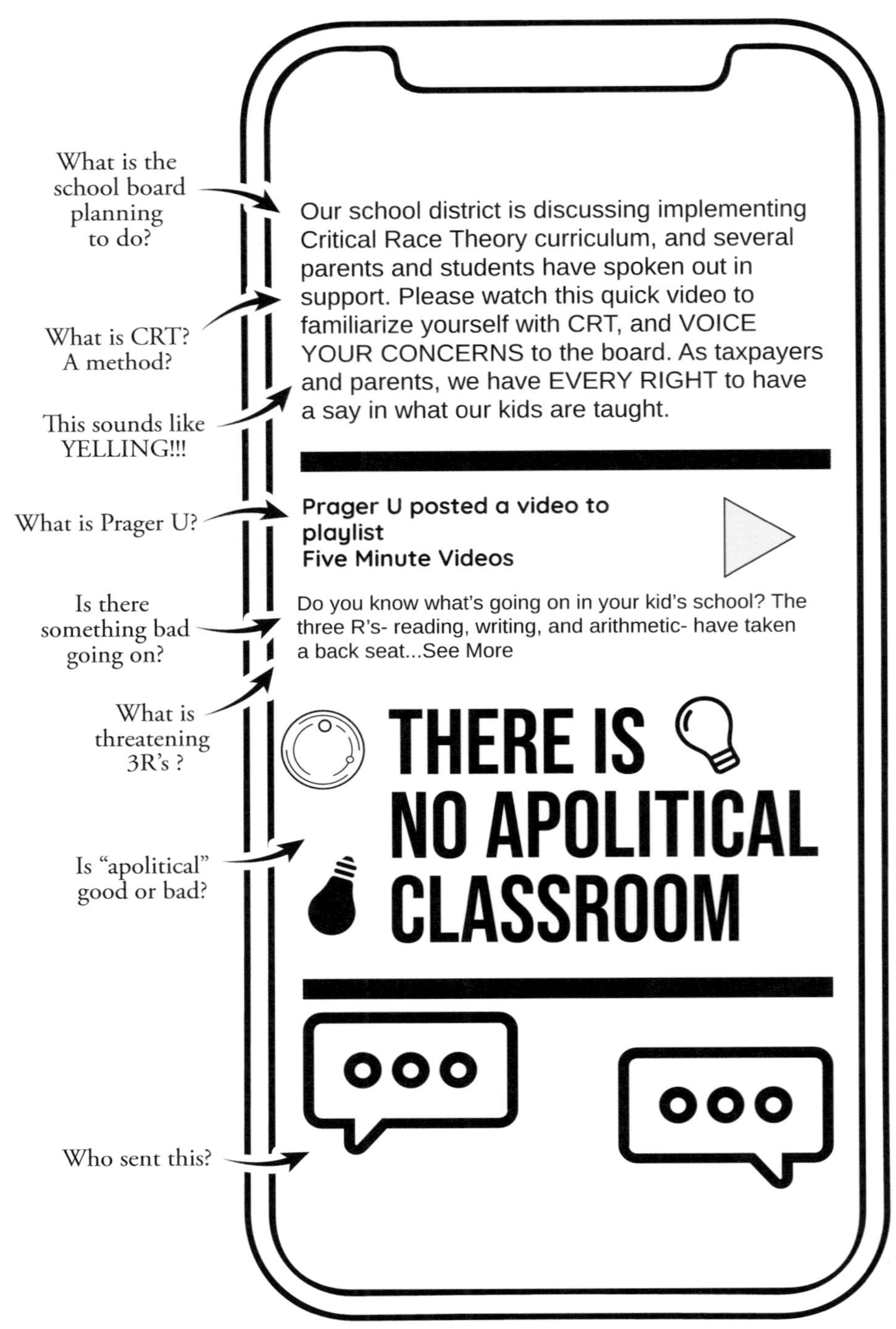

What is the school board planning to do?
What is CRT? A method?
This sounds like YELLING!!!
What is Prager U?
Is there something bad going on?
What is threatening 3R's ?
Is "apolitical" good or bad?
Who sent this?
Our school district is discussing implementing Critical Race Theory curriculum, and several parents and students have spoken out in support. Please watch this quick video to familiarize yourself with CRT, and VOICE YOUR CONCERNS to the board. As taxpayers and parents, we have EVERY RIGHT to have a say in what our kids are taught.
Prager U posted a video to playlist
Five Minute Videos
Do you know what's going on in your kid's school? The three R's- reading, writing, and arithmetic- have taken a back seat...See More
THERE IS NO APOLITICAL CLASSROOM

**Figure 62**

When we review their comments as an entire class, questions typically fall into these categories:

Questions about modality/platform:

> Who sent this? Who reads it?
>
> Why is this text message and link to a social media post effective or ineffective?
>
> How do these modalities limit or expand information?
>
> What are the advantages and disadvantages of a 5-minute video?
>
> How do the choices of a text message and link to a 5-minute video reflect expectations for obtaining information about any topic in the news?

Questions about context:

> What are the current issues being discussed in this school district?
>
> What exactly is CRT (its origins, applications, and results)?
>
> What curricular policies based on CRT are proposed?
>
> What is PragerU?

Questions about symbols (language and images):

> How do certain words evoke emotional reactions?
>
> How are tone, voice, credibility conveyed?
>
> Why are certain words highlighted in upper case? What information is omitted? What does the question "Do you know what's going on in your kid's school?" imply?

Some of the answers to these questions depend on individual interpretations, and others require lateral research such as searches of primary or outside sources. This is the stage at which most students make the mistake of following an embedded link, believing it provides enough context or confirmation (Breakstone et al., 2021). Instead, students need to find sources that will give them deeper context, history, and multiple perspectives. Depending on the students' experience, you may have to guide them in their research. In this case, to find out more about the meaning of this social media post, we brainstorm and list potential sources together:

- the school board website (meeting notes, video recordings of media, reports from the curricular committee are all publicly available);

- local, regional, national news sources (newspapers, television, radio, podcasts, magazines, etc.) that have covered controversies in this school district and in other places;

- a variety of academic journals, books, and other sources that explain the history, meaning, and application of CRT;

- multiple sources that evaluate the ownership, credibility, and purpose of PragerU;

- interviews with teachers and administrators working in the district.

This deeper interrogation and lateral research can be divided up among the class (one topic per group), followed by a presentation of their findings on the topics to the class. This outside research gives students the opportunity to question and verify information that easily spreads through communities and can have a deep impact on their lives (as teachers or students).

Another way to approach interrogation of this text and many others is through the lens of a propaganda checklist. You can find several checklists online (see Learn More at the end of the chapter). A good place to start, however, is by looking out for four common techniques described by Hobbs in *Media Literacy in Action* (2021, p. 128–130). I summarize and build on Hobbs in this propaganda checklist (figure 63).

Let's revisit the post now, with the propaganda checklist in mind. This can be done as a class or in small groups. Once again, encourage students to write notes on a handout or mark up an electronic version as depicted in figure 64. Prompt class discussion with questions:

Are emotions activated? If so, how?

Are ideas and information simplified? If so, what is left out?

Are values and needs of a particular audience addressed or exploited?

Are opposing points of view challenged or attacked?

While observation and interrogation of this text message are based on exploring what you see and uncovering more information, interpretation and reflection are the stages in which students bring their own experiences and interests into the process. A journal entry or other writing assignment is a good pedagogical option as it gives students time to think about the information they

| Activation of strong emotions | Propaganda uses words and images that appeal to human emotions such as sympathy, hope, loyalty, patriotism, frustration, fear, resentment, and anger. When strong emotions are activated, emotional responses can suppress critical thinking. | ✓ |
|---|---|---|
| Simplification (of ideas and information) | Simplification is a way to take a complex issue and reduce it to a few core facts. These facts might be accurate, but they are often not meaningful because they do not tell the whole story. Simplification involves reducing information into fragmented, repeated, and easily shared and packaged phrases. Ideas are often presented as simple binaries—yes/no, good/evil, either/or, us/them. Simplification aligns well with modalities that are limited in the amount of data that can be shared. | ✓ |
| Appeals to values and needs | Appeals to a specific (or universal) audience, in order to establish an emotional connection, can be achieved in many different ways. Language, sound, and imagery can appeal to age groups, ethnicities, interests, hopes, desires, beliefs, and values. This technique is used to create a sense of affiliation, belonging, and relevancy. | ✓ |
| Attacks opponents | Strong signals of propaganda include direct attacks on opposing points of view. These are often explicit comments that vilify, question character or credibility of, and strategically discredit opponents. Attacks are often strongly worded and obvious, but not always. Attacks can be more subtle by causing doubt or arousing suspicion. | ✓ |

Figure 63

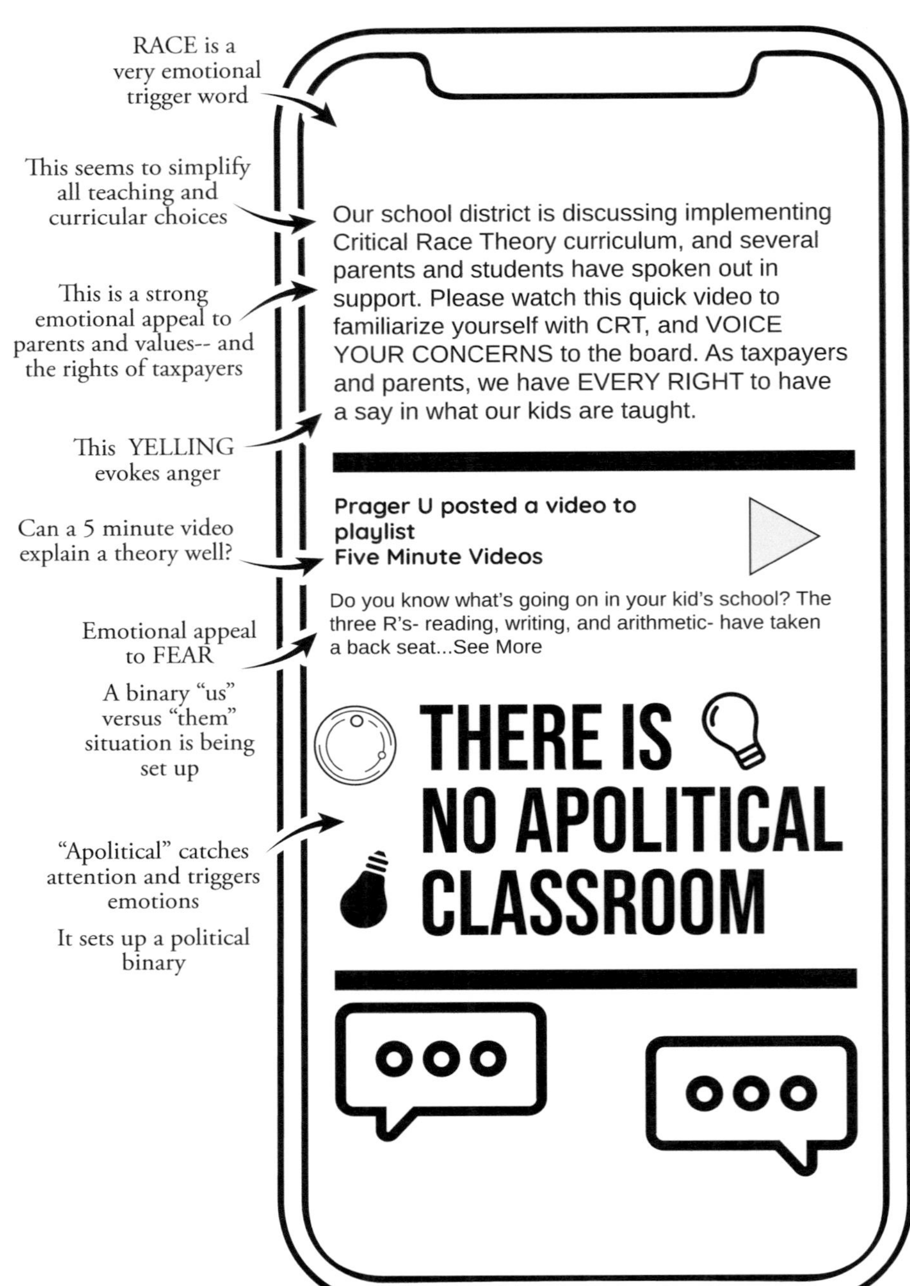

RACE is a very emotional trigger word

This seems to simplify all teaching and curricular choices

This is a strong emotional appeal to parents and values-- and the rights of taxpayers

This YELLING evokes anger

Can a 5 minute video explain a theory well?

Emotional appeal to FEAR

A binary "us" versus "them" situation is being set up

"Apolitical" catches attention and triggers emotions

It sets up a political binary

Our school district is discussing implementing Critical Race Theory curriculum, and several parents and students have spoken out in support. Please watch this quick video to familiarize yourself with CRT, and VOICE YOUR CONCERNS to the board. As taxpayers and parents, we have EVERY RIGHT to have a say in what our kids are taught.

Prager U posted a video to playlist
Five Minute Videos

Do you know what's going on in your kid's school? The three R's- reading, writing, and arithmetic- have taken a back seat...See More

THERE IS NO APOLITICAL CLASSROOM

**Figure 64**

have discovered. I also give a list of questions to students as a wrap-up to the assignment (see figure 65). After having time in class to talk and time outside of class for research, I ask students to respond to the questions in writing and share then their answers in class.

Students' written responses, class discussions, or journal entries about the questions presented in figure 65 could be the final stage of this media work, but extended responses are also an option. The following examples can be adapted to any timely topic in education that the students want to address.

1.  Prepare a speech for the open public forum at the next school board meeting. You are only allowed to speak for 3 minutes. The meeting will focus on hearing public opinions before the school board considers curricular proposals.
2.  Work with a partner to create a five-minute video that explains CRT. How do you decide what to include? What do you have to leave out? What is the best modality that can be used to convey what CRT is and how it might be applied? How do you convey credibility?
3.  In small groups, create and record a podcast in which you discuss if, how, and when race should be discussed and integrated in educational contexts. Each student can represent a different perspective. Each discussant must cite valid and up-to-date resources to support their claims. You are not required to agree on your perspectives, but you should model constructive feedback, active listening, and lateral research skills.

CRT is just one example of an issue that was particularly relevant to the time and place of my teacher education class. For classes that focus more on communication skills and language awareness, media about other controversial topics offer the same opportunities for unraveling messages, digging deeper, and giving students space to formulate and express their ideas. Following the same processes as the CRT example, with emphasis on a propaganda checklist, many memes, announcements, billboards, texts, blogs, news articles, advertisements, posters, and so forth offer abundant opportunities.

*Example 2: Public Funding and Services*

Other controversial issues that have gained media attention in the United States concern the role and funding of police. For example, a sign posted in New York City (Sableman, 2016) made a strong emotional appeal and included a hashtag to "Shut Down City Hall" at the bottom of the poster (see

# Understanding who, where, and what we teach

Use your research to discuss the social media post about Critical Race Theory and its relationship to our local school. Write down your thoughts about the following questions:

Based on your research of CRT, how do you think it relates to K-12 classrooms? Is it a curricular choice? If so, how would it be implemented? Does CRT pose a danger to students? If so, how?

Propaganda can be harmful or beneficial. What propaganda techniques are used in this text message? Is this an example of beneficial or harmful propaganda? Why?

What words or phrases in this message evoke emotional responses? What kinds of emotions are appealed to?

Compare the 5-minute video from Prager U about CRT to other media sources that explain CRT. How do different producers and platforms impact the what you learn about CRT?

Why is the statement "There is no apolitical classroom" highlighted in this post? How is it meant to be interpreted? How do you interpret it?

Where does this social media post fit into the discourse of the larger community and schools? What values, beliefs, desires, and fear are represented here, and how do these relate to the community?

How does this controversy over CRT relate to language teaching and learning? What could it mean for teachers and students?

**Figure 65**

figure 66). This poster, like the CRT posting, is directly connected to current events related to a specific time and place. (Although it first appeared in 2016, the photo of the poster has been reposted, and many versions of signs, memes, and other "defund the police" media have been created over the years). This poster uses strategies of propaganda to tap into strong emotions that are linked to racism, civic order, and morality. The choice of the words "liberate" and "abolish" tie into the history of the United States and ideals of freedom; they are part of a national identity or imagination. In addition, these words simplify the issue by equating freedom to abolishment of police. This poster can be used as a model for students to take their own pictures or screenshots of more recent media. Since the murder of George Floyd in 2020, the Black Lives Matter and Defund Police movements have garnered both support and resistance from community members. In language classrooms, media associated with these movements can be closely analyzed. In addition, the history of these topics can be laterally researched.

**Figure 66**

### Example 3: Protecting our Environment

Media work that involves lateral research and identification of propaganda strategies, can also be applied to the plethora of media messages about the environment. Without great effort, students can find signage in their schools and communities that promotes sustainability. Most of the media reminds individuals of how to behave—what to recycle and where to do it. Some of the media addresses the cynics by reminding them that what they do matters. This media also merges with advertisements in which companies use their commitment to environmental issues as a selling point. Students are typically quick to call out "greenwashing"—the phenomenon in which corporations make themselves look as if they are saving the environment despite the harm that their manufacturing and other processes might be doing. Greenwashing is a mixture of disinformation, public relations, advertising, and propaganda. But it isn't the only kind of propaganda associated with media messages about environmentalism. There are also examples of simplification, binary thinking, and emotional appeals. A common emotional appeal targets an individual's sense of guilt or duty to save the environment, such as slogans that tell us to RECYCLE! REUSE! REPURPOSE! Though these messages call for positive individual actions, they might also distract from more widespread public initiatives.

A similar appeal to individual actions began in the 1970s as part of the "Keep America Beautiful" campaign with a famous public service announcement (PSA) that showed a Native American man with a tear running down his cheek as a reaction to littering. The ownership of this PSA, used on television until 1983, was recently given to the National Congress of American Indians Fund who retired its use as a PSA because of its misrepresentation of Indigenous culture (Schmall, 2023). Moreover, the PSA's slogan "People start pollution. People can stop it," put responsibility on individuals, rather than addressing policies and environmental regulations. When students discover this kind of information by doing lateral research, they learn not only about language but also about policies and practices that relate to their daily activities.

In both cases, environmentalism and defunding the police, students can learn about language, voices of authority, emotional appeals, simplification of ideas and issues, and social contexts. For deeper analyses and research skills development, both topics open up a wealth of questions.

Questions about modality/platform:

> Where do we see most media about defunding/environmentalism?
>
> What platforms seem to be the most popular for these topics?
>
> Who creates these media, and what positions do they hold in society?
>
> How do these modalities limit or expand information?

Questions about context:

> Where and when did policing/environmentalism begin to gain attention in media?
>
> How have media messages about these issues changed over the years?
>
> What controversies about these topics have evolved over the years?
>
> Whose voices are most powerful or authoritative?

Questions about symbols (language and images):

> How do certain words and/or images evoke emotional reactions to these topics?

How does emotional language enhance, confuse, or negate factual information?

How are semiotic choices used to convey credibility?

What information is simplified or omitted?

When appropriate for students, extended research can address how Indigenous culture and history is represented in media, how different communities in the United States have reacted to team mascots that depict Indigenous peoples, and how language loss, preservation, or revitalization occurs in Indigenous communities around the world. Discussions of environmental issues can also expand in various directions. Who do media campaigns target? How are stories about environmental policies and practices conveyed through media? How effective are they? For issues such as defunding the police, research can take a historical perspective of policing in the United States. This topic also highlights the power of language choices because the word "defund" has become a point of contention even among proponents of the message. Should "defund" be replaced with "reform?" Is the use of "defund" necessary to bring attention to the issue? What other examples of calls for radical reform have used provocative language? Is this strategy effective? Rather than avoiding controversial issues, give students opportunities to explore meaning, engage in research, and learn to talk to their peers.

## From Challenge to Opportunity

At the beginning of this chapter, I mentioned that the challenges we face when incorporating media literacy education into language learning and teaching are real, but not without opportunities. The opportunities are ultimately to engage our students in communication skills that support critical thinking, collaboration, and problem-solving, but opportunities exist for us too, as educators, to reflect on our own values and beliefs. There is no one perfect method for discussing controversial topics in classrooms, but we can employ our teaching strategies, decision-making skills, and expertise. Get to know your students to best understand how to help them engage in productive, intellectually challenging discussions. No one can tell you the best way to do that; but I can tell you that media work brings form and structure to discussions by directing focus to the understanding of language and symbolic meanings.

KEY IDEAS

misinformation

disinformation

fake news

propaganda

lateral reading

lateral research

bias

truth

credibility

blurred boundaries

emotional appeals

simplification

decontextualization

REFLECT

1.  What controversial topics do you avoid in your social and professional conversations? Which ones do you wish you could talk about more? Which issues do you have a strong opinion about? About which issues are you the best informed? What do you wish you were more informed about?

2.  What media do you use to get information about the news that you care about (and what do you care about)? Are you confident that your sources are accurate and reliable? Do you fact-check information? What biases are reflected in your sources? Do you seek out news or information from sources that represent other biases or points of view? Why or why not?

EXPLORE

1.  Fact-checking
List the media sources you rely on for your daily news. How would you rank each of these sources on the statements in figure 67 (1= strongly agree, 5= strongly disagree)?

| The facts reported in this source are accurate. | 1 | 2 | 3 | 4 | 5 |
|---|---|---|---|---|---|
| This source contextualizes topics well. | 1 | 2 | 3 | 4 | 5 |
| This is a consistently reliable source. | 1 | 2 | 3 | 4 | 5 |
| This source does not rely on propaganda techniques. | 1 | 2 | 3 | 4 | 5 |
| This source considers different perspectives. | 1 | 2 | 3 | 4 | 5 |

**Figure 67**

Next, check out some of the following websites to see how your sources and the stories they present are evaluated by media watchers and fact checkers.

https://adfontesmedia.com/interactive-media-bias-chart/
This captivating media bias chart shows on a scatterplot where many sources lie on the axis of bias and reliability. You can download a static chart for no cost, but subscriptions are required for more detailed information. It is a good site to explore, even if you do not subscribe.

https://www.factcheck.org/ Go to FactCheck.Org from The Annenberg Public Policy Center at The University of Pennsylvania. This site monitors factual accuracy of published news stories in the United States.

https://www.snopes.com/fact-check/ Snopes.com provides tabs with the "latest" and "top" stories that circulate in news and social media, including memes. Their tab on "media literacy" has useful resources for teachers. You have to look beyond the annoying ads on this site.

2.  Proofreading for bias
Take a close, systematic look at some of your teaching materials (syllabus, lesson plans, assignments, slides, worksheets). Apply the media work processes (observation, interrogation, interpretation, reflection, and response), giving particular attention to the biases that can be revealed in the materials. Ask yourself and then others in a group:

How much knowledge about specific topics is assumed? (sports, celebrities, foods, history, etc.)

Do instructions assume prior knowledge of school routines and procedures?

Does my course content make assumptions about family structure, language, religious beliefs, cultural values, ability and disability, gender, ethnicity, or social class?

Talk through these questions with colleagues or classmates. We often cannot see biases in our materials ourselves. It's okay to help make them visible to each other. We all know the value of proofreading and having a second pair of eyes reading essays, manuscripts, and reports, right? Apply this to classroom materials.


LEARN MORE

Organizations, educational institutions, and government agencies around the globe curate resources and collaborate to develop projects and make media literacy education accessible worldwide.

The Media Literacy Network brings together educators from European and African countries (https://www.mediaenmaatschappij.nl/international/media-literacy-network).

The United Nations sponsors the Global Media and Information Literacy Week (https://www.un.org/en/observances/media-information-literacy-week).

The UNESCO Media and Information Literacy Alliance promotes international collaborations to develop media and literacy information competencies (https://www.unesco.org/en/media-information-literacy/alliance).

Some organizations based in North America are listed below. Keep in mind that their resources for questioning media credibility and analyzing propaganda are not exclusively applicable to media produced in English and in North America. Moreover, teachers and students should explore and utilize media literacy education resources in languages other than English.

Media Literacy Now: https://medialiteracynow.org/

Center for Media Literacy: https://www.medialit.org/

National Association for Media Literacy Education: https://namle.org/

Common Sense Media: https://www.commonsense.org/education

The Media Education Lab: https://mediaeducationlab.com/

The News Literacy Project: https://newslit.org/

NewseumED: https://newseumed.org/medialiteracy

International Council for Media Literacy: https://ic4ml.org/journal-of-media-literacy/

# CHAPTER 7

# Opportunities

There are days when I want to ignore media, when I want to retreat to a world without updates, notifications, email, texts, or the internet. I don't want to create another account with a password that I will forget, answer a survey about my experience paying an online bill (why would that ever be pleasant?), or be reminded that I should be afraid of everything (unless I buy a product that will make me feel better). For many of us, our personal tasks and professional lives depend on our connections to media, so cutting ourselves off is not really an option, nor is it the best idea. We need to know what is going on in the world around us. Who is making important and life-altering decisions that will affect us directly and indirectly? We need to have access to information, but we do not have to let the "dings" of notifications pull us away from conversations with people in front of us. Rather than avoiding media, we can use it as a tool for teaching and learning. In this final chapter I want to situate media work as an opportunity. I will highlight opportunities for learning afforded by media work as a way of reviewing the main points of this book.

## Learning Opportunities

Engagement in media work is predicated on the ideas that media are fluid and responsive to continually changing contexts. Media that we use in the classroom naturally reflect changes in language and culture and respond to transforming communities and evolving pedagogies. This mutability means that media work is a constant developmental process that includes taking a self-reflective position as teachers. The questions and assignments shared in earlier chapters approach media through a lens that observes, interrogates, interprets, reflects, and responds to local mediascapes. I envision media work playing out in different classrooms in innovative ways, and by providing guidelines and structure that you can adapt to your needs, I hope that this book helps

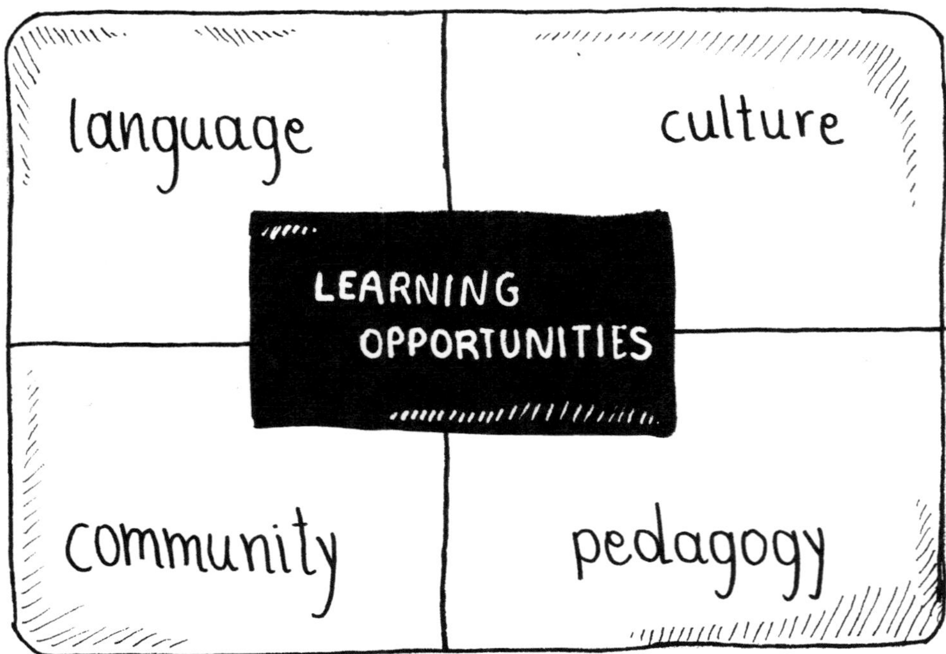


**Figure 68**

you to create new opportunities for your students. Zooming out to the larger picture, I see media work as providing learning opportunities that connect to language, culture, community and pedagogy (see figure 68).

## Language

Language learning is at the forefront of my media work approach. But language learning is not only about grammar. I think of language learning opportunities in media work as multilayered. One layer includes linguistic features that align with and build on your lessons with both familiar and new material. You might be working on content-based vocabulary but also introduce local expressions or variations. Another layer might include how specific language choices create different tones and express different voices. These sociolinguistic perspectives can focus on language varieties as well as the presence of bias, disinformation, and propaganda. Other layers can address contextualized interpretations, linguistic hierarchies, and language policies. And, as an added benefit, media work can tap into different languages that students know and encourage them to use their full linguistic repertoires. The shared target language of the classroom might be a tool for discussing cross-cultural interpretations, reflections, and responses, but the use of several languages can be a natural part of media work (García & Li W., 2014; Li W., 2018).

## Culture

What opportunities for learning about culture does media work open up? One obvious answer lies within the interpersonal interactions that occur in the classroom. As students share their observations and interpretations of both local and global media, they learn from each other. By sharing their ideas and contrasting media from different communities, they learn that heritage language groups are heterogeneous, that multilingualism is not a deficit, and that the dominant language of the school is not superior to other languages. Additionally, discussions of media from across the globe or across the city help students to connect unfamiliar places to familiar people.

More opportunity for cultural learning takes place when media work leads to conversations in which students gradually open up to one another. Given the chance to talk about mediated images of people, places, and ideas, students talk in depth about texts and images; they do not have to tell their own stories or rely on one story to represent a larger group. Mediated representations offer a certain distance from personal experiences that some students might need or prefer.[1] Many students, however, are comfortable sharing their stories; their stories frame culture as a multilayered, fluid process rather than a fixed entity. They talk to each other about being bullied because of their accent and of being placed in an ESL class when English was one of their native languages. They talk about their experiences as an outsider in their adopted country and as an outsider when they visit their birth home. They talk about the joy of being able to talk to their family members in their home languages, the layers of identity that they encompass, and the insights they have gained through their intercultural relationships. The lessons I give on intercultural communication and culture pale in comparison to the power of these conversations.

Another opportunity for cultural learning takes place through media work that tells stories about culture in the public realm. This refers to policies and practices that are created, sustained, or disrupted through media in public spaces. In this broader context, media work opens up an opportunity to explore how multilingualism, intersectionality, and other cultural practices are positioned as a norm, a deviation, or a commodity. You might look at how institutions (schools, libraries, museums, hospitals, big box stores, local shops, etc.) represent their commitment to inclusivity and how they manifest it in their actions. Students can investigate what kinds of actions disrupt linguistic and cultural hierarchies in meaningful ways, and how these

---

1. Some students may have experienced traumatic events as refugees, displaced persons, or migrants. No students should feel pressured or obliged to speak about or for groups with whom they identify.

actions cultivate behaviors or intercultural interactions that are sustainable. By looking at school-based media, for example, teachers came to realize that the signage and other messages did not reflect the dual language identity of their schools. How could permanently changing some of this media impact attitudes toward languages and cultures? How could bilingual signage that gives equal space to English and Spanish reinforce intercultural communication as a norm for everyone? In some public spaces, such as museums, the text on placards that describe art and artifacts is being rewritten to acknowledge histories of colonization, enslavement, and racism. In public spaces such as these, students can document and comment on the intercultural learning that these revisions encourage, or write revised signage, descriptions, or policies themselves. Media are cultural storytellers.

## Community

Media work that draws on students' experiences in their neighborhoods, workplaces, or hometowns not only focuses on meaningful and relevant messages, but it may also provide chances for students to learn more about their own communities and participate in local organizations and events. Media work can be connected to topics addressed in school assemblies, field trips, service learning, music, sports, theater, or other events, to give students the chance to contextualize and explore a topic and then participate in a related activity. Responses to media can include assignments that reach out to communities, such as informative blogs or reports that share lateral research and dispel disinformation.

Another dimension of community learning concerns recognition of the histories of places. Media is not static, nor are the communities in which media is found. Students who conduct a media work assignment on Chinatown, for example, might share some of the same media content, but they might process it differently from one another. Where one might see comfort and affiliation, another might see tourism and gentrification. Where one sees preservation of tradition, another sees commodification. Chinatown before, during, and after COVID-19 quarantines was not the same. Media work must allow for such variations over time and for different interpretations. In fact, discussions of change and instability remind students of the importance of contextualizing information. Moreover, discussing unpredictability can be challenging, but it can also open up the imagination for possible futures.

Not all media work assignments will directly result in community-oriented actions, but reflection and responses can encourage a civic mindset (Friesem, 2016). Media scholar Paul Mihailidis (2019) asserts that media literacy education needs civic intentionality based on caring, imagining a better world, and connecting knowledge to action. This caring dimension of media literacy can sometimes be overshadowed by the urgency of identifying disinformation and fake news. Caring for and imagining better communities, therefore, needs to be an intentional pedagogical act. Civic intentionality in media work can be implicit or explicit, and it can emerge at any point in the process. Resulting actions can range from peer-to-peer learning to participation in community events or organizations. Figure 69 describes a few examples of outcomes of media work that brought students closer to their immediate communities.

In some cases, a specific action such as creating a resource or writing to a policy maker can be an explicit part of a media work assignment. At other times, actions emerge when students take the initiative to join a club, sign a petition, or talk to someone who they do not know. You can also add media work to larger projects that are based on community involvement or service. Brian Morgan describes projects in English for academic purposes (EAP) classes called "Language in Public Life" and "Get Involved;" the former requires students to critique media coverage of a social issue or current event,

| Media work assignments | What students did after media work... |
|---|---|
| Examination of media in public spaces, emphasis on public services such as transportation, healthcare, and municipal services | Community services:<br>Student created a list of translation services available to learners of English in Philadelphia. For another class, this student wrote a paper about language policy in healthcare, expanded the list of services, and shared this resource with local organizations that serve immigrants and newcomers. |
| Examination of characters in popular media who speak with non-dominant American English accents | Workplace settings:<br>Student who supervised workers in a warehouse started to say hello to workers from non-English speaking backgrounds. This led to increased daily interactions between him and other employees and served as a model for other supervisors. The student reflected on his inaccurate assumptions that people from different cultures did not want to interact with each other, or had nothing in common. |
| Examination of media found in educational settings such as classrooms, schools, campuses, and websites | Educational settings:<br>Students decided to accept invitations to attend meetings of student clubs affiliated with cultural groups other than their own,<br><br>A student teacher presented alternative ways to communicate with students' families to in-service teachers.<br><br>Noticing a lack of media addressing issues and space for returning adult students, one student lobbied for the creation of a student lounge for returning adult students. |

**Figure 69**

and the latter asks students to research and critique the work of NGOs. Both activities organically incorporate dimensions of media work (Morgan, 2009; Morgan & Ahmed, 2023). Morgan comments in his duoethnography with Anwar Ahmed that in the "Get Involved" project:

> there is the issue of language and additional language/semiotic awareness underpinning the content-based EAP setting. The assignment can draw attention to the dominant and contested meanings and affective/emotive symbols currently in circulation, fostering the kinds of language skills and strategies students need in order to participate effectively in public life if they choose to do so (Morgan & Ahmed, 2023, p. 883).

Civic or community engagement may also overlap with political issues. As I pointed out in Chapter 6, politics are a part of our teaching world. To ignore the political nature of what we do is to ignore the lived experiences of our students and their communities. Language teaching, especially teaching English as a dominant language, must acknowledge the complex histories and current policies that create, maintain, or disrupt linguistic hierarchies and discrimination. For example, media work that looks at communities' monolingual and multilingual signage or at representations of language learners on screens are catalysts for conversations about language in society. Media work makes room for class discussions about whose languages and cultures are valued—where, when, and how. My greatest concern is not that we (teachers and students) might say the wrong thing or make a mistake, but that classrooms will become spaces where we are unable to discuss, make mistakes, forgive, and learn from each other.

Students need to develop voices that are heard, valued, and rewarded in their communities and outside of their communities. So why not build on this? Why not teach students to navigate the world they live in? Why not give them the tools to engage in productive conversations that can move them forward? You don't have to tackle an issue such as CRT, but there are plenty of issues that all students can relate to, such as what it means to "belong." You can ask students to take notes or photos of signs in school common areas that make them feel welcomed, happy, valued, or motivated. This is a good opportunity to see how and if students feel included, and it might provide insights into their interests and concerns. Students can respond by making posters or signs that they would like to see in their schools. A classroom collage of these signs can teach vocabulary and remind students of the ways in which they are valued. More advanced students can do a similar activity that takes their observations further out into their communities. They can interrogate and interpret what makes them feel good/valued, what makes them feel excluded/inferior, and what they would like to see added to their mediascapes.

Then, they can produce media of their own (websites, artwork, theater, music, signage, podcasts, blogs, videos, etc.) Students can generate topics that matter to them, and teachers can give them the tools to explore and talk about issues that are important to their communities.

## Pedagogy

Media work also helps us to be more critically engaged with our own teaching. I experience this engagement in two ways: first, I think more critically about the design and purpose of my class assignments; second, I am more aware of the biases and accessibility of different media modalities (media ecology) that I choose as resources. Let's begin with media work assignments. Approach media work with a critical mindset. Ask yourself questions as you begin to design your lessons (see figure 70).

Even though students will be able to choose media that they want to explore, as teachers we need to show them examples and model what we want them to do. To introduce media work, I use examples that contain obvious cultural references, stereotypes, and interesting language. I want to show them how easy it is to find media in their local environments, that it can be digital or analog, and that media contain layers of messages. These initial examples can set the tone and expectations for the assignment. For my undergraduate classes I want media messages to be somewhat complex and tap into identities of people and places. I have a growing collection of photos taken in neighborhoods in Philadelphia and its surrounding suburbs and towns. I share examples in English, Spanish, Chinese, Korean, Vietnamese, Polish, Arabic, Haitian Creole, and other languages I see displayed on my walks. After we explore those photos together, students take photos in their own neighborhoods. If walking through public spaces is not possible (due to quarantines, time, or mobility issues, for example), students can visit websites of local businesses, neighborhood organizations, and town halls. Let them explore. A student once asked if she could document the media in her best friend's living room. She had noticed the variety of books, magazines, and artifacts from around the world that seemed to tell a story about this family and their immigrant identity. She was fascinated by this, and she shared her enthusiasm when she presented her detailed (and excellent) analysis to the class.

Ask students to select and collect media content. Establish boundaries of pedagogical appropriateness for your classes, but be open to a broad range of sources and genres. The almost endless possibilities do not mean that all media are of pedagogical value. You and your students are the ones to decide what is meaningful, relevant, and pedagogically valuable. Be careful to not imply

# Where do I begin?

**Questions for designing a student-centered media work activity**

What do I see and take note of in my mediated environments,
and do others notice the same things?

Is access to various media and modalities equitiable among my students?

How will I avoid expressing a preference for certain media
(i.e. digital over analog)?

How will I avoid expressing preferences for specific languages
(target, heritage), genres (entertainment, informative),
and content (politics, sports, anime, fashion, science, music, etc.)?

How will this asssignment connect to current social issues in ways
that encourage dialogue over divisiveness?

How will this assignment motivate students to examine media
that is relevant to their lives?

How will I show students how to document objective observations,
noticing what is and what is not present in the media?

How many examples will I expect students to find, and will anyone be
at a disadvantage in the data collection process?

How will we move through the processes of media work? Do I want
these processes to be similantaneous or in a particular order? Do we need
to include them all?

How structured or flexible will I make this assignment?

What do I want students to learn about language, culture, and media from
this assignment, and how will I know what they have learned?

**Figure 70**

hierarchies of sources or content. A living room turned out to be as interesting as a bustling urban neighborhood. Encourage topics that students connect to that will give them room to think, reflect, and challenge themselves to see something new in their everyday settings. Modeling media work without prescribing or imposing preferences is possible with some forethought.

Design lessons that ask students to connect meaning to observable data and discuss multiple interpretations. Give opportunity for reflection and response through modalities that encourage reflection and response. I find that small-group online written discussions elicit thoughtful and insightful comments, perhaps because the format gives students time to think. Responses can take on many forms, and you may need to let them emerge. Overall, you should remain adaptable to students' needs by framing assignments through probing questions that draw out students' voices and making space for intellectual curiosity.

Designing media work has also made me more critically engaged with other aspects of my teaching, in particular with the changing media platforms for teaching and learning. The experiences of our students echo a rapidly changing world. It doesn't seem too long ago that we relied on chalkboards, whiteboards, overhead projectors, and occasionally a television wheeled into the classroom on a cart. Computer podiums, smartboards, projectors, cameras, and microphones have opened up a new world. The possibilities are immense! However, it is sometimes easy to lose track of pedagogical purpose when a new, exciting platform is introduced. Educational software, course management platforms, and online programs are all useful tools. But the tools must match the purpose, otherwise the tools become the focus of attention. Remember from Chapter 2—"the medium is the message" (McLuhan, 1964)? It is important to ask questions about how media define what is worth knowing and how media define opportunities to interact with knowledge.

- Does this medium/platform highlight the content of the lesson and provide opportunities for learning and application? Or, does it mostly present the content in an entertaining way?

- Does this medium narrowly define content? If so, how can other media be incorporated into the lesson to provide a wider perspective?

- Am I using platforms and media that tap into a wide range of learning styles, abilities, and interests?

- Do we assume that all students are familiar with or have easy access to this medium/platform?

- Does this medium/platform offer a way for students to meaningfully demonstrate their understanding of the content?

These questions can apply to specific lessons or to the goals and objectives of our classes. I interrogate, for example, my class syllabi as media work. A syllabus for a university course in the United States typically follows a traditional format and includes mandatory components such as objectives, outcomes, assignments, grading rubrics, assessments, expectations for participation, academic integrity, and several other policies. The syllabus is a contract that outlines the responsibilities of the students and teachers. On one hand, I understand the need to have this in print because expectations for learning outcomes must be clear. On the other hand, I struggle with the presentation of a class as a static list of things to do and rules to follow.

Succumbing to the "ooohs and aaahs" of technology, I recently created a "liquid syllabus" that presents content in a more visually attractive and dynamic way, but I found that students spent very little time looking at this syllabus, especially compared to the number of hours it took to create it. One reason for this underwhelming reception might be the fact that the format of the syllabus for decades has taught students to think of classes as a list of items to complete and points to earn. This reward mindset is echoed in many other contexts today, such as gaming and consumerism. Several students have told me that they do not look at the syllabus or course calendar at all and depend on the to-do list that is generated by the course management system. When I give an assignment in class that emerges from the day's discussion and it does not appear on that list, it creates a problem. Students wonder if it is a required assignment. Some forget to complete it because they did not get a reminder. Some don't see it at all. This is an example of media ecology in which the presentation of information through certain media shapes meaning. How, then, can I present my class in a way that defines it as a space for learning, rather than a box to check off?

There is no single answer to this question, but thinking about it opens up room for new ideas to emerge. I have given students a drawing in which I sketched out the main ideas of the class, the assignments corresponding to these ideas, and the connections among them all. I typically make drawings like this as I design my courses each semester, but I had never shared these drawings with the students before. When I did, students said that they could see connections among the content, assignments, and outcomes, and that the course didn't seem so "boxed in" by requirements. I still had to provide the traditional pages of polices and course expectations, but drawing the first page of the syllabus redefined the class and my role as a teacher.

We should also apply questions of media ecology in a more general way to the landscapes of our teaching—our classrooms, offices, and other learning spaces. As a college professor, I cannot decorate my classroom, and many items are fixed in place; however, I can change a few things by thinking about the use of screens or other media. Even if I am in a high-tech classroom where students can work in groups and post their collaborative outcomes on different screens, there are still some circumstances in which this is not the best option. Sometimes it is better to give students dry-erase markers and ask them to write their ideas on a whiteboard. Why? Because they tend to pass the marker around to all group members, erase and revise, and interact with other groups when they are out of their seats. The classroom becomes lively. There are other times when more research-oriented tasks are better suited to the students creating an infographic or other image on screen to share with the class. Media and platforms should match the intent of the lesson, rather than the lesson being built around the media.

The spaces we can decorate with various media, our offices or classrooms, also tell stories. Posters, maps, photographs, artifacts, arrangement of furniture all shape conceptualizations of what knowledge encompasses and what success entails. Take a look around your classroom or office and ask yourself, what does a successful language learner look like? Sound like? Who speaks the target language, where, and what varieties (dialects, styles)? How are cultures and identities represented? If these conceptualizations are narrow and hierarchical, ask yourself how you can change the media to expand the stories you want to tell.

## A Few (Never Final) Thoughts on Integrating Media Work into Your Classrooms

Finding what works for you and your students takes time and constant revisions. I don't have foolproof answers or step-by-step instructions, but I can share a few tips from over three decades of experience. This experience includes mistakes, successes, miscalculations, surprises, frustration, satisfaction, and most of all, an ongoing desire to do better. Here are a few teaching tips that are gleaned from my work with young teachers and college students but applicable to other teaching contexts.

### *Avoid the Smart-Device Vacuum*

Every so often I see or hear news stories that stereotype young people as digital natives who have short attention spans and want to do everything online. These claims make it seem as if digital media and devices are the only media or modality in our students' lives and that they want all aspects of their lives to be online. This isn't true. Their personal and social lives with friends may revolve around screens, but young people do not necessarily want their school work to be online (Pechenkina & Aeschliman, 2017). Nevertheless, schools are compelled to adopt new technologies as a way of keeping up, without always considering whether the tools are the best match for students or learning goals. We do not have to be complicit in digital supremacy in every domain of our lives.

Media work does not necessarily need to add to screen time. Digital technology is not the right mode for all tasks. Human connections are proving to be the most important factor in studies on happiness, and we are lucky to be in a profession that still values and nurtures face-to-face communication. Media work supports these connections by asking students to look more closely at the messages they encounter as they navigate their daily lives and relationships. Some messages will be on screens and some will not. Encouraging students to explore local settings outside of cyberspace leaves less room for them to cut and paste internet images, browse for answers, and ask artificial intelligence (AI) for help. And when media work does focus on messages conveyed through screens, the interrogation, interpretation, reflection, and response processes should offer chances to look away from screens and talk to peers.

### Focus on Language and Stories

When students tell me that they want to look at media connected to a controversial social movement or political issue, I want to encourage their exploration in the most productive way possible. First, this means reminding the student to focus on language and how stories are told. The processes of media work are meant to engage the student with content and context, but they need to be reminded to first see and document what is really there before arriving at conclusions about meaning. Remind students to consider how language and semiotic choices frame an issue through a certain lens. Second, media work on controversial issues should also inspire productive conversations in the classroom. If a student is sharing their work and not everyone is in agreement about the topic (which is the norm), it is my responsibility as an educator to direct the conversation back to language and storytelling. I might ask:

> "What does this media tell us about the issue? How is it supposed to make us feel?"

> "Is this issue presented as a binary (either/or) dilemma? Or is it presented as a complicated issue? What language reflects this?"

> "Does the language used make it seem as if the two sides are irreconcilable? Why or why not? Do you agree with that?"

> "What did you learn from this media about the history or context of the issue?"

Thank students for bringing up difficult topics or perspectives, then, if necessary, move the conversation to larger social (not personal) levels, focusing on how stories are conveyed through various media. This keeps conversation centered on the issue and different ways of seeing it without targeting an individual opinion. You can ask students to find examples from media that portray different points of view and bring them to the next class or post them on a course website. This allows students to talk about the ideas and language from media examples without having to express their own opinions if they are not ready or willing to do so. If a controversial topic arises in an assigned media work activity, ask *specific* questions about the observation and interrogation stages of the activity. Prompt students to clarify their ideas:

> "How do *specific* examples of language and imagery support different perspectives on this issue?"

> "Do any of the language choices leave room for multiple interpretations? Which ones?"

> "What did you decide to research more? Why? What did you find?"

> "What surprised you the most in your (lateral) research of the topic?"

Make students accountable for their opinions. Ask questions what will help them to establish credibility and be open to more questions.

> "What specific evidence did you observe that led you to that conclusion?"

> "How easy/difficult was it to find reliable sources? Tell us how you did it."

> "Are you satisfied with that evidence, or do you want to know more?"

> "What should people know about this issue to make an informed decision about it?"

> "How can fact-checking and lateral research help us to understand this topic better?"

*Accept that "Teachable Moments" Are Not Always Possible.*

We do not have the ability to turn every encounter into a teachable moment. We have to do our best to sense potential hostility and hurtful comments and make the decision to deescalate tension. Without ignoring a problem, or pretending that something wasn't said, I try to move the class on to something else. Later, I might reach out to individual students to see if they need to talk more, outside of class. I mentioned in Chapter 6 that there is tension between creating an intellectual challenge (going out of one's comfort zone) and preventing psychological or emotional discomfort. Sometimes in order to avoid the latter, we need to defuse and move on. I try to have a few responses at the ready:

> "The expertise needed for this conversation is beyond the scope of this class. I encourage you all to research more about it if you want to know more."

> "I hear what you are saying, and I appreciate your contribution to the discussion, but we have to move on."

> "So, we can agree on . . . but not on . . . That's where we need to leave it right now so we can move on to other things."

These conversations are not easy. On a daily basis, we encounter people who hold values and beliefs that have little in common with our own. At best, our differences are interesting and respected, sometimes they are barriers to communication, and at worst they incite harm. We have to make on-the-spot decisions about how to handle each situation as it arises. This requires careful semantic choices, interpretations of verbal and nonverbal cues, and choosing appropriate responses. We might have to respond to a student who intentionally or unintentionally insults other students, or to someone who complains to us that their neighbors aren't learning English fast enough! There is no manual for dealing with these situations. We look, listen, and decide whether it is a "teachable moment," an opportunity to find common ground, or a potentially hostile interaction that should be managed outside of class. This negotiation and decision-making is part of interacting in our media-saturated worlds, and the ways teachers react can serve as models for students. Although there is no solution that works for all situations, we are all better equipped to deal with challenging situations when we are committed to disagreeing without inciting hostility.

*Play with Media Work*

Media work can be many different things. Whether you look at greeting cards, menus, bus schedules, websites, videos, or historical documents, think about how you will provide both structure and flexibility for the assignment. At the end of this chapter you will find a worksheet that leads you through developmental stages for designing media work. Before you dive into the details, though, think about what you want to accomplish with media work. Play with it. The processes of observation, interrogation, interpretation, reflection, and response can be used in different configurations and applied to various focal points. You might need to emphasize vocabulary or grammatical structures, and you can do this through material such as a school or community newsletter that also tells stories about people and places. You may use advertisements to explore cultural values (or stereotypes of cultures) and find that the use of metaphors and idioms also provides a language lesson.

Media work is a flexible approach that you can draw on to provide structure for what you want to teach. If you want to teach about health-related vocabulary, for example, think about where students might encounter this vocabulary in the media of their daily lives. They might see letters sent home from school about mandatory physicals, pamphlets about services and programs in their communities, and food items at grocery stores that promise health benefits. You might focus on these observations and word choices and then link this media work to other parts of the curriculum, such as science, nutrition, or self-care. Or, you might extend this work into a research project that interrogates health claims of products found in different kinds of media. Have a structure in mind, but be open to creativity.

Because we live in a data-driven world, we may need to evaluate media work while also preserving the playfulness of it. I break media work down into small steps that involve multiple homework assignments. Each assignment might be worth the same points, but it is more likely that some parts are more involved than others and merit additional points. By breaking it down into stages, students concentrate on one assignment at a time and think about the process rather than how to get to a final product in a hurry. This also allows me to adapt the different stages as needed. I might revise when students should work individually, in pairs, or in groups depending on how they are responding. I might add a journal reflection to check on students' progress. Don't be afraid to play with media work.

## Back to the Beginning

It makes sense to think of going "back to the beginning," because I want to emphasize the fact that the processes of media work constitute a continual reflective cycle of observing, questioning, and responding to our mediascapes. We may need to look again at original observations and ask new questions as language and contexts around us change. In Chapter 1, I interrogated and interpreted my observations of text and imagery on the paper packaging of a falafel wrap. I described the market where I bought it and the social dynamics of the community. If I go back to that market today, would my observations and interpretations be the same? How could I find out more about the business and its owners? I can think of many more questions to ask, and this is true of every example of media work that I shared in this book. We can always go back to the beginning and see how language, imagery, and stories have changed or remained the same. The market stand where I bought my falafel wrap has changed its logo to a bigger, bolder, and less stylized font. The vendors in the market seem to be more culturally diverse, but the customers are not. I still hear only one language, but that doesn't mean there is only one story to be told. The entire market is a rich mediascape, and it would be fascinating to compare it with markets in other areas of the city. There are so many stories to discover!

Media are, of course, just one conduit through which stories are transmitted, but they provide such a rich resource of language, imagery, sounds, content, and contexts. Media are chaotic, full of contradictions, both predictable and unpredictable—a reflection of the people who create, critique, and consume them. Media amplify our hopes and fears and define what is important to know and to do.

My intention is that media work inspires a "hmmm" in both you and your students and that as you look closely at and question the media in your everyday environments your students say "aha" (figure 71), and learn to express their own stories.

**Figure 71**

KEY IDEAS

language engagement

intercultural engagement

community engagement

pedagogical engagement

civic intentionality

media ecology in the classroom

teachable moments

"playing" with media

QUESTION, EXPLORE, and MORE

1.  As you begin to think about and design media work assignments or projects for your students, keep the following questions in mind:

    What media would be valuable for your students to explore?

    -   How will they access and document this media?

    -   How many alternative formats will be available to them?

    -   What are the learning outcomes (linguistically, culturally, and socially)?

    How will the students interrogate, interpret, and reflect?

    -   Will they work individually, in groups, or both?

    -   How will they interact and share ideas (discussions, essays, journals, presentations, podcasts, videos, posters, blogs, artwork, etc.)?

    How do you want them to respond to the media messages?

    -   Sharing their ideas with people in their communities?

    -   Taking action to support learning or change?

    Other pedagogical considerations

    -   What parts of the media work process are most relevant to your teaching goals and objectives?

- How will you evaluate students' work at different stages of media work?

- How will you provide opportunities for reflection and revisions?

- How will you incorporate and value diverse perspectives and languages?

2. Experiment with different media work assignments. Create assignments according to the criteria below (review Chapter 5 for ideas):

   - Design a short homework assignment in which students watch their favorite movies or programs and document characters and their different qualities. Create a chart for the students to complete.

   - Create an assignment that asks students to document media in their local communities, interpret meanings, and then share their ideas with the class. Include opportunities for students to respond to each other's work.

   - Ask students to research a topic (climate change, for example) and find media that tell different, or opposing, stories. Create an assignment that encourages students to interrogate and research these different media stories.

   - Choose a word or phrase and ask students to find media that they connect to it. Create a multi-stage lesson in which they apply media work processes to their media collections. Examples of a word or phrase might be:

     "multilingualism," "The American Dream," "The US as a melting pot," "community," "identity," "home," "adventure," "tradition"

3. Curate a collection of photographs, print media, and other ephemera to keep in a digital or analog file (see figure 72).

**Figure 72**

I have collections in both formats and have spent a great deal of time looking for "that perfect photo of . . ." because it was not labeled and filed away methodically. My excuse for this lack of organization was that media work was an evolving process that I began long before I recognized the theory and structure behind it. Moreover, the flexible and adaptable nature of media work meant that I used it for many different classes and workshops in many different contexts. The files were all over the place. I have since made improvements, but you can begin with better organization (see figure 73) and then easily find the media samples you need.

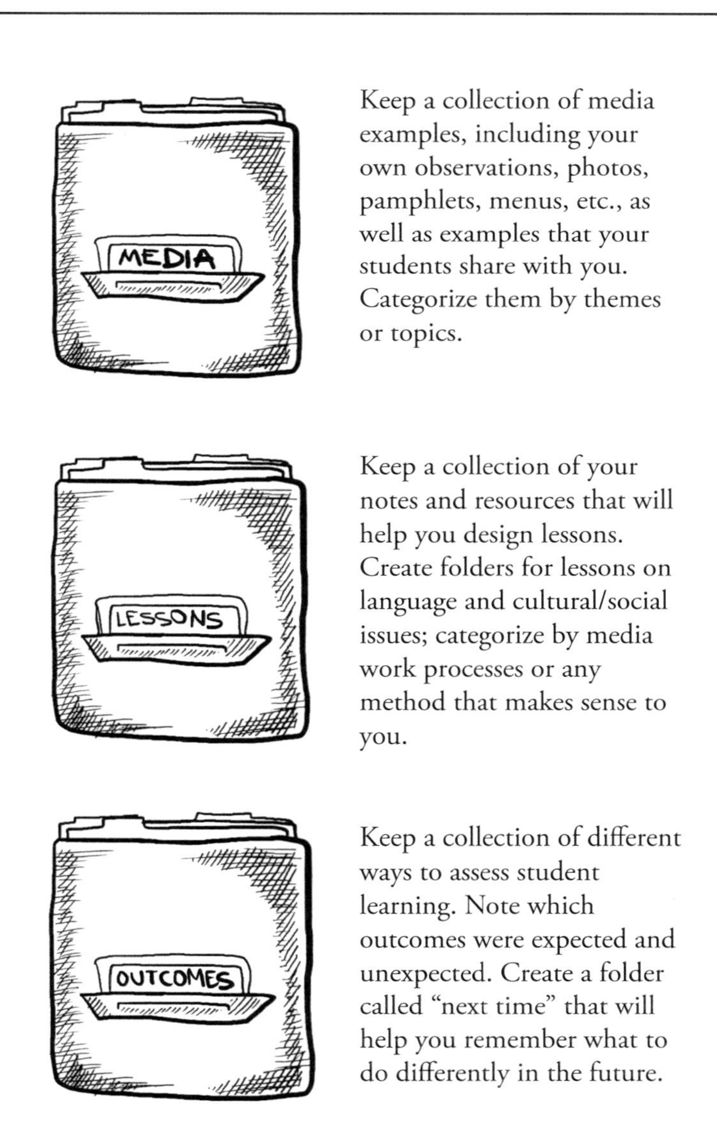


Keep a collection of media examples, including your own observations, photos, pamphlets, menus, etc., as well as examples that your students share with you. Categorize them by themes or topics.

Keep a collection of your notes and resources that will help you design lessons. Create folders for lessons on language and cultural/social issues; categorize by media work processes or any method that makes sense to you.

Keep a collection of different ways to assess student learning. Note which outcomes were expected and unexpected. Create a folder called "next time" that will help you remember what to do differently in the future.

**Figure 73**

# References

Alim, H. S., & Paris, D. (2015). Whose language gap? Critical and culturally sustaining pedagogies as necessary challenges to racializing hegemony. *Journal of Linguistic Anthropology, 25*(1), 79.

Alim, H. S., Rickford, J. R., & Ball, A. F. (2016). *Raciolinguistics: How language shapes our ideas about race.* Oxford University Press.

Alvarez, Brenda. (2023, May 26). The Pride flag flies again: A union and a community worked together to reinstate pride flags in a Connecticut school. *NEA Today.*

Amin, N. (1997). Race and the identity of the nonnative ESL teacher. *TESOL Quarterly, 31*(3), 580. https://doi.org/10.2307/3587841

Baranova, V. (2023). Linguistic in/exclusion in medicine: Multilingual COVID-19 communication in Russia. *Journal of Eurasian Studies, 14*(2), 106–117. https://doi.org/10.1177/18793665231185792

Baranova, V. (2024). The linguistic landscape of the war: Minority languages, language activism, and contesting identities in Russia. *Linguistic Landscape, 10*(1), 55–78. https://doi.org/10.1075/ll.23006.bar

Berg-Nordlie, M. (2018). New in town. Small-town media discourses on immigrants and immigration. *Journal of Rural Studies, 64*, 210–219. https://doi.org/10.1016/j.jrurstud.2018.05.007

Berger, A. A. (2019). *Media analysis techniques* (Sixth edition). Sage.

Best, J., & Horiuchi, G. T. (1985). The razor blade in the apple: The social construction of urban legends. *Social Problem, 32*(5), 488–499. https://doi.org/10.2307/800777

Bhatia, T. K., & Kathpalia, S. S. (2019). World Englishes and cross-cultural advertising. *World Englishes, 38*(3), 348–351. https://doi.org/10.1111/weng.12419

Billig, M. (2005). *Laughter and ridicule: Towards a social critique of humour* (1st ed.). Sage. https://doi.org/10.4135/9781446211779

Birnie, I. (2022). The social linguistic soundscape and its influence on language choice in Stornoway. In D. Smakman, J. Nekvapil, & K. Fedorova, *Linguistic choices in the contemporary city* (pp. 141–153). Routledge. https://doi.org/10.4324/9780429348037-12

Blackwood, R., & Dunlevy, D. A. (2021). *Multilingualism in public spaces: Empowering and transforming communities.* Bloomsbury. https://doi.org/10.5040/9781350186620

Block, D. (2014). *Social class in applied linguistics.* Routledge. https://doi.org/10.4324/9781315871141

Blommaert, J. (2013). *Ethnography, superdiversity and linguistic landscapes: Chronicles of complexity*. Multilingual Matters. https://doi.org/10.21832/9781783090419

Boerhout, L., & Van Driel, B. (2013). Memory walk: An interaction-oriented project to interrogate contested histories. *Intercultural Education, 24*(3), 211–221. https://doi.org/10.1080/14675986.2013.799804

Bori, P. (2021). Neoliberalism and global textbooks: A critical ethnography of English language classrooms in Serbia. *Language, Culture and Curriculum, 34*(2), 183–198. https://doi.org/10.1080/07908318.2020.1797082

boyd, d. (2014). *It's complicated: The social lives of networked teens*. Yale University Press.

Breakstone, J., Smith, M., Wineburg, S., Rapaport, A., Carle, J., Garland, M., & Saavedra, A. (2021). Students' civic online reasoning: A national portrait. *Educational Researcher, 50*(8), 505–515. https://doi.org/10.3102/0013189X211017495

Brutt-Griffler, J., & Samimy, K. K. (1999). Revisiting the colonial in the postcolonial: Critical praxis for nonnative-English-speaking teachers in a TESOL program. *TESOL Quarterly, 33*(3), 413–431. https://doi.org/10.2307/3587672

Brutt-Griffler, J., & Samimy, K. K. (2001). Transcending the nativeness paradigm. *World Englishes, 20*(1), 99–106. https://doi.org/10.1111/1467-971X.00199

Canada's Center for Digital Media Literacy. (n.d.). *Media Smarts*. Representation of diversity in media. https://mediasmarts.ca/digital-media-literacy/media-issues/diversity-media/representation-diversity-media-overview

Canagarajah, A. S. (1999). *Resisting linguistic imperialism in English teaching*. Oxford University Press.

Canagarajah, A. S. (2008). The politics of English language teaching. In *Encyclopedia of Language and Education* (pp. 213–227). Springer US. https://doi.org/10.1007/978-0-387-30424-3_16

Canale, M., & Swain, M. (1980). Theoretical bases of communicative approaches to second language teaching and testing. *Applied Linguistics, 1*(1), 1–47. https://doi.org/10.1093/applin/I.1.1

Canelli, R. (2006, September 6) English instruction strains school budgets. *Bucks County Courier Times*, 1A.

Carey, J. W. (1989). *Communication as culture: Essays on media and society*. Unwin Hyman.

Carroll, S., & Swain, M. (1993). Explicit and implicit negative feedback: An empirical study of the learning of linguistic generalization. *Studies in Second Language Acquisition, 15*, 357–386. http://dx.doi.org/10.1017/S0272263100012158

Center for Media Literacy Education (n.d). Educational philosophy. Retrieved September 20, 2024, from https://www.medialit.org/about-cml#education

Chamberlin, C. (2021). On the street where I live: Mapping a spectrum of antiracist messages and meanings. *Journal of Media Literacy Education, 13*(2), 15–28. https://doi.org/10.23860/JMLE-2021-13-2-2

Chamberlin, C., & Khan, M. (2022). Critical media work as antiracist pedagogy in language learning classrooms. *CATESOL Journal, 33*(1), n1. https://eric.ed.gov/?id=EJ1365669

Chamberlin, C., & Torigoe, C. (2016). *Helpless and illegal "others:" Immigrant identity in local newspaper articles in the U.S. and Japan."* Conference on Education Theory and Practice in Challenging Times: Cultivating an Ethos of Social Justice, Respect and Diversity. International Association for Intercultural Education. Angers, France.

Chamberlin-Quinlisk. C. (2003). Media literacy in the ESL/EFL classroom: Reading images and cultural stories. *TESOL Journal, 12*(3), 35–39. https://doi.org/10.1002/j.1949-3533.2003.tb00141.x

Chamberlin-Quinlisk, C. (2012a). Critical media analysis in teacher education: Exploring language-learners' identity through mediated images of a non-native speaker of English. *TESL Canada Journal, 29*(2), 42. https://doi.org/10.18806/tesl.v29i2.1099

Chamberlin-Quinlisk, C. (2012b). TESOL and media education: Navigating our screen-saturated worlds. *TESOL Quarterly, 46*(1), 152–164.

Chun, C. (2019). Methodological issues in critical discourse studies. In McKinley, J. & H. Rose (Eds.). *The Routledge handbook of research methods in applied linguistics,* 199–210. Routledge.

Chun, C. (2015) *Power and meaning making in an EAP classroom: Engaging with the everyday.* Multilingual Matters.

Cohen, M., & Glover, J. (Eds.). (2014). *Colonial mediascapes: Sensory worlds of the early Americas.* University of Nebraska Press.

Cope, B., & Kalantzis, M. (Eds.). (2017). *E-Learning ecologies: Principles for new learning and assessment.* Routledge.

Cummins, J. (1997). Cultural and linguistic diversity in education: A mainstream issue? *Educational Review, 49*(2), 105–114. https://doi.org/10.1080/0013191970490202

Cummins, J. (2001). Empowering minority students: A framework for intervention. *Harvard Educational Review, 71*(4), 656–675.

Cummins, J. (2010). *Language, power and pedagogy: Bilingual children in the crossfire.* Multilingual Matters.

Curran, N. M., & Chesnut, M. (2022). English fever and coffee: Transient cosmopolitan-ism and the rising cost of distinction. *Journal of Consumer Culture, 22*(2), 551–570. https://doi.org/10.1177/1469540521990869

Davies, A. (2003). *The native speaker: Myth and reality.* Multilingual Matters.

Delpit, L. (1996). *Other people's children: Cultural conflict in the classroom.* Norton.

Delpit, L. D. (2012). *"Multiplication is for white people:" Raising expectations for other people's children.* Perseus.

de Saussure, F. (1966). *Course in general linguistics.* McGraw-Hill.

DiGiacomo, D. K., Hodgin, E., Kahne, J., Alkam, S., & Taylor, C. (2023). Assessing the state of media literacy policy in U.S. K-12 schools. *Journal of Children and Media, 17*(3), 336–352. https://doi.org/10.1080/17482798.2023.2201890

Drakett, J., Rickett, B., Day, K., & Milnes, K. (2018). Old jokes, new media – Online sexism and constructions of gender in internet memes. *Feminism & Psychology, 28*(1), 109–127. https://doi.org/10.1177/0959353517727560

Dubreil, S., Malinowski, D., & Maxim, H. H. (2023). *Spatializing language studies: peda-gogical approaches in the linguistic landscape.* Springer.

Duff, P. (1993). Tasks and interlanguage performance: An SLA [second language acquisition] research perspective. In G. Crookes & S. Gass (Eds.), *Tasks in language learning: Integrating theory and practice* (pp. 57–95). Clevedon, UK: Multilingual Matters.

Dugan, D. (Director). (1999) *Big Daddy* [Film]. Columbia Pictures.

Egbert, J. & Huff, L. (2013). "You're a winner:" An exploratory study of the influence of exposure on teachers' awareness of media literacy. In B. Zou (Ed.), *Explorations of language teaching and learning with computational assistance* (pp. 263–279). IGI Global. https://doi.org/10.4018/978-1-4666-1855-8.ch017

Egbert., J. & Neville, C. (2015). Engaging K-12 language learners in media literacy. TESOL Journal, 6(1), 177–187. https://doi.org/10.1002/tesj.182

Edge, J. (2006). *(Re-)locating TESOL in an age of empire*. Palgrave Macmillan. https://doi.org/10.1057/9780230502239

Faez, F. (2011). Are you a native speaker of English? Moving beyond a simplistic dichotomy. *Critical Inquiry in Language Studies, 8*(4), 378–399. https://doi.org/10.1080/15427587.2011.615708

Fairclough, N. (1989). *Language and power*. Longman.

Fairclough, N. (2010). *Critical discourse analysis: The critical study of language*. Routledge. https://doi.org/10.4324/9781315834368

Fairclough, N. (2011). *Media discourse*. Bloomsbury.

Ferris, D. (2002). *Treatment of error in second language student writing*. University of Michigan Press.

Flannery, M. E. (2024, January 10). Educators fight book bans through their union. *NEA Today*. https://www.nea.org/nea-today/all-news-articles/educators-fight-book-bans-through-their-union

Foucault, M. (1972). *The archaeology of knowledge*. Pantheon Books.

Freire, P. (1970/2000). *Pedagogy of the oppressed*. Continuum.

Freire, P. (1985). *The politics of education: Culture, power, and liberation*. Bergin & Garvey.

Friesem, E. (2016). Question-based dialogue on media representations of social problems: Enhancing civic engagement by uncovering implicit knowledge accumulated from the media. *Journal of Communication Inquiry, 40*(1), 46–66. https://doi.org/10.1177/0196859915594204

Friesem, E. (2021). *Media is us: Understanding communication and moving beyond blame*. Rowman & Littlefield.

Fromm, M. (2024). *Media literacy snapshot 2024: The state of media literacy education in the United States*. National Association for Media Literacy Education.

Gabriel, M., & Goldberg, E. (Directors). (1995). *Pocahontas* [Film]. Walt Disney Pictures.

Garcia, A. (2019). Centering analog literacy in an era of digital harm. *Research in the Teaching of English, 54*, 192–194.

Garcia, A., & de Roock, R. S. (2021). Civic dimensions of critical digital literacies: Towards an abolitionist lens. *Pedagogies, 16*(2), 187–201. https://doi.org/10.1080/1554480X.2021.1914058

García, O. (2009). *Bilingual education in the 21st century: A global perspective.* Wiley-Blackwell.

García, O., & Kleifgen, J. A. (2020). Translanguaging and literacies. *Reading Research Quarterly, 55*(4), 553–571. https://doi.org/10.1002/rrq.286

García, O., & Li, W. (2014). *Translanguaging: Language, bilingualism and education.* Palgrave Macmillan. https://doi.org/10.1057/9781137385765

Gay, G. (2002). Preparing for culturally responsive teaching. *Journal of Teacher Education, 53*(2), 106–116. https://doi.org/10.1177/0022487102053002003

Gay, G. (2018). *Culturally responsive teaching: Theory, research, and practice.* Teachers College Press.

Gee, J. P. (2014a). *An introduction to discourse analysis: Theory and method.* Routledge. https://doi.org/10.4324/9781315819679

Gee, J. P. (2014b). *How to do discourse analysis: A toolkit.* Routledge. https://doi.org/10.4324/9781315819662

Gerbner, G., Gross, L., Signorielli, N., & Morgan, M. (1980). Television violence, victimization, and power. *The American Behavioral Scientist, 23*(5), 705–716. https://doi.org/10.1177/000276428002300506

Gerbner, G., Jhally, S., & Morgan, M. (Directors). (2014). *The electronic storyteller: TV & the cultivation of values* [Film]. Media Education Foundation.

Giroux, H. A. (1994). *Disturbing pleasures: Learning popular culture.* Routledge.

Giroux, H. A., & Purpel, D. E. (1983). *The hidden curriculum and moral education: Deception or discovery?* McCutchan.

Glaser, B. G., & Strauss, A. L. (1967). *The discovery of grounded theory: Strategies for qualitative research.* Aldine de Gruyter. https://doi.org/10.4324/9780203793206

Glassner, B. (2009). *The culture of fear: Why Americans are afraid of the wrong things.* Basic Books.

González-Carriedo, R. (2014). Ideologies of the press in regard to English language learners: A case study of two newspapers in Arizona. *Critical Inquiry in Language Studies, 11*(2), 121–149. https://doi.org/10.1080/15427587.2014.906808

Gordon, E., & Mihailidis, P. (Eds.). (2016). *Civic media: Technology, design, practice.* MIT Press.

Gorter, D. (Ed.). (2006). *Linguistic landscape: A new approach to multilingualism.* Multilingual Matters. https://doi.org/10.21832/9781853599170

Gorter, D., & Cenoz, J. (2015). Translanguaging and linguistic landscapes. *Linguistic Landscape,* (1–2), 54–74. https://doi.org/10.1075/ll.1.1-2.04gor

Gorter, D., Marten, H. F., & Van Mensel, L. (2019). Linguistic landscapes and minority languages. In G. Hogan-Brun & B. O'Rourke (Eds.), *The Palgrave handbook of minority languages and communities* (pp. 481–506). Palgrave Macmillan. https://doi.org/10.1057/978-1-137-54066-9_19

Hall, B. J. (2005). *Among cultures: The challenge of communication* (2nd ed.). Thomson Wadsworth.

Hall, B. J., Covarrubias, P. O., & Kirschbaum, K. A. (2022). *Among cultures: The challenge of communication* (4th edition). Routledge.

Hall, S. (1997). *Representation: Cultural representations and signifying practices*. Sage.

Hall, S., & Du Gay, P. (1996). *Questions of cultural identity*. Sage.

Hallett, R. W., & Quiñones, F. M. (2023). The linguistic landscape of an urban Hispanic-serving institution in the United States. *Social Semiotics, 33*(3), 645–659. doi: https://doi.org/10.1080/10350330.2021.1916391

He, H. (2019). Media literacy education and second language acquisition. In R. Hobbs & P. Mihailidis (Eds.), *The international encyclopedia of media literacy* (pp. 1–7). Wiley. https://doi.org/10.1002/9781118978238.ieml0125

Heller, M. (2006). *Linguistic minorities and modernity: A sociolinguistic ethnography*. Continuum.

Herman, E. S., & Chomsky, N. (1988). *Manufacturing consent: The political economy of the mass media*. Pantheon Books.

Higdon, N. (2020). *The anatomy of fake news: A critical news literacy education*. University of California Press.

Hobbs, R. (2005). The state of media literacy education. *Journal of Communication, 55*(4), 865–871. https://doi.org/10.1111/j.1460-2466.2005.tb03027.x

Hobbs, R. (Ed.). (2016). *Exploring the roots of digital and media literacy through personal narrative*. Temple University Press.

Hobbs, R. (2020). *Mind over media: Propaganda education for a digital age*. W. W. Norton & Company.

Hobbs, R. (2021). *Media literacy in action: Questioning the media*. Rowman & Littlefield.

Hobbs, R., He, H., & Robbgrieco, M. (2015). Seeing, believing, and learning to be skeptical: Supporting language learning through advertising analysis activities. *TESOL Journal, 6*(3), 447–475. https://doi.org/10.1002/tesj.153

Hobbs, R., & Jensen, A. (2009). The past, present, and future of media literacy education. *The Journal of Media Literacy Education, 1*(1), 1–11. https://doi.org/10.23860/jmle-1-1-1

Hobbs, R., & Mihailidis, P. (2019). *The international encyclopedia of media literacy*. John Wiley & Sons. https://doi.org/10.1002/9781118978238

Horisk, C. (2024). *Dangerous jokes: How racism and sexism weaponize humor*. Oxford University Press. https://doi.org/10.1093/oso/9780197691496.001.0001

Horrigan, J. (2021). *Philadelphia's digital divide by the numbers*. City of Philadelphia. https://www.phila.gov/documents/connecting-philadelphia-2021-household-internet-assessment-survey/

Jenkins, H. (2006). *Convergence culture: Where old and new media collide*. New York University Press.

Jewitt, C., & Kress, G. R. (Eds.). (2003). *Multimodal literacy*. Peter Lang.

Johnson, E. (2005). War in the media: Metaphors, ideology, and the formation of language policy. *Bilingual Research Journal, 29*(3), 621–640. https://doi.org/10.1080/15235882.2005.10162855

Kellner, D., & Share, J. (2005). Toward critical media literacy: Core concepts, debates, organizations, and policy. *Discourse, 26*(3), 369–386. https://doi.org/10.1080/01596300500200169

Kellner, D., & Share, J. (2007). Critical media literacy is not an option. *Learning Inquiry*, *1*(1), 59–69. https://doi.org/10.1007/s11519-007-0004-2

Kincheloe, J. L. (1993). *Toward a critical politics of teacher thinking: Mapping the postmodern*. Bergin & Garvey.

Krashen, S. D. (1985). *The input hypothesis: Issues and implications*. Longman.

Kress, G. (2003). *Literacy in the new media age*. Routledge.

Kress, G. (2010). *Multimodality: A social semiotic approach to contemporary communication*. Routledge. https://doi.org/10.4324/9780203970034

Kress, G. (2000). Multimodality, in B. Cope & M. Kalantzis, *Multiliteracies: Literacy learning and the design of social futures*. Routledge.

Kubota, R. (2020). Confronting epistemological racism, decolonizing scholarly knowledge: Race and gender in applied linguistics. *Applied Linguistics*, *41*(5), 712–732. https://doi.org/10.1093/applin/amz033

Kubota, R. (2021). Critical antiracist pedagogy in ELT. *ELT Journal*, *75*(3), 237–246. https://doi.org/10.1093/elt/ccab015

Kubota, R., & Lin, A. (2006). Race and TESOL: Introduction to concepts and theories. *TESOL Quarterly*, *40*(3), 471–493. https://doi.org/10.2307/40264540

Kubota, R., & Lin, A. (2009). *Race, culture, and identities in second language education: Exploring critically engaged practice*. Routledge. https://doi.org/10.4324/9780203876657

Ladson-Billings, G. (1995). Toward a theory of culturally relevant pedagogy. *American Educational Research Journal*, *32*(3), 465–491. https://doi.org/10.3102/00028312032003465

Ladson-Billings, G. (1998). Just what is critical race theory and what's it doing in a nice field like education? *International Journal of Qualitative Studies in Education*, *11*(1), 7–24. https://doi.org/10.1080/095183998236863

Ladson-Billings, G. (2014). Culturally relevant pedagogy 2.0: A.k.a. the remix. *Harvard Educational Review*, *84*(1), 74–84. https://doi.org/10.17763/haer.84.1.p2rj131485484751

Ladson-Billings, G. (2021). Three decades of culturally relevant, responsive, & sustaining pedagogy: What lies ahead? *The Educational Forum*, *85*(4), 351–354. https://doi.org/10.1080/00131725.2021.1957632

Lankshear, C., & Knobel, M. (2006). New literacies: Everyday practices and classroom learning. Open University Press.

Lee, J. S. (2014). English on Korean television. *World Englishes*, *33*(1), 33–49.

Lessenski, M. (2023). *Bye, Bye Birdie: The challenges of disinformation. The Media Literacy Index 2023 Measuring Vulnerability of Societies to Disinformation*. Open Society Institute. https://osis.bg/wp-content/uploads/2023/06/MLI-report-in-English-22.06.pdf

Levitan, S., Lloyd, C., Morton, J., Corrigan, P., O'Shannon, D., Walsh, B., Zucker, D., Wrubel, B., Richman, J., Higginbotham, A., Lloyd, S., Ko, E., Tatham, C., Chandrasekaran, V., Pollack, J. & J. Burditt (Executive Producers). (2009-2020). *Modern Family*. [TV series]. Lloyd-Levitan; Picador; Steven Levitan; 20th Century Fox Television.

Lewis, J., & Jhally, S. (1998). The struggle over media literacy. *Journal of Communication, 48*(1), 109–120. https://doi.org/10.1111/j.1460-2466.1998.tb02741.x

Li, W. (2018). Translanguaging as a practical theory of language. *Applied Linguistics, 39*(1), 9–30. https://doi.org/10.1093/applin/amx039

Li, W. (2020). Multilingual English users' linguistic innovation. *World Englishes, 39*(2), 236–248. https://doi.org/10.1111/weng.12457

Li, W., & García, O. (2022). Not a first language but one repertoire: Translanguaging as a decolonizing project. *RELC Journal, 53*(2), 313–324. https://doi.org/10.1177/00336882221092841

Lin, A. (2014). Critical discourse analysis in applied linguistics: A methodological review. *Annual Review of Applied Linguistics, 34*, 213–232. doi:10.1017/S0267190514000087

Lippi-Green, R. (2012). *English with an accent: Language, ideology and discrimination in the United States*. Routledge.

Long, M. H. (1983). Native speaker/non-native speaker conversation and the negotiation of comprehensible input. *Applied linguistics, 4*(2), 126–141.

*Looney Tunes*. (1944-present). Warner Brothers Cartoons.

López, F. A., & Sleeter, C. E. (2023). *Critical race theory and its critics: Implications for research and teaching*. Teachers College Press.

Lorenz, E. P., & Frisby, C. M. (2022). Disability on drama TV: How attitudes about disability in the US relate to viewing frequency and identification with a character with a disability on "Glee." *Media Education, 13*(1), 81–91. https://doi.org/10.36253/me-12641

Lotherington, H. (2004). What four skills? Redefining language and literacy standards for ELT in the digital era. *TESL Canada Journal, 22*(1), 64–78. https://doi.org/10.18806/tesl.v22i1.166

Lotherington, H. (2011). *Pedagogy of multiliteracies: Rewriting Goldilocks*. Routledge.

Lum, C. M. K. (2006). *Perspectives on culture, technology, and communication: The media ecology tradition*. Hampton Press.

Macedo, D. P. & Steinberg, S. (Eds.) (2007). *Media literacy: A reader*. Peter Lang.

Malinowski, D., Maxim, H. H., & Dubreil, S. (2020). *Language teaching in the linguistic landscape: Mobilizing pedagogy in public space*. Springer.

Martens, H., & Hobbs, R. (2015). How media literacy supports civic engagement in a digital age. *Atlantic Journal of Communication, 23*(2), 120–137. https://doi.org/10.1080/15456870.2014.961636

Masterman, L. (1985). *Teaching the media*. Routledge. https://doi.org/10.4324/9780203359051

McArdle, E. (2023, November 6). Book Bans and the librarians who won't be hushed: How educators are speaking out in response to recent—and increasing—book bans. *Ed. Magazine, Harvard Graduate School of Education*. https://www.gse.harvard.edu/ideas/ed-magazine/23/11/book-bans-and-librarians-who-wont-be-hushed

McCullough, G. (2019). *Because internet: Understanding how language is changing.* Penguin Random House.

McDougall, J. (2019). *Fake news vs media studies: Travels in a false binary.* Springer International Publishing. https://doi.org/10.1007/978-3-030-27220-3

McGrew, S. (2024). Teaching lateral reading: Interventions to help people read like fact checkers. *Current Opinion in Psychology, 55,* 101737. https://doi.org/10.1016/j.copsyc.2023.101737

McLuhan, H. M. (1964). *Understanding media: The extensions of man.* New American Library.

Meehan, K., Friedman, J., Baêta, S., & Magnusson, T. (2023). *Banned in the USA: The mounting pressure to censor.* PEN America. https://pen.org/report/book-bans-pressure-to-censor/

Melo-Pfeifer, S. (Ed.). (2023). *Linguistic landscapes in language and teacher education: Multilingual teaching and learning inside and beyond the classroom.* Springer. DOI: 10.1007/978-3-031-22867-4

Meyrowitz, J. (1998). Multiple media literacies. *Journal of Communication, 48*(1), 96–108. https://doi.org/10.1111/j.1460-2466.1998.tb02740.x

Mihailidis, P. (2019). *Civic media literacies: Re-imagining human connection in an age of digital abundance.* Routledge.

Mihailidis, P., & Thevenin, B. (2013). Media literacy as a core competency for engaged citizenship in participatory democracy. *The American Behavioral Scientist, 57*(11), 1611–1622. https://doi.org/10.1177/0002764213489015

Mills, K. A. (2016). *Literacy theories for the digital age: Social, critical, multimodal, spatial, material and sensory lenses.* Multilingual Matters.

Moeller, S., Joseph, A., Lau, J., & Carbo, T. (2010). Towards media and information literacy indicators. UNESCO.

Molina-Guzmán, I. (2010). *Dangerous curves: Latina bodies in the media.* New York University Press.

Morgan, B. (2009). Revitalising the essay in an English for academic purposes course: critical engagement, multiliteracies and the internet. *International Journal of Bilingual Education and Bilingualism, 12*(3), 309–324.

Morgan, B., & Ahmed, A. (2023). Teaching the Nation(s): A duoethnography on affect and citizenship in a content-based EAP Program. *TESOL Quarterly, 57*(3), 859–889.

Morgan, B., & Ramanathan, V. (2005). Critical literacies and language education: global and local perspectives. *Annual Review of Applied Linguistics, 25,* 151–169. doi:10.1017/S0267190505000085

Morgan, M. (2012). *George Gerbner: A critical introduction to media and communication theory.* Peter Lang.

Morgan, M., & Shanahan, J. (2010). The state of cultivation. *Journal of Broadcasting & Electronic Media, 54*(2), 337–355. https://doi.org/10.1080/08838151003735018

Morozov, E. V. (2014). *To save everything, click here: The folly of technological solutionism.* PublicAffairs.

Motha, S. (2006a). Decolonizing ESOL: Negotiating linguistic power in U.S. public school classrooms. *Critical Inquiry in Language Studies, 3*(2/3), 75–100. https://doi.org/10.1080/15427587.2006.9650841

Motha, S. (2006b). Racializing ESOL teacher identities in U.S. K-12 public schools. *TESOL Quarterly, 40*(3), 495–518. https://doi.org/10.2307/40264541

Motha, S. (2014). *Race, empire, and English language teaching: Creating responsible and ethical anti-racist practice.* Teachers College.

Nambu, S. (2021). Linguistic landscape of immigrants in Japan: A case study of Japanese Brazilian communities. *Journal of Multilingual and Multicultural Development, 45*(5), 1–17. https://doi.org/10.1080/01434632.2021.2006200

Nelson, C. D. (2006). Queer inquiry in language education. *Journal of Language, Identity, and Education, 5*(1), 1–9. https://doi.org/10.1207/s15327701jlie0501_1

Nelson, C. D. (2009). *Sexual identities in English language education: Classroom conversations.* Routledge. https://doi.org/10.4324/9780203891544

New London Group (1996). A pedagogy of multiliteracies: designing social futures, *Harvard Educational Review, 66*(1), 60–92.

Nieto, S. (1992). *Affirming diversity: The sociopolitical context of multicultural education.* Longman.

Nieto, S. (1999). *The light in their eyes: Creating multicultural learning communities.* Teachers College.

Nieto, S. (2010). *Language, culture, and teaching: Critical perspectives* (2nd ed.). Routledge. https://doi.org/10.4324/9780203872284

Oliver, M. B., Raney, A. A., & Bryant, J. (Eds.). (2019). *Media effects: Advances in theory and research.* Routledge. https://doi.org/10.4324/9780429491146

Ong, W. J. (1982). *Orality and literacy: The technologizing of the word.* Methuen.

Paakspuu, K. (2009). "Writing the body:" The hypertext of photography. *International Journal of Media and Cultural Politics, 5*(3), 183–197. https://doi.org/10.1386/macp.5.3.183/1

Paris, D. (2012). Culturally sustaining pedagogy: A needed change in stance, terminology, and practice. *Educational Researcher, 41*(3), 93–97. https://doi.org/10.3102/0013189X12441244

Paris, D. (2021). Culturally sustaining pedagogies and our futures. *The Educational Forum, 85*(4), 364–376. https://doi.org/10.1080/00131725.2021.1957634

Paris, D., & Alim, H. S. (2014). What are we seeking to sustain through culturally sustaining pedagogy? A loving critique forward. *Harvard Educational Review, 84*(1), 85–100. https://doi.org/10.17763/haer.84.1.982l873k2ht16m77

Paris, D., & Alim, H. S. (Eds.). (2017). *Culturally sustaining pedagogies: Teaching and learning for justice in a changing world.* Teachers College.

Pechenkina, E., & Aeschliman, C. (2017). What do students want? Making sense of student preferences in technology-enhanced learning. *Contemporary Educational Technology, 8*(1), 26–39. https://doi.org/10.30935/cedtech/6185

Peck, A., & Stroud, C. (2015). Skinscapes. *Linguistic Landscape, 1*(1/2), 133–151. https://doi.org/10.1075/ll.1.1-2.08pec

*PEN America.* (n.d.). PEN America: The freedom to write. https://pen.org

Pennycook, A. (2001). *Critical applied linguistics: A critical introduction.* Erlbaum.

Pennycook, A. (2021). *Critical applied linguistics: A critical re-introduction.* Routledge.

Pennsylvania State Legislature (2021). Teaching Racial and Universal Equality Act., 1532, https://www.legis.state.pa.us/CFDOCS/Legis/PN/Public/btCheck.cfm?txtType= PDF&sessYr=2021&sessInd=0&billBody=H&billTyp=B&billNbr=1532&pn=1679

Phillipson, R. (2009). *Linguistic imperialism continued.* Routledge. https://doi.org/10.4324/9780203857175

Piller, I. (2016). *Linguistic diversity and social justice: An introduction to applied sociolinguistics.* Oxford University Press. https://doi.org/10.1093/acprof:oso/9780199937240.001.0001

Piller, I. (2017). *Intercultural communication: A critical introduction.* Edinburgh University Press.

Postman, N. (1986). *Amusing ourselves to death: Public discourse in the age of show business.* Penguin Books.

Ricento, T. (2014). *Language policy and political economy: English in a global context.* Oxford University Press. https://doi.org/10.1093/acprof:oso/9780199363391.001.0001

Ricento, T. (2019). *Language politics and policies: Perspectives from Canada and the United States.* Cambridge University Press. https://doi.org/10.1017/9781108684804

Rideout, V., Peebles, A., Mann, S., & Robb, M. B. (2022). *Common Sense census: Media use by tweens and teens, 2021.* https://www.commonsensemedia.org/sites/default/files/research/report/2020_zero_to_eight_census_final_web.pdf

Risager, K. (2021). Language textbooks: Windows to the world. *Language, Culture and Curriculum, 34*(2), 119–132. https://doi.org/10.1080/07908318.2020.1797767

Rodriguez, C. E. (2018). *America, as seen on TV: How television shapes immigrant expectations around the globe.* New York University Press.

Rubdy, R., & Ben Said, S. (Eds.). (2016). *Conflict, exclusion and dissent in the linguistic landscape.* Palgrave Macmillan.

Ruecker, T. (2011). Challenging the native and nonnative English speaker hierarchy in ELT: New directions from race theory. *Critical Inquiry in Language Studies, 8*(4), 400–422. https://doi.org/10.1080/15427587.2011.615709

Sableman, P. (2016). *Liberate New York City* [photograph]. Flickr. Accessed September 20, 2024. https://www.flickr.com/photos/pasa/28829658330/

Schmall, E. (2023, February 27). 'Crying Indian' ad that targeted pollution to be retired. *New York Times*. https://www.nytimes.com/2023/02/27/us/native-american-pollution-ad.html?login=email&auth=login-email

Scollon, R., & Scollon, S. B. K. (1981). *Narrative, literacy and face in interethnic communication*. Ablex.

Scollon, R., & Scollon, S. B. K. (1995). *Intercultural communication: A discourse approach: Language in society, Vol. 21*. Blackwell.

Scollon, R., & Scollon, S. B. K. (2003). *Discourses in place: Language in the material world*. Routledge.

Selinker, L. (1972). Interlanguage. *International Review of Applied Linguistics in Language Teaching, 10*(3), 209–231.

Selinker, L., & Lamendella, J. T. (1981). Updating the interlanguage hypothesis. *Studies in Second Language Acquisition, 3*(2), 201–220. https://doi.org/10.1017/S0272263100004186

Shohamy, E., Ben-Rafael, E., & Barni, M. (Eds.). (2010). *Linguistic landscape in the city*. Multilingual Matters. https://doi.org/10.21832/9781847692993

Skutnabb-Kangas, T. (2000). *Linguistic genocide in education—or worldwide diversity and human rights?* L. Erlbaum Associates. https://doi.org/10.4324/9781410605191

Sleeter, C. E. (Ed.). (1991). *Empowerment through multicultural education*. State University of New York Press.

Sleeter, C. E. (2012). Confronting the marginalization of culturally responsive pedagogy. *Urban Education, 47*(3), 562–584. https://doi.org/10.1177/0042085911431472

Sleeter, C. E., & McLaren, P. L. (Eds.). (1995). *Multicultural education, critical pedagogy, and the politics of difference*. State University of New York Press.

Story, L. (2007, January 15). Anywhere the eye can see, it's likely to see an ad. *The New York Times*. https://www.nytimes.com/2007/01/15/business/media/15everywhere.html

Strate, L. (2014). *Amazing ourselves to death: Neil Postman's brave new world revisited*. Peter Lang.

Strate, L. (2017). *Media ecology: An approach to understanding the human condition*. Peter Lang.

Street, B.V. (2017). New literacies, new times: Developments in literacy studies. In Street, B., May, S. (Eds) *Literacies and language education* (pp. 3–15). Springer, Cham. https://doi.org/10.1007/978-3-319-02252-9_1

Street, B. V. (1993). *Cross-cultural approaches to literacy*. Cambridge University Press.

Stroud, C., & Jegels, D. (2014). Semiotic landscapes and mobile narrations of place: Performing the local. *International Journal of the Sociology of Language*, 228, 179–199. https://doi.org/10.1515/ijsl-2014-0010

Tanenbaum, M. (2021, April 8). Philly iceberg meme will test your obscure knowledge of the city. *Philly Voice*. https://www.phillyvoice.com/philly-iceberg-meme-history-odb-mcdonalds-gritty-boner4ever-cave-kelpius/

The series at a glance. (2006, September 6). *Bucks County Courier Times.*

Thevenin, B. (2022). *Making media matter: Critical literacy, popular culture, and creative production.* Routledge.

Turkle, S. (2011). *Alone together: Why we expect more from technology and less from each other.* Basic Books.

Turner, B., Turner, T., Mandabach, C., Carsey, M., & Werner, T. (1998-2006). *That 70's Show.* The Casey-Werner Company.

UNESCO. (2023). *Media and Information Literacy.* UNESCO. https://www.unesco.org/en/media-information-literacy

Valdés, G. (2001). *Learning and not learning English: Latino students in American schools.* Teachers College.

van Dijk, T. A. (1993). Principles of critical discourse analysis. *Discourse & Society, 4*(2), 249–283. https://doi.org/10.1177/0957926593004002006

Vandrick, S. (2009). *Interrogating privilege: Reflections of a second language educator.* University of Michigan Press.

Vygotsky, L. (1986). *Thought and Language.* MIT Press.

Wang, G., & Ma, X. (2021). Representations of LGBTQ+ issues in China in its official English-language media: A corpus-assisted critical discourse study. *Critical Discourse Studies, 18*(2), 188–206. https://doi.org/10.1080/17405904.2020.1738251

Warschauer, M. (2006). *Laptops and literacy: Learning in the wireless classroom.* Teachers College.

Warschauer, M. (2011). *Learning in the cloud: How (and why) to transform schools with digital media.* Teachers College.

Widdowson, H. (2021). English beyond the pale: The language of outsiders. *ELT Journal, 75*(4), 492–501. https://doi.org/10.1093/elt/ccab043

Widdowson, H. G. (2012). The ownership of English. In *Negotiating academic literacies* (pp. 237–248). Routledge.

Wineburg, S., Breakstone, J., McGrew, S., Smith, M. D., & Ortega, T. (2022). Lateral reading on the open internet: A district-wide field study in high school government classes. *Journal of Educational Psychology, 114*(5), 893–909. https://doi.org/10.1037/edu0000740

Wodak, R. (2012). Language, power and identity. *Language Teaching, 45*(2), 215–233. https://doi.org/10.1017/S0261444811000048

Wodak, R. (2013). *Critical discourse analysis.* Sage. https://doi.org/10.4135/9781446286289

Wodak, R., & Meyer, M. (2016). *Methods of critical discourse studies.* Sage.

Woo, A., Diliberti, M. K., & Steiner, E. D. (2024). *Policies restricting teaching about race and gender spill over into other states and localities: Findings from the 2023 state of the American teacher survey.* (RRA1108-10.). RAND Corporation.

Yoon, I. (2016). Why is it not just a joke? Analysis of internet memes associated with racism and hidden ideology of colorblindness. *Journal of Cultural Research in Art Education, 33*(1), 92–123. https://doi.org/10.2458/jcrae.4898

Yosso, T. J. (2002). Critical race media literacy: Challenging deficit discourse about Chicanas/os. *The Journal of Popular Film and Television, 30*(1), 52–62. https://doi.org/10.1080/01956050209605559

Yosso, T. J. (2006). *Critical race counterstories along the Chicana/Chicano educational pipeline.* Routledge.

Yosso, T. J. (2020). Critical race media literacy for these urgent times. *International Journal of Multicultural Education, 22*(2), 5–13. https://doi.org/10.18251/ijme.v22i2.2685

# Index